CONSTRUCTION SPECIFICATIONS PRACTICE GUIDE

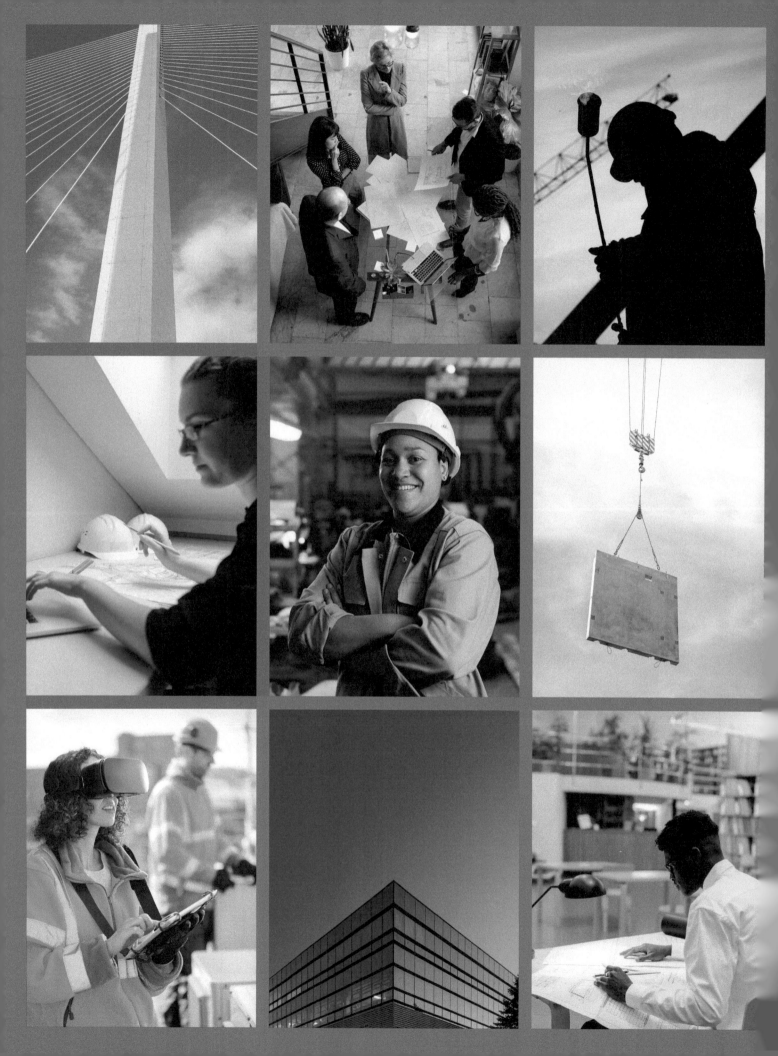

CONSTRUCTION SPECIFICATIONS

PRACTICE GUIDE

Construction Specifications
Practice Guide

2nd Edition

For general information about our other products and services, please contact CSI within the United States at (800) 689-2900 or at www.csiresources.org.

Library of Congress Control Number: 2020924177

ISBN: (electronic) 978-1-7349654-7-6

ISBN: (print) 978-1-7349654-6-9

Third Printing, 2023

Printed in the United States of America 10 9 8 7 6 5 4 3

PREFACE |

Introduction

Beginning with the publication of the first *CSI Manual of Practice (MOP)* in 1967 and continuing through the publication of this second edition of the *Construction Specifications Practice Guide (CSPG)*, the Construction Specifications Institute (CSI) has worked to ensure that these essential learning and reference tools convey practice competency areas for the professional delivery of construction projects. This revised version of the *CSPG* focuses on the authoring and use of specifications in a construction project, and how the specifications define the requirements to be met by all participants on the project team. Overall, the specifications allow the basis of design to be reflected in the facility's performance and satisfy the owner's and occupants' needs and wants. CSI's practice guides are the primary source materials for the organization's various certification exams. The *CSPG*, in particular, is the primary reference for the CSI Certified Construction Specifier (CCS™) certification.

To help supplement other sources of professional practice knowledge, CSI conducts job analysis research regularly to reinforce the relevance of content presented in the practice guides and included in the certification examinations, and to define the knowledge, skills, and abilities needed by any CSI certification holder. Practice guide content is based on the outcomes of this research and is organized into knowledge domains that reflect competencies and learning objectives. This information forms a body of knowledge and aligns the content in the certification exams with the other CSI materials that convey that knowledge.

What's New in the 2nd Edition?

In addition to updated content and improved readability, the *CSPG 2nd Edition* has been reorganized to improve application in practice and ease of use in instruction. The book follows the sequence of the knowledge domains described as follows.

Online Materials

Included with the book are five appendices that you can access from your account on ebooks.csiresources.org.

Appendix A: Comparisons of Standard
General Conditions

Appendix B: CSI Forms

Appendix C: MasterFormat® Numbers and Titles

Appendix D: UniFormat®

Appendix E: SectionFormat®/PageFormat®

The Six CCS Knowledge Domains

The knowledge domains constitute the job analysis and body of knowledge for the CCS examination as follows:

Planning, Development, and Organization—Evaluate the scope of the project and identify anticipated specifications; manage the specifications production schedule; develop and maintain the project files for the proposed systems, products, and materials; identify a tracking system for questions, substitutions, and related bidding items; develop a detailed document production plan; maintain version control of the specifications; and develop and maintain the office master guide specifications.

Coordination—Collect, track, and coordinate the specification information; coordinate the alignment of the architect/engineer (A/E) team's proposed choices with the project requirements; coordinate the specification information with the project team; obtain and verify the owner procurement and contract requirements; integrate sustainable design and construction requirements; evaluate and verify the compatibility of products and materials; coordinate the specifications across the project team disciplines; evaluate the specifications to confirm alignment with the contract documents; compile the available project information into the project manual; mentor the project team on how to produce and use the project manual; and coordinate with the project team to specify alternates.

Procurement, Contracting, and General Requirements—Edit specifications to conform to owner procurement and contract requirements; coordinate Division 01—General Requirements with all other specifications; incorporate project-specific requirements into the Division 01 section; specify the project measurement and payment procedures, substitution requirements and procedures, RFI requirements and procedures, construction administrative requirements, submittal requirements and procedures, methods of quality control and quality assurance, temporary facilities and controls, and project closeout requirements and procedures; evaluate the acceptability of substitution request submittals; coordinate pre-construction mock-ups and associated testing; and prepare performance and life cycle specifications.

Research—Research materials and systems for the product selection, availability and lead time for selected products, sourcing for selected products, applicable code requirements, and applicable product standards; evaluate product suitability for the project conditions; and review key product selections with the product representatives.

Analysis and Evaluation—Align the specifications to the project delivery method and schedule; evaluate the proposed systems, assemblies, and materials being proposed for the project and verify that they meet the project requirements; analyze drawings for their inclusion; evaluate products for code requirements; assess the interior climate conditions and exterior environmental conditions for impact on the materials and methods; evaluate products and systems for constructability and sequencing in the project locale; evaluate and select products for compliance with the design intent; obtain and evaluate standards and information from technical and professional societies; review standards for appropriateness and verify that necessary reference standards options have been selected; review and incorporate the results of value engineering decisions; and verify the proposed construction meets the manufacturer's warranty requirements.

Production—Organize the project documents according to CSI Formats; develop the outline specifications and project manuals; translate the design narratives into specifications and the graphic information from drawings into succinct written form; determine what submittals are required to ensure quality installation and adequate project documentation; include sustainable design and construction procedures in specifications; specify preparation and finishing requirements for the product; review and comment on any specification sections written by others; and prepare and edit specifications sections and documents for publication and distribution.

What This Book Offers

The Construction Specifications Practice Guide 2nd Edition is an ideal resource for specifiers and design professionals to gain greater knowledge of construction specifications and the methods for their research and creation. This book also will benefit the other project teams (owner, contractor, and supplier), as greater knowledge of specification content will help the specifications communicate design intent and be understood. It provides essential project knowledge that can both streamline the execution of any project and mitigate risk for individual practitioners and their firms.

The CSPG is an essential resource for professionals in practice—helping them not only clarify their understanding but also correct bad habits. It also is an excellent instructional textbook for those who have just started their professional career or who are studying in anticipation of pursuing a career in the construction industry.

Use in CCS Exam Preparation

Though the *CSPG* is the primary resource for CCS examination items, it is not the sole source for the knowledge and abilities tested by the certification examination. CCS candidates are expected to have enough practical professional experience to supplement their studying, ensuring that their knowledge is based on both study and practice.

About the Authors

This CSI practice guide would not exist without the tireless and expert contributions of the *CSPG 2nd Edition* Author Team:

Ronald Geren, FCSI Lifetime Member, AIA, CCS™, CCCA™, CDT®, CSC, SCIP, and *CSPG 2nd Edition* Lead Author

Basit Baig, CSI-EP

Benjamin Burroughs, CCS™, CDT®, CCCA™

Kurt Schwarm, CSI, CCS™, CDT®, CCCA™, AIA

In addition, CSI wishes to thank the following individuals for their technical review of the *CSPG 2nd Edition*:

Steve Doub, CSI, CCS™, CDT®

Brynolf Peterson, CSI, CCS™, CCCA™, CDT®, AIA

James Robertson, FCSI, CCS™, CDT®, FAIA, NCARB

Joseph Scarpa, CCS™, CDT®, CCCA™, CPSM, LEED AP

Rondi Werner, CSI, CCS™, CDT®, CCCA

Anne Whitacre, FCSI, CCS™, LEED AP

CSI also wishes to thank the following for their contributions:

American Institute of Architects

ConsensusDocs Coalition

Construction Management Association of America

Design Build Institute of America

Engineers Joint Contract Documents Committee

Greg Ceton, CDT®

Kathryn Malm Bourgoine, CDT®, UXC, CSPO

Rebecca W. Ayers

Adaobi Tulton

IPS Technical Publishing

Silva Brand

CSPG STRUCTURE |

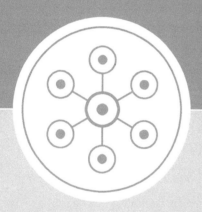

DOMAIN 1

Planning,
Development,
& Organization

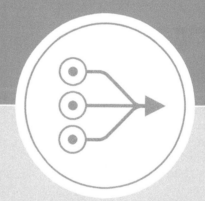

DOMAIN 2

Coordination

DOMAIN 3

Procurement,
Contracting,
& General
Requirements

The Knowledge Domains reflected in this book represent the foundational content of the CSI construction specification certification and learning programs. Other exam preparation materials provided by CSI that correspond to the Certified Construction Specifier (CCS™) certification also follow this arrangement of Knowledge Domains.

The order of these *Construction Specifications Practice Guide* Knowledge Domains roughly corresponds to the stages and issues presented by developing and use of specifications, as explained more fully in this publication.

DOMAIN 4

Research

DOMAIN 5

Analysis
& Evaluation

DOMAIN 6

Production

CONTENTS |

Chapter 4: Modifications 58

Chapter 5: Specifying for Purchase of Goods 68

Chapter 6: Federal Agencies 84

Chapter 7: Construction Bonds & Insurance *100*

DOMAIN 4: RESEARCH

Chapter 8: Product Research & Selection *124*

DOMAIN 5: ANALYSIS & EVALUATION

DOMAIN 6: PRODUCTION

Chapter 11: Project Manual Production *172*

Chapter 12: Outline & Shortform Specifications *184*

Chapter 13: Organizing Using Formats

Chapter 14: Specification Methods

Chapter 15: Preparing the Specifications 250

INDEX 268

APPENDICES

**DOMAIN 1:
PLANNING, DEVELOPMENT,
& ORGANIZATION**

Chapter 1
PLANNING, DEVELOPMENT, & ORGANIZING THE PROJECT MANUAL

1.1 Planning the Project Manual

The specifier's role extends beyond the mere editing of master specification sections for a given design project — the role requires extensive knowledge in all matters regarding the preparation of construction documents, including drawings, procurement requirements, and contract requirements. The term *specifications* is often misused to indicate the book that accompanies the set of contract drawings. The specifications are just a part of the written requirements prepared for a construction contract. The more accurate term for this "book" is the *project manual*. It is the collection of procurement requirements, contract forms, conditions of the contract, procedural and administrative requirements, and technical specifications needed for a construction project. More detailed information on the *project manual concept* can be found in Chapter 11 — Project Manual Production.

Planning the project manual requires thorough knowledge of conceptual or preliminary design drawings, project requirements for the work covered in each section, and preliminary project descriptions or outline specifications. The architect/engineer (A/E) continually asks questions, suggests alternatives, and reviews proposed design solutions with the owner and the consultant team. When the team includes a specifier, that individual becomes an active team member in the design process. Knowing the project's scope and complexity, contract type, and project delivery method can help in the early decision-making process for preparing the project manual. Determining the type of specifications and the specifying method, understanding formats, and choosing the right format set the stage to organize and communicate the project requirements to those that bid/propose, permit, and construct the project.

1.1.1 The Influence of Project Scope and Complexity

Choosing whether to prepare full-length, shortform, or outline specifications depends a lot on the project's complexity. The specifier should review early design documents or meet with the design team to discuss the project's complexity to determine what form of

Construction
Specifications
Practice Guide

DOMAIN 1
Planning,
Development,
& Organization

DOMAIN 2
Coordination

DOMAIN 3
Procurement,
Contracting,
& General
Requirements

DOMAIN 4
Research

DOMAIN 5
Analysis
& Evaluation

DOMAIN 6
Production

specifications to prepare. The project requirements might also dictate the specifying method or methods that can or should be used. If a project is for a government agency, for instance, nonrestrictive methods are generally required, and it is essential to be aware of this requirement before beginning to prepare specifications.

Full-length specification sections should be used for larger, more complex projects or projects where the liability risk is high. *Outline specifications* are typically prepared early in the design process to convey basic product and material requirements while the design may still be fluid. (See Chapter 12 — Outline and Shortform Specifications.)

Shortform specifications are appropriate for limited scope projects that may need less-detailed descriptions than those provided by typical full-length specifications. Similarly, for projects with a limited scope of work, a specification with concise, streamlined descriptions of the work may be appropriate. In particular, projects without exterior envelopes, roofing, or waterproofing may be constructed with more streamlined documentation. Shortform specifications may also be used when the project calls for specifications to be placed on the drawings instead of using a project manual.

Combining full-length and shortform specification sections in a project manual sometimes occurs; however, combining shortform and full-length sections should be avoided to keep consistency between sections. If you are specifying a product or system lacking comprehensive information, you may need to use the shortform version if the missing information cannot be developed independently. Coordination of section titles and numbers is necessary when combining shortform and full-length specification sections. Coordinate the specification titles and numbers with the various consultants who may provide content that overlaps other sections. More detailed information on shortform specifications can be found in Chapter 12 — Outline and Shortform Specifications.

When the result is most important, *performance specifications* provide the flexibility that allows optional solutions that meet the same requirements or provides the same results. *Project descriptions* for the design-build project delivery method are another example where performance specifying may be utilized. More detailed information on performance specifications can be found in Chapter 14 — Specification Methods.

When the work is limited to the delivery of goods and no construction or installation is involved, *purchasing specifying* and *purchasing contracts* are appropriate. More detailed information on specifying for purchase of goods can be found in Chapter 5 — Specifying for Purchase of Goods.

1.1.2 The Influence of Contract Types and Project Delivery Methods

Construction documents prepared for a project using the design-bid-build project delivery method differ from those prepared for a project using the design-build or other project delivery method. Chapter 5 — Project Analysis and Evaluation provides a detailed discussion on how the specifications are influenced explicitly by each project delivery method.

The typical project delivery methods are as follows:

- Design-Bid-Build (D-B-B)
- Construction Manager at Risk (CMAR)
- Integrated Project Delivery (IPD)
- Design-Build (D-B)
- Owner-Build (O-B)

Refer to the Construction Specifications Institute's (CSI's) *Project Delivery Practice Guide (PDPG)* for more detailed information on the project delivery methods. In addition, refer to Chapter 10 — Specification Variations for Project Delivery Methods for discussion on how the different project delivery methods affect the specifications.

Some projects may be simple and straightforward, requiring only a single set of drawings and one project manual. In contrast, other projects may include multiple project manuals and separate packages of drawings, especially if the project is using the fast-track scheduling technique (refer to the *PDPG* for more information on the fast-track scheduling technique).

Another influence on the preparation of the project manual is the type of contractual arrangement. Many projects have a single contractor that performs the work with the assistance of subcontractors. This arrangement is referred to as a *single-prime contract*. Single-prime contracts typically require one project manual and one set of drawings.

On the other hand, some projects use the *multiple-prime contract* arrangement that involves the owner individually procuring separate contracts to perform portions of the overall work (e.g., electrical, plumbing, landscaping, building envelope). With separate contracts come separate sets of contract documents issued to each contractor that address their work portion. Each one of these contracts has its own set of drawings and a project manual. Using multiple project manuals on a single project significantly changes the specifier's scope of work.

1.1.3 Managing the Specifications Production Schedule

In addition to having a thorough understanding of construction materials, systems, and methods, the A/E must be proficient in the management and organization techniques required to meet

scheduled commitments. This proficiency includes incorporating information from multiple consultants (e.g., checking specification format and verifying that there is no duplication or omissions in specification content).

1.1.3.1 Reviewing the Project Schedule

The project schedule should include ample time to review comments received after each design submittal, whether from the owner or another reviewing authority. When the construction management as advisor/agent (CM-Advisor/Agent) method is used for a multiple-prime contract, the A/E usually produces construction document packages identified by the CM-Advisor/Agent to implement the multiple-prime contracts and fast-track the scheduling technique. Though the entire project schedule may be reduced by utilizing these techniques, the overall document preparation time is usually longer. The construction documentation process is usually staggered to produce separate bid/ proposal packages based on the required scheduling.

Section 01 32 00 — Construction Progress Documentation should include requirements for using the critical path method (CPM) network analysis with updating requirements or the more

DOMAIN 1
Planning,
Development,
& Organization

DOMAIN 2
Coordination

DOMAIN 3
Procurement,
Contracting,
& General
Requirements

DOMAIN 4
Research

DOMAIN 5
Analysis
& Evaluation

DOMAIN 6
Production

straightforward Gantt method depending on the project's complexity. Additionally, the specifications should identify long-lead items and milestone dates to ensure compliance with the overall project schedule.

1.1.3.2 Coordinating the Production Schedule with Consultants

Most design consultants prepare the specifications that address their portion of the project. Each consultant must be aware of the production schedule, including the delivery dates for the various specification documents. Understanding the schedule ensures the A/E receives all sections on time and nothing is missing when it is submitted to the owner.

1.2 Project Manual Development and Organization

Once a plan has been established and a thorough understanding of the scope of work has been obtained from the design documents, the A/E begins developing the project manual. Staying organized is essential to managing the information and maintaining a structure to retrieve the information quickly.

1.2.1 Reviewing Project Requirements

The specifier should review project requirements for the work covered in each specification section. Preliminary project descriptions (PPDs) or outline specifications prepared during the early design phases may be helpful. It is also important to thoroughly review the drawings, details of construction, and drawing schedules. Local conditions and governing codes must also be considered, as both proprietary and master guide specifications may not address local project conditions or may contain references that do not apply. Prepare a preliminary table of contents for the project manual by identifying the specification sections from MasterFormat® that are needed to cover the project's scope.

1.2.2 Developing a Detailed Document Production Plan

Producing a project manual requires the development of a plan for acquiring information systematically and comprehensively to fully understand the scope of the work, the project delivery method, form of agreement between owner and builder, insurance and bonding requirements, format for specifications, and other relevant characteristics of the project.

1.2.2.1 Producing a Project Manual

Preparing project manuals varies with individual firm practice. Regardless of who prepares the project manual (principal of a small firm, specifier, or project A/E in a larger firm), the following tasks should be performed:

- Establish the format to be used for the specifications and coordinate with consultants as required.

- Review the Owner-A/E Agreement.

- Understand the type of construction contract, insurance requirements, and bonds required.

- Review the Owner-Contractor Agreement (if this is available for review).

- Review the General Conditions of the Contract for Construction.

- Review supplementary conditions when available. (The construction contract may have already been executed before the architect comes on board; the general and supplementary conditions may not be available for modification. Additionally, public entities may have general and supplementary conditions that cannot be modified.)

- Prepare the draft Division 01 — General Requirements sections.

- Send the proposed conditions of the contract and Division 01 sections to the owner and consultants for review.

- Prepare drafts of technical specifications in Divisions 02 through 49 with the A/E team and consultants.

- Make decisions about the quality of materials and equipment to be installed and the workmanship requirements.

- Review the drawings and specifications together to eliminate conflicts in terminology or assemblies.

- Revise the specifications based on final review comments received and decisions made.

- Receive the final specifications prepared by consultants.

- Compile and reproduce the project manual for distribution.

Figure 1.1 provides a flow diagram for developing the project manual compared to the development of the contract drawings.

Refer to Chapter 15 — Preparing Specifications for detailed guidance on producing specification sections.

1.2.3 Developing and Maintaining Project Files

Decisions made on product selections, evaluations of similar or equivalent performance characteristics, and availability in local markets should be recorded and archived for easy access or retrieval. Systematic and progressive compiling of information is essential, beginning as soon as early design drawings or sketches become available.

1.2.3.1 Assembling and Recording Information

There are no set rules or instructions for assembling and recording product installation and workmanship characteristics. Develop methods that work for you. Some common approaches include compiled project notes, a communication log of all emails from the project A/E to the specifier, a project notebook or project folders organized by MasterFormat® divisions, or checklists. More examples of assembling and recording project information are included in Chapter 11 — Project Manual Production.

1.2.3.2 Tracking Questions, Substitutions, and Related Items During Procurement

Questions, substitution requests, and changes occur throughout the procurement phase of a project. Managing the flow of information in an organized and deliberate fashion adds significantly to the clarity of purpose and design intent. The A/E has many organizational tools and processes for handling these necessary revisions, clarifications, and modifications.

Email communication is the most widely used form of written communication, and this situation is not likely to change. However, sifting through the hundreds, maybe thousands, of emails in a single project is overwhelming.

CSI Form 7.0A "Communication Record" and CSI Form 7.0B "Communication Log" are simple and effective forms for recording questions about the specifications during procurement (see Appendix B for samples of these forms). Some A/E offices may have company forms, which can vary by office practice, client, or project type. Online collaboration and project management applications can also be an effective means of tracking incoming questions and substitution requests during procurement. Regardless of how the questions and substitution requests are received, verbal responses without written confirmations are entirely improper. Responses should be issued in written form, such as an addendum during the procurement phase.

1.2.4 Maintaining Version Control of Specifications

It is vital to ensure that the A/E coordinates changes in the specifications so the entire project team (owner, contractor, suppliers, A/E, and consultants) are working with the latest specification version and can see what changes have been made. Maintaining version control includes identifying revisions after the project team has formally accepted the specifications and during the plan review process by the authorities having jurisdiction, not just during procurement and construction.

The specifier should maintain a record of all modifications made to the project manual after its

DOMAIN 1
Planning,
Development,
& Organization

DOMAIN 2
Coordination

DOMAIN 3
Procurement,
Contracting,
& General
Requirements

DOMAIN 4
Research

DOMAIN 5
Analysis
& Evaluation

DOMAIN 6
Production

Figure 1.1
Project Manual
Development

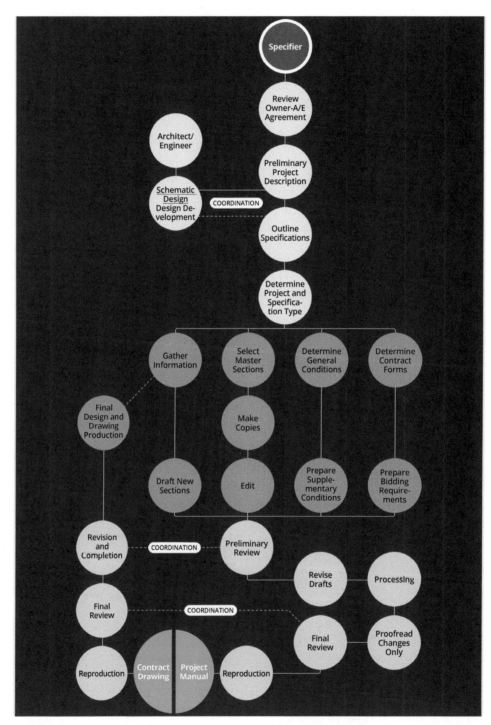

publication (see Chapter 4—Modifications for more information on modifications). These modifications include the following:

    Addenda. Addenda are written or graphic instruments issued to clarify, revise, add to, or delete information in the procurement

documents or previous addenda. Typically, addenda are issued before the opening of bids/proposals.

    Substitution Requests. Except for closed proprietary specifications, substitutions are often allowed and often desirable to a client who wants to take advantage of the contractor's knowledge of alternative materials, products, or assemblies that, if accepted by the A/E and owner, could save time, money, or both. It is important to note that approval of substitutions requires the A/E's acceptance of the substitution as an equivalent to the specified materials, products, or assemblies.

Requirements for processing requests for substitutions are included in Division 01 — General Requirements and are covered in detail in Chapter 3 — General Requirements. The use of forms and logs to document and track requests for substitutions allows convenient access to the entire project team, including the owner and authorities having jurisdiction. See CSI Form 1.5C "Substitution Request (During the Bidding/Negotiating Phase)," CSI Form 13.1A "Substitution Request (After the Bidding/ Negotiation Phase)," and CSI Form 13.1B "Substitution Request Log" in Appendix B.

Contract Modifications. Requirements and procedures for contract modifications (changes after the execution of the owner/ contractor agreement) are included in the general conditions of the contract and Division 01 — General Requirements (see Chapter 4 — Modifications). These requirements and procedures must be followed to ensure conformity with the construction contract and provide a structure for evaluating requests for additional cost, additional contract time, or both.

Requests for Information (RFI). A standardized request for information (RFI) form with space for requesting an interpretation and another space for a response aids the A/E in answering questions during construction. A copy of the form should be placed in the project manual. See CSI Form 13.2A "Request for Information" in Appendix B.

1.2.4.1 Revision Methods

The A/E needs to coordinate all revisions to the specifications after the final version is completed, or typically after the procurement documents have been issued. Common methods of documenting revisions are as follows:

- Revision numbers
- Delta symbols
- Clouds
- ~~Strikethrough~~, **bold**, <u>underline</u>, or *italic* text (or a combination of these)

Word processing and specification editing software applications may provide features that allow the tracking of changes.

To ensure consistency across all contract documents, coordinate the revision identifiers used in specifications with the drawings, addenda, and modifications.

Bidders and proposers often need to forward copies of addenda to sub-bidders and sub-proposers within compressed timeframes; thus, the use of electronic formats allows for quick distribution of document revisions. Additionally, electronic formats may have security features that prevent a document's modification after distribution, such as the portable document format (PDF).

1.2.4.2 Methods of Issuing Revisions to Procurement and Contract Documents

There are two basic methods for preparing written changes to procurement and contract documents: the narrative method and the revised page method.

Narrative Method. In the narrative method, modifications are described in writing. When using the narrative method, the following criteria should be observed:

- Brevity: Give only enough information to make the change clear, but avoid over-simplification.

- Clarity: Give enough information to communicate the required changes. When modifying written documents, repeat enough of the original text to make each change self-explanatory.

- Cross-references: Express a change only once, and then refer to it wherever necessary. If a change in the specifications requires a change to the drawings, explain

DOMAIN 1
Planning,
Development,
& Organization

DOMAIN 2
Coordination

DOMAIN 3
Procurement,
Contracting,
& General
Requirements

DOMAIN 4
Research

DOMAIN 5
Analysis
& Evaluation

DOMAIN 6
Production

all related changes in the addendum or modification. After that, refer the reader to the addendum or change order rather than repeat the instructions. One correction properly expressed should serve for all repetitive changes. Verify that changes do not contradict or make some other part of the work impossible to accomplish.

Revised-Page Method. Depending on the number and type of changes, the revised-page method may be a more effective means of communicating changes to the project manual or the drawings. In this method, the change is made to the specification section or drawing sheet using one of the revision methods discussed in Section 1.2.4.1, which is then reissued. Each section reissued may include the revision date and identifier (e.g., "CO-01" or "Change Order No. 1") in the footer or header.

1.2.4.3 Version Control for Multiple Work Packages

Many project delivery methods permit using the fast-track scheduling technique, which condenses the traditional linear project design and construction schedule into a series of overlapping design and construction activities. This method allows one construction activity on a project to begin while subsequent activities are in various design or procurement stages. The scope of work for each activity must be clearly delineated to make this technique perform correctly.

The scope of work issued is called a *work package*. A work package is defined by CSI's document "Multiple Work Package Projects" as

> *a group of specifications, drawings, and schedules prepared by the design team to describe a portion of the work for pricing, permitting, and construction.*

As one work package begins construction, another might follow that is currently in procurement, and the one following that may be in construction documents preparation, followed by another in design. This phased situation creates the problem of managing the various documents that have been previously issued with the documents that are being developed for subsequent work packages.

There are two approaches described in the "Multiple Work Package Projects" document for managing partial sets of contract documents:

Standalone Method. Each work package issued is a complete and separate package from all other work packages. It consists of drawings and specifications that only address the scope of that work package. Although standalone work packages make it easier to determine each package's extent, it is more complicated to manage as more work packages are issued. As standalone contract documents, revisions to work packages must be tracked separately, further complicating the control of documents within each work package.

Cumulative Method. As work packages are issued, subsequent packages include revised drawings and specifications by adding to the drawings and specifications issued in previous work packages. The changes made to the specifications in the most recent work package are delineated using one of the methods in Section 1.2.4.1. This method is preferred to the standalone method since it progresses toward developing a single comprehensive set of contract documents and makes revisions more manageable.

For more information about multiple work packages, refer to CSI's document "Multiple Work Package Projects."

1.3 Developing and Organizing Office Master Guide Specifications

Office master guide specifications are not the same as a project manual. Master guide specifications are available from many sources and are commonly used to develop specifications for project manuals. Office master guide specifications are developed to capture information common to an office, owner, or building type.

DOMAIN 1
Planning,
Development,
& Organization

DOMAIN 2
Coordination

DOMAIN 3
Procurement,
Contracting,
& General
Requirements

DOMAIN 4
Research

DOMAIN 5
Analysis
& Evaluation

DOMAIN 6
Production

1.3.1 Introduction to Master Guide Specifications

Most A/E firms, government agencies, and large corporations use master guide specifications as a basis for their construction documents. Developing and using master guide specifications is an efficient way of producing project specifications. However, preparing and updating an office master is a task separate from preparing a project manual. Suppose the office master uses the Veteran Administration (VA) or Housing and Urban Development (HUD) specifications. In that case, the A/E would not make long-term changes to those documents but make only project-specific edits.

For any given specification section, there are two basic methods of preparing text: write the text from scratch, or edit prewritten text.

Option two is usually less time-consuming, but it has its drawbacks, too. When using prewritten text, A/Es have many sources to draw from, including commercial master guide specification services, office master guide specifications or text, manufacturer-furnished specifications, and previous project specifications. Each guide specification source has its pros and cons (see Table 1.1). However, the most effective and efficient source is a set of specifications

pre-edited to the A/E's principal project types and specification requirements.

The term *master specifications* refers to the documents used as guides for preparing project specifications. The US Department of Defense (DOD) and HUD refer to their specifications as *guide specifications*. These manuscripts facilitate the preparation of project specifications by standardizing products, materials, processes, and formats. These specifications allow editing to adapt the guide specification to specific project requirements. These two terms (*master specifications* and *guide specifications*) are combined to form the term *master guide specifications*, used in this manual for prepared specification sections intended to be edited and used as project specifications.

The term *office master specifications* is also used to distinguish an A/E's master specification from commercial master guide specifications. The office master specification may be derived from commercial master guide specifications that were used as its basis.

A master guide specification ideally would include the types of items typically utilized for most projects. Each master guide specification section should include text written in a consistent style covering

Table 1.1
Comparison of
Available Guide
Specifications

SOURCE	PROS	CONS
Commercial master guide specifications	Regularly updated	Contains far more information than project requires, making extensive editing necessary
Office master guide specifications	Contains vetted office knowledge	Can often become outdated if not vigilantly maintained
Manufacturer-furnished specifications	Product manufacturer's information is reliable	Proprietary language requires editing for competitively bid projects
Previous project specifications	For identical projects can be a time-saver	Very few projects are identical. Can be more time-consuming to edit out nonapplicable content.

typical requirements and list possible options and choices. Instructional notes may be included and should provide direction, guidance, and notice of required decisions. The A/E edits selected master guide specification sections to suit the particular project. Paragraphs and articles that do not apply in word-processor-based master guide specifications are deleted unless the "track changes" feature is on. In database master guide specifications, paragraphs are never permanently deleted. They are instead unselected in order to exclude the content from a specification section.

Master guide specifications have evolved from the need to compile a concise, centralized, and quick-to-edit source of information from the sometimes overwhelming amount of data and options available to the A/E. When new project experience is systematically incorporated into the master for future use, the master guide specification becomes a significant repository of knowledge for the firm that serves as a part of the "corporate memory." A master guide specification prepared and maintained with an emphasis on consistency and editing speed makes project specifications more accurate and quicker to prepare. Investments in the firm's master guide specification are returned through lower project specification preparation costs.

Using a master guide specification does not eliminate the need to understand the principles of specification writing. Master guide specifications are only tools. They require competence, skill, and project experience for their proper use. Although master guide specifications can be extensive, they might not cover every necessity of a specific project. These additional needs require custom specifications to be written consistent with the master guide specifications. The use of a master guide specification requires an understanding of the basis of the conditions of the contract and general requirements for which they were prepared.

1.3.2 Content of Master Guide Specifications

A complete master guide specification system should consist of carefully coordinated elements that together form a comprehensive information library, including the following:

- Master guide specification sections themselves
- Provisions for coordination of drawings and specifications
- List of frequently specified products and additional required information
- Checklist for each specification section, identifying principal decisions needed for an individual project
- Information and evaluation about products, materials, systems, codes, and standards, utilized or referenced in the master guide specification section

1.3.3 Reasons for Using a Master Guide Specification

The reasons for developing and using a master guide specification or purchasing a commercially available system for a firm's project specifications include the following:

Easier updating and maintenance of specification data. A master guide specification is an efficient method for incorporating and recording changes in product data and administrative procedures needed to keep specification sections current.

Improved efficiency in specifying. The use of a master guide specification can save a lot of project time. Repetitive development of the same specifications for multiple projects is virtually eliminated. Although overhead costs for developing (or purchasing) and maintaining the office master guide specification must be charged against project savings, a net saving can easily be realized. Whether purchased or developed in-house, time-saving tools are feasible only with carefully coordinated and consistently formatted documents.

Expanded decision-making capability. A master guide specification that presents a wide range of standard options enables the A/E to make the best possible choice for each item in a project.

Reduced delays in project development. The use of a master guide specification allows

DOMAIN 1
Planning,
Development,
& Organization

DOMAIN 2
Coordination

DOMAIN 3
Procurement,
Contracting,
& General
Requirements

DOMAIN 4
Research

DOMAIN 5
Analysis
& Evaluation

DOMAIN 6
Production

specification production concurrent with drawings, avoiding the delay, confusion, and misuse caused by last-minute preparation and production.

Minimized repetitive work. A master guide specification can free personnel from developing a specification from scratch for each project, allowing them to concentrate on more critical technical requirements.

Reduced errors and omissions. The use of a carefully developed and maintained office master specification system can minimize inadvertent mistakes and omissions. A/Es become familiar with the location of specific topics in the specification. Alterations to published guide specifications may be undertaken to conform with the firm's insurer or legal counsel requirements. New projects are started from the definitive databank that records feedback from projects and updates from other sources, such as commercial subscription services. By reducing the time required to prepare project specifications, personnel can concentrate on properly addressing critical issues. Electronic tools can further reduce errors and omissions by performing programmed operations. The office master specification provides a vehicle for capturing past projects' experience and developing an essential part of the overall corporate knowledge base.

Reduced exposure to liability. By reducing errors and omissions, a master guide specification may minimize the potential for litigation.

Use of the owner's guide specifications. If an owner has guide specifications required for use on their projects, it is essential to verify conflicts between owner specifications and the specifying firm's standard practice. These issues must be resolved and clarified before project completion.

Standardized office policies and procedures. A master guide specification system can be instrumental in standardizing technical terminology, service scope to clients, and office policy on a wide range of technical considerations. Office unified technology should be based on Construction Specifications Institute (CSI)

formatted documents, including MasterFormat®, UniFormat®, the United States National CAD Standard (NCS), and other industry efforts to standardize and organize information.

Improved office practices. A master guide specification can be used to train inexperienced personnel and establish a standard production procedure. Expanding and updating the master guide during slow periods can level the workload and initiate systematic office improvements. Many firms use the master guide specifications in their in-house educational programs.

Electronic technology to enhance production and improve efficiency. Master guide specifications can enhance production by incorporating internal software linkages that provide coordination. They can also assure that choices selected in a section do not contain contradictory information. The Department of Defense Unified Facilities Guide Specifications and some commercial guide specification systems provide options for generating tables of contents, listings of submittals, reference standards, and other reports. Specification software can enable efficiencies through macros and hyperlink features that can provide additional production benefits. The same technology can provide tools for the coordination of specifications and drawings and reduce the potential for errors and omissions. Additional considerations for the use of technology are included at the end of this chapter.

Building Information Modeling (BIM). Systems and programs incorporate building models and objects into three-dimensional representations of the project. These systems assist with the coordination of the assemblies and components as the A/E and consultants design them. The supporting documentation and specifications require additional document management to be incorporated into the project.

The same specifying techniques described for project specifications apply to master guide specification preparation with the additional considerations relating to the following:

- Use for more than one project type, client or client type, location, or code jurisdiction

- Alternative products for similar applications, one or more of which may be used on a particular project

- Editing notes, explaining options and procedures

1.3.4 Strategies for Developing and Organizing an Office Master Guide Specification

A master guide specification should be developed by an experienced individual or a team of individuals thoroughly familiar with specification principles and formats and current software capabilities. The office master specification may be prepared as a separate effort following an established office procedure and drawing from all available resources. The text can be developed in two ways: (1) by compiling and editing sections from previous project specifications and industry association guide specifications or (2) by utilizing commercially available master guide specifications, edited to suit office practice. In planning and preparing office master specifications, carefully analyze the various technologies and methods of editing, storing, and retrieving text

currently in use for the required sections and for producing the final project manual.

When using commercial master guide specifications as an office master, the A/E should ensure that all users have the latest release or updated version of the commercial master guide specifications. Office masters based on commercial master guide specifications should include the latest updates to either office edits or the commercial base specification.

1.3.5 Master List of Section Numbers and Titles

When starting the development of an office master specification, prepare a master list of section numbers and titles needed and a scope statement for each section. During development, a comprehensive list facilitates coordination, avoids duplication, and helps prevent the omission of required sections. The master list can also be used as a checklist for project specifications. Section numbers and titles should be per those listed in MasterFormat®. The office master list should designate the following:

- The number and title assigned to each section, with gaps in the numbering of Level 3 and

DOMAIN 1
Planning,
Development,
& Organization

DOMAIN 2
Coordination

DOMAIN 3
Procurement,
Contracting,
& General
Requirements

DOMAIN 4
Research

DOMAIN 5
Analysis
& Evaluation

DOMAIN 6
Production

Level 4 sections to allow the addition of other sections that may be needed for a specific project

- A brief description of the work included in each section and related work specified in other sections

- The current status of the development of each section

- The date of the initial preparation and the date of the latest revision of each section

- The name of the individual responsible for preparing and updating each section

- The order of priority for the completion of incomplete or unedited sections

The most commonly used sections should be prepared first, with other sections postponed until needed for a particular project or available labor permits development.

Using commercial master guide specification as the initial basis of the office master specification is more time-efficient, but it also presents some issues that need to be considered. For example, a checklist should identify which sections have been edited to suit the practice, and which have not, in order to avoid the assumption by novices that unedited sections are acceptable for use.

When setting up the master list of section titles from scratch, as opposed to using the list provided by a commercial master guide specification, determine the required scope of each section, based on the work to be covered and the ultimate size (number of pages) of a typical project section. A master guide specification may contain any combination of sections at MasterFormat® Level 2 or Level 3. Each firm must make its judgment based on its practice. The following are some suggestions for the scope of master sections:

- A single section may be written covering the entire scope of a division. For example, a single section for a division such as concrete can be useful for small projects.

- Separate sections for Level 2 titles listed in MasterFormat® can divide the extent into more manageable pieces.

- If a Level 2 section is too broad for general use because it contains too many types of products or would be unwieldy in size, several Level 3 sections may be written in place of the single Level 2 section.

- It may be useful to prepare both a Level 2 section and corresponding Level 3 sections for the same scope in some instances. The Level 2 section can be used for less complicated projects, and the Level 3 sections can be used for more detailed requirements.

- Level 3 sections permit a detailed subdivision of the specifications, making a considerably more modular system. Sections for which decisions have already been made can be started very early in the project without delay until other related product selections have been made.

- Level 4 sections may be used for particular work results that require specialized or unique requirements that a Level 3 section cannot provide.

1.3.6 Standard Formats and Language

Standard section and page formats should be used to develop a master guide specification to promote consistency from section to section. The easiest way to do this is to create a master section template from which new master guide specification sections or custom project specifications are developed. The template should follow CSI's SectionFormat® and PageFormat® and contain the standard articles, paragraphs, and statements used most often to make it easy to use consistent language throughout the master guide specification system. Refer to Figure 1.2 for an example of a partial template for a section. Master guide specifications and the master section template should follow the principles of specification language and streamlining for brevity, as discussed in Chapter 15 — Preparing Specifications.

Figure 1.2
Example Partial
Section Template

SECTION [NUMBER]
[SECTION TITLE]

****

SECTION INCLUDES [_____]

EDIT ENTIRE MASTER TO SUIT PROJECT EQUIREMENTS: MODIFY AS NECESSARY. DELETE ITEMS WHICH ARE NOT APPLICABLE.

♣ SYMBOL IN LEFT MARGIN INDICATES ACTION IS REQUIRED: EDIT/SELECT/ADD/DELETE TO SUIT PROJECT REQUIREMENTS. INFORMATION BETWEEN BRACKETS [ ] WILL BE DELETED AUTOMATICALLY UNLESS SPECIFIC INDICATION IS MADE TO RETAIN INFORMATION.

****

PART 1 - GENERAL

1.01 SUMMARY

♣   A.   Section Includes: [_____]

****

EDIT PARAGRAPH BELOW TO SUIT PROJECT REQUIREMENTS: ADD SECTIONS AS APPLICABLE.

****

    B.   Related requirements:
♣   1.   Section [_____] - [_____]
♣   2.   Section [_____] - [_____]

****

RETAIN ARTICLE BELOW IF APPLICABLE.

****

♣ **[1.02 PRICE AND PAYMENT PROCEDURES**
      1.   Allowances: refer to Section 01 21 00 for allowances involving Work of this Section.]

****

ITEMS LISTED UNDER FOLLOWING ARTICLE HAVE BEEN USED WITHIN OTHER PORTIONS OF THIS SECTION. IF PARAGRAPHS CONTAINING THESE REFERENCES ARE DELETED IN PROCESS OF EDITING, DELETE ITEMS HERE ACCORDINGLY.

****

1.03 REFERENCES

    A.   American Society for Testing and Materials International (ASTM)
♣   1.   Section [_____] - [_____]

****

DEPENDING ON SCOPE OF WORK, APREINSTALLATION CONFERENCE MAY NOT BE NECESSARY. RETAIN ARTICLE BELOW AND EDIT ACCORDINGLY.

****

1.04 ADMINISTRATIVE REQUIREMENTS

    A.   Pre-installation Meetings
      1.   Conduct pre-installation meeting in accordance with Section 01 31 19.
♣   2.   Convene pre-installation meeting [one week] [_____] prior to commencing work of this Section [prior to purchasing materials for field sample [mock-up]].

****

INCLUDE SUBMITAL REQUIREMENTS BELOW WHICH ARE CONSISTENT WITH SCOPE OF PROJECT AND EXTENT OF WORK OF THIS SECTION. ONLY REQUEST SUBMITTALS WHICH ARE ABSOLUTELY NECESSARY.

****

1.05 SUBMITTALS

    A.   General: Submit in accordance with Section 01 33 00
    B.   Product Data:

[Project Name/Number/Date]   [Page Number]   [Section Title]

DOMAIN 1
Planning,
Development,
& Organization

DOMAIN 2
Coordination

DOMAIN 3
Procurement,
Contracting,
& General
Requirements

DOMAIN 4
Research

DOMAIN 5
Analysis
& Evaluation

DOMAIN 6
Production

Figure 1.2
Example Partial
Section Template
(continued)

        1. Submit manufacturer's descriptive literature and product **specification** for each product.

♣   2. Include data to indicate [_____]

    C. Shop Drawing:

♣   1. Indicate typical layout including dimensions and
           [_____]

♣   2. Submit detail drawings of [_____]

♣   [3. Submit drawings showing **field** measured dimensions.]

      [4. Submit drawings of special accessory components not included in manufacturers product
        data.]

****

INCLUDE QUALITY ASSURANCE REQUIREMENTS CONSISTENT WITH SIZE AN SCOPE OF PROJECT
AND EXTENT OF WORK OF THIS SECTION. EDIT ARTICLE BELOW ACCORDINGLY.

****

1.06   QUALITY ASSURANCE

♣   A. Manufacturer **Qualifications:** Comany specializing in manufacturing products **specified**
       in this section with minimum [5][____] years [documented] experience.

♣   B. Fabricator Qualidications: Company specializing in fabricating products **specified** in this
       Section with minimum [5][____] years [documented] experience.

    C. [Installer] [Applicator] [Erector] **Qualifications:** Acceptable to manufacturer with
       [docmented] experience on at least [5][____] projects similar scope in past [5][____]
       years.

****

INCLUDE DELIVERY, STORAGE, AND HANDLING REQUIREMENTS CONSISTENT WITH SIZE AND
SCOPE OF PROJECT AND EXTENT OF WORK OF THIS SECTION. EDIT ARTICLE BELOW ACCORDINGLY.

****

1.07   DELIVERY, STORAGE, AND HANDLING

    A. Comply with requirements of Section 01 65 00 and Section 01 66 00.

****

COORDINATE LENGTH OF WARRANTY PERIOD WITH ADJACENT CONSTRUCTION AND OWNER
REQUIREMENTS TO OBTAIN UNIFIED SYSTEM WARRANTY. VERIFY AVAILABLE WARRANTY TIME
PERIODS FROM SPECIFIED MANUFACTURERS. EDIT ARTICLE BELOW TO COMPLY WITH PROJECT
CONDITIONS AND/OR OWNER'S INSTRUCTIONS. IF STATUTORY ONE-YEAR WARRANTY PERIOD IS
SUFFICIENT, DELETE ARTICLE BELOW.

****

1.08   WARRANTY

    A. Comply with provisions of Section 01 78 00.

♣   B. Warrant installed units [_____] to be free from defects in material and
       workmanship for [_____] years.

♣   C. Include coverage for [against][_____].

PART 2 - PRODUCTS

****

EDIT LIST OF MANUFACTURERS BELOW TO SUIT PROJECT REQUIREMENTS.

****

2.01   MANUFACTURERS

    A. Manufacturers' Names: [_____]

***** OR *****

[Project Name/Number/Date]   [Page Number]   [Section Title]

Continued

Figure 1.2
Example Partial
Section Template
(continued)

2.02   MANUFACTURERS AND PRODUCTS

♣   A.   Products and Manufactures: [_____]

****

RETAIN PARAGRAPH BELOW IF SUBSTITUTIONS WILL BE ALLOWED.

****

♣   [B.   Subsitutions: Under provisions of Section 01 25 00.]

****

EDIT DESCRIPTIVE SPECIFICATIONS IN ARTICLE BELOW TO IDENTIFY PROJECT REQUIREMENTS AND
TO ELIMINATE ANY CONFLICT WITH SPECIFIED MANUFACTURER'S PRODUCTS.

****

♣ **2.03   MATERIALS [MANUFACTURED UNITS][EQUIPMENT][COMPONENTS]**

****

SELECT AND SPECIFY/EDIT COLORS AND FINISHES IN ARTICLE BELOW TO SUIT PROJECT
REQUIREMENTS. DELETE INAPPLICABLE ITEMS.

****

♣ **2.04   [FINISHES][SHOP [FACTORY] FINISHING]**

        A.   [_____] Finish: Color and finish as selected by Architect from sample submitted

             [_____].

2.05   ACCESSORIES

        A.   Products and Manufactures: [_____]

PART 3 - EXECUTION

3.01   EXAMINATION

        A.   Examine conditions and proceed with work in accordance with Section 01 71 00.

3.02   PREPARATION

♣ **3.03   ERECTION [INSTALLATION][APPLICATION]**

♣   A.   Install [Erect][Apply][Place] in accordance with manufacturers printed instructions,
             [State[Municipality] of [_____] standards].

♣   B.   Install unit [___] _ plumb, level, square and free from warp or twist while maintaining
             dimensional tolerances and alignment with surrounding construction [adjacent
             surfaces].

3.04   FIELD QUALITY CONTROL

        A.   General: Comply with requirements of Section 01 45 13.

♣   B.   Tests: [_____].

♣   C.   Inspections: [_____].

3.05   ADJUSTING

        A.   Adjust parts for smooth, uniform operation.

3.06   CLEANING

♣   A.   Clean as recommended by manufacturer. Do not use materials or methods which may
             damage finish [surface] or surrounding construction.

END OF SECTION

DOMAIN 1
Planning,
Development,
& Organization

DOMAIN 2
Coordination

DOMAIN 3
Procurement,
Contracting,
& General
Requirements

DOMAIN 4
Research

DOMAIN 5
Analysis
& Evaluation

DOMAIN 6
Production

1.3.7 Preparing Master Guide Specification Sections

A master guide specification section should cover the items, products, materials, methods, and alternatives that an A/E encounters most frequently. Also, each section should conform to standard terminology, the designation of options, and appropriate workmanship. The procedures followed for developing a master guide specification section are similar to those discussed earlier for writing specification sections.

The basic steps in preparing a master guide specification section are as follows:

1. Assemble and review resource material from available sources.

2. Determine the specification information necessary for the section. This determination depends on the type and size of projects anticipated. Judgment and experience must be exercised to prepare master guide specifications adaptable to the various projects and types of construction contracts involved.

3. Confirm that the information designated for the individual section is appropriate and manageable. If the information options are too complicated or the scope too broad, consider subdividing the section into two or more narrower scope sections. Conversely, straightforward and uncomplicated information from several related sections may be combined into a single broader scope section.

4. Place information in the section per the three-part SectionFormat®. A skillfully arranged master guide specification should be relatively easy to read and use.

5. Ensure that each article in the three-part SectionFormat® is restricted to a single topic; strict conformance to this principle makes the section easier to read and use.

6. Arrange choices so decisions can be made logically with no time wasted in editing. Each option must be arranged to be identified, easily referenced, modified, or deleted without disturbing other text. Consistent sequencing also enables quicker scanning by readers.

7. Determine the method of handling and identifying optional requirements for each choice. Where numerous options could exist, blank spaces may be provided for information to be inserted. The two main alternatives for multiple-choice options are using brackets or using alternative paragraphs. The decision for handling options usually hinges on how easy it is to read and understand the options, plus the specification software or system being used. For instance, mutually exclusive options in individual paragraphs can be more quickly edited by deletion than can options embedded with brackets. However, a word processing macro may make the in-line bracketed options just as easy and quick to edit. The A/E should carefully study how choices are presented in the master guide specification. The information storage and retrieval system used affects how choices are made available for evaluation and selection or rejection for inclusion in a project specification. Some choices, such as those required by reference standards or brand-name products listed, may be adopted as permanent decisions. Each of these decisions should be listed separately, identified as such, and reviewed periodically to ensure that the decision is still appropriate.

8. Physically arrange the presentation of the specification text according to CSI's PageFormat® (see Appendix E).

9. Include notes and instructions to assist the persons editing the section. This information should be distinguishable from the specification text, so the two are not confused. This type of information may be labeled as "Editing Notes" or set apart from specification text by some notation, such as indentation, separation, a text box or a line of asterisks above and below the note, a font change, hidden text, or a combination of several schemes. Specification notes affecting an entire article usually are located immediately after the article title and before the affected text. Notes affecting individual paragraphs should generally appear just before the affected paragraph. Notes are used to:

   • Provide a brief overview of the content.

   • Bring options to the attention of the A/E.

- Identify needed selections and options.

- Provide supplementary information to aid in decision-making. This aid could include commentary on reference standards and options within those standards.

- Point out coordination and cross-reference requirements.

- Match the wording and terminology used on the drawings.

Some options needed in project specifications should not be included in the master guide specifications. Either there are too many options to consider (e.g., color, pattern, and texture), or they are project-specific (e.g., engineering design data). Additionally, other information essential to proper specifying never appears in the project specifications and therefore is never included in the master text. This information notably includes detailed cost information and the actual text of trade association and other referenced standards. The master guide specification system must allow for efficient retrieval of all these external information types for specific projects, such as hyperlinks embedded in the master guide specification, either in the text or in the notes.

1.3.8 Commercially Available Master Guide Specifications

There are currently several producers of full-length commercially available master guide specifications based on US products and standards; these include the following:

- American Institute of Architects (AIA)/ Deltek MasterSpec

- Deltek SpecText

- Building Systems Design (BSD) SpecLink

Most commercial master specifications are based on MasterFormat® section numbers and titles. These products are available on a subscription basis and can vary significantly from one another in organization, extent, flexibility, language style, history, and automation features. These master specification systems generally operate using a proprietary software application for individual computers, office network, or internet cloud-based systems. The successful use of a commercial master guide

specification by an A/E depends mainly on how well it matches the firm's needs and preferences.

A commercial master guide specification is designed to accommodate various construction types, geographic locations, code jurisdictions, and client types. Some provisions may be too restrictive or costly for typical firm applications and should be excluded. The inclusion of inapplicable provisions often results in increased cost simply because the specified content is not typical for the project site and customary practice. Failure to omit or edit such provisions could result in unnecessary increases in construction time and cost. If entire specification sections or significant portions of a section are not expected to be used, then they should be omitted when the master is adapted for the firm. Further, sections not relevant to the standard work of the firm can be eliminated. When portions are removed, the excluded portions should be clearly identified and remain available for future use if appropriate. For this reason, content should not be permanently deleted.

1.3.9 Updating Master Guide Specification Sections

Updating is a crucial aspect affecting the effectiveness of a master guide specification. Out-of-date information can cause construction and liability problems, which, in turn, cost time and money. Master guide specifications should be updated on a regular schedule following an established policy. The commercially available master guide specifications previously listed are updated for differing reasons. However, updates are typically on a predefined schedule and as needed when problems are identified or when a significant change has occurred concerning the information contained in a given section. Subscribers to commercial specifications should update their master guide specification sections as the revised material is received.

The process of updating master guide specifications should include the following:

- Revising text that has caused problems on a previous project (An investigation should be taken to determine if the problems were project-specific or representative of a more considerable, industry-wide change.)

Construction
Specifications
Practice Guide

DOMAIN 1
Planning,
Development,
& Organization

DOMAIN 2
Coordination

DOMAIN 3
Procurement,
Contracting,
& General
Requirements

DOMAIN 4
Research

DOMAIN 5
Analysis
& Evaluation

DOMAIN 6
Production

- Changing text and designations to reflect current referenced standards

- Reviewing choices that have been adopted as permanent

- Reviewing the continuing appropriateness of proprietary, descriptive, and performance-specifying methods and changing to other methods if necessary

- Adding new sections

- Inserting additional options and choices in specification clauses

- Eliminating typographical and other errors

- Updating terminology to be consistent with the CSI formats and office practice

1.3.10 Shortform Master Guide Specifications

Shortform master guide specifications are commercially available or created by the A/E from a traditional full-length master guide specification (refer to Chapter 12—Outline and Shortform Specifications for detailed information about shortform specifications). A separate shortform master guide specification may be prepared for each project type commonly designed, such as residential, light commercial, or tenant improvement. The resulting shortform master guide specification can then be efficiently edited to create the project specification. A shortform specification may be created by other methods, such as expanding a project description, editing an existing specification, developing a section from industry reference standards, or writing a section from scratch. However, it is recommended that shortform specifications should be developed from a master guide specification.

1.3.11 Additional Considerations

Master guide specifications have improved significantly over the past several years. These improvements include an expanded number of available sections and sophisticated technology to edit them. However, with these improvements come other issues that users need to consider when integrating them into the design practice.

1.3.11.1 Electronic Technology

Current technology can provide further enhancements for master guide specifications. The use of various types of software and features can provide improved efficiencies and productivity. Such software may involve word processing, spreadsheets, databases, computer-aided design (CAD), building information modeling (BIM), and cloud-based technology. Features may include the following:

- Notes and instructions that do not require deletion and are maintained as hidden text or tags that do not print (except when desired)

- The ability to track or record changes, such as insertions and deletions

- Incorporation of web-based hyperlinks to additional data or resources, such as manufacturer or reference standard websites

- Inclusion of embedded objects such as charts, photos, and graphic images

- Shared linkages to other software for CAD, BIM, cost estimating, and scheduling

- Dynamic changes between files, such as needed data, cross-referencing, and compilation of listings

- Publishing to a neutral format, such as portable document format (PDF) or other formats for internet-based posting, increasing accessibility and usability

- Security features to prevent modification of contract documents by anyone other than those expressly designated

1.3.11.2 Additional Information

A master guide specification, in itself, is not a complete system. The question of how much additional information is needed depends, in part, on how comprehensive the master guide specification is intended to be. The master guide specification user still needs to refer to product data, project-specific design information, building codes, and referenced standards.

1.3.11.3 Sections on Demand

Usually, each master guide specification section used on a project is copied to be edited, thus leaving the master guide specification section intact for others to copy and use. Current files should be readily available in a central location. For example, files are usually stored electronically in a cloud-based system or on an office server.

For cloud-based master specification systems, the software typically does not allow editing of the master guide specification sections; therefore, specifiers select sections needed for a project, and copies are automatically added to a project file. Most cloud-based systems allow the creation of office masters from the cloud-based sections, and users can select using either the office master or the master guide specifications. Some design offices may restrict users to using only the office masters. Office masters created using the cloud-based master specifications can also be given restricted access so only those authorized can make revisions to the office masters.

1.3.11.4 Review Before Distribution

Final project specifications culminate in the distribution of procurement documents for most project delivery methods. Before distribution, reviewing the project specifications by comparing the project section text to the master section text or tracking changes made to the master specification text can ensure that all applicable content is retained and unnecessary content is deleted. Copies of project specification files should also be published in a secure medium and shared among team members by distributing within a computer network, posting to a project website, or shared via a web-based collaboration application. National and international companies and government agencies usually have specific policies and procedures relative to their expected regional and local office practice.

**DOMAIN 2:
COORDINATION**

Chapter 2

PROJECT MANUAL
COORDINATION

2.1 Coordination Overview

Successful performance of a construction project requires fulfilling the stakeholders' needs and expectations. Implementing a coordination process is an efficient solution to avoiding weak performance in a construction project. Each project team member has a role in ensuring the successful completion of a project at all project stages.

In the past 50 years, the construction industry has changed tremendously in terms of the size and complexity of construction projects. Currently, many construction projects have an intricate design of electrical and mechanical installations, employ sophisticated structural systems, and serve the diversified requirements of different end-users. The project complexity is a result of industry fragmentation, which requires effective coordination between the project parties. Additionally, construction projects are unique and involve a myriad of interrelated activities and work packages. Project parties deal with large amounts of information derived from various stakeholders, such as owners, designers, contractors, subcontractors, suppliers, banks, and governmental units. Thus, accessing the required information at the right time and location is rather difficult in such circumstances. Therefore, construction projects have commonly suffered from low quality, reduced productivity, and overruns in cost and time.

The coordination process must be applied as an essential function in project management to efficiently oversee a building project. The purpose of the coordination process is to add value to project delivery and to improve efficiency by dealing with the dependencies between project tasks and parties; in other words, "managing dependencies between activities."

2.2 Coordination of the Construction Documents

The ultimate responsibility for coordinating the construction documents should be with the

DOMAIN 1
Planning,
Development,
& Organization

DOMAIN 2
Coordination

DOMAIN 3
Procurement,
Contracting,
& General
Requirements

DOMAIN 4
Research

DOMAIN 5
Analysis
& Evaluation

DOMAIN 6
Production

architect/engineer's (A/E's) project manager; however, the project manager may assign the coordination responsibility to another design team member. The designated coordinator should review the consistency between the drawings and the project manual. Good coordination policies, including establishing effective intra-office and inter-team communication procedures, are essential. In preparing drawings and the project manual, the specifier and project A/E should work together, keeping in mind the difficulties faced by estimators, bidders, contractors, inspectors, and product representatives.

As the project design stage begins, a meeting should be held to address the project's coordination procedures. This meeting should include the A/E, consultants, computer-aided drafting (CAD) or building information modeling (BIM) drafters, and the specifier. A preliminary project description or outline specifications should be developed as a checklist, and additional meetings should be held as the design progresses.

Project manual preparation should proceed concurrently with design, and coordination should become a continuous process from the beginning of the project.

2.2.1 Project Coordination Checklists

The designated coordinator should use standard office checklists to ensure that necessary items are included in the construction documents and that specified items are consistent with the drawings and do not duplicate the specifications. The location of some scheduled items (e.g., lists of equipment, finishes, toilet accessories) may vary according to the project's size and can be published either in the drawings or the project manual. Checklists are recommended to ensure that necessary items are included in the specifications, that specified items are consistent with the drawings, and that drawings do not duplicate the specifications.

A checklist format varies depending on its purpose. Some project management software may include standardized checklists that can be adapted for each office.

A coordination checklist designed to avoid omissions in the identification of essential items noted in the drawings might have lists of materials, systems, and products by specification section. Checkmarks may be used to indicate inclusion in the design, and space should be provided for notes regarding coordination with other work and other items requiring special attention. MasterFormat® provides a sound basis for establishing a practical coordination checklist.

Specialized forms may be used to address specific office problems, such as omissions, discrepancies, or duplications. For example, rather than put overly specific or detailed notes on a drawing, designers can keep a list of catalog references used in preparing details of particular products and equipment. These lists should be communicated to the specifier using an outline organized by the project manual table of contents that the specifier can later consult when preparing each specification section.

2.2.2 Other Coordination Tools and Methods

BIM coordination applications identify clashes and how to avoid them. Clashes can be filtered by the model, discipline, or user. Collaborating with other design team members using this clash technology minimizes time-consuming meetings and costly construction changes in the field.

Cost management allows the review of potential change items and establishes control thresholds. For instance, if the project is behind schedule, cost management includes determining the amount of budget variance to get back on track and the corrective actions required. The cost management function is typically conducted by the owner's internal project management team or a hired project management firm. Cost management includes the processes required to maintain financial control of projects, including the economic evaluation that initiates the project, estimating, organizing, controlling, analyzing, reporting, forecasting, and taking the necessary corrective action. The cost management function maintains its important focus at every stage throughout the life cycle of a project and involves all project team roles. In listing the reasons for a project's success, cost management is the most important, as all project aspects affect this function. What counts for the owner is the "bottom line."

2.2.3 Preliminary Coordination

Construction documents are generally reviewed at set milestones such as Schematic Design, Design Development, and Construction Documents at the 50 percent and 90 percent completion stages. Drafts of interim specification sections and copies of interim drawings from consultants should be collected, published, and reviewed to coordinate information. This effort should involve coordinating the following information:

- Within the project manual
- Within the drawings of each separate discipline
- Between the drawings of separate disciplines
- Within the specifications of each separate discipline
- Between the specifications of separate disciplines
- Between the project manual and drawings

Consultants should review the drawings and specifications of other disciplines and forward corrections and comments to the A/E for communication to the other project team members.

In addition to obvious graphical, dimensional, and typographical errors, documents should be carefully checked and compared to eliminate the following:

- Omissions
- Overlaps and duplications between disciplines
- Noncompliance with laws and regulations
- Conflicts and discrepancies with locations of equipment and components
- Incompatible materials and components
- Difficult or impossible construction methods
- Inconsistent terminology and abbreviations
- Inconsistent units of measure
- Incorrect or unspecified materials, components, or equipment
- Errors in the extent of alternates
- Errors in defining areas of construction phasing
- Errors in defining limits of work
- Errors in identifying work by the owner or work that is not in the contract
- Errors in designating work of separate contracts or packages
- Inaccurate or unnecessary cross-referencing

Construction
Specifications
Practice Guide

DOMAIN 1
Planning,
Development,
& Organization

DOMAIN 2
Coordination

DOMAIN 3
Procurement,
Contracting,
& General
Requirements

DOMAIN 4
Research

DOMAIN 5
Analysis
& Evaluation

DOMAIN 6
Production

Checking construction documents is not the same as coordinating the separate portions. A drawing may be found correct unto itself but inconsistent with other parts of the construction documents. Particular attention should be given to coordinating Division 01 sections with the conditions of the contract. The level of specification detail should complement the level of drawing detail. Early coordination with sufficient time devoted to the task helps achieve design intent and eliminate problems during the construction stage.

2.2.4 Final Coordination

Final construction documents should receive final coordinating and checking before issuance. Final coordination should include the following:

- Verifying all previously noted inconsistencies, errors, and inaccuracies have been corrected

- Verifying the construction documents are complete, with a final check of the project manual table of contents and drawing table of contents

- Verifying consistency of all schedules

2.2.5 Terminology and Abbreviations

Use consistent terminology and abbreviations throughout the construction documents to avoid confusion among the various users. The "service sink" in the specifications should not become the "janitor's sink" on the drawings, nor should "bituminous surface course" become "asphalt topping."

The use of inconsistent terminology and abbreviations may create confusion in preparing specifications. It can quickly raise construction costs, cause delays, and may even result in faulty construction.

The A/E should take responsibility for enforcing consistent terminology and abbreviations. Inconsistent and inappropriate terminology is perpetuated by such poor practices as the indiscriminate reuse of detailed drawings and poorly edited specifications from previous projects.

2.2.6 Precedence

Questions of precedence often arise between drawings and specifications. However, the use of statements in the project manual to establish the various contract documents' precedence is not recommended because they are complementary. The conditions of the contract should only state that in a case of conflict between drawings and specifications, the A/E makes a documented interpretation. If necessary, for bidding purposes only, a precedence listing may be prepared.

2.3 Preliminary Review and Coordination of the Project Manual

Office quality control/quality assurance procedures will most typically mandate document review at specific stages of document development. Submitting preliminary documents (schematic design, design development, and 60 percent construction documents are typical stages) provides draft sections for review and coordination with the entire team. If using cloud-based project specifications, this review can be ongoing. Copies of edited sections should be reviewed by design team members familiar with the design and drawing details to identify errors, oversights, and new or changed decisions. Draft specification sections from consultants should be collected and reviewed to coordinate the entire project manual.

Sections should be checked and compared to eliminate omissions, overlaps, duplications, and inaccurate cross-referencing. Division 01 sections should be provided for owner review and coordinated with their requirements. If the owner is providing Division 01, the A/E should prepare additional sections as necessary to perform the A/E's contractual responsibilities. Coordinate these documents with applicable specification sections, alternates, allowances, and unit prices related to the bid/proposal form. Cross-reference these to the instructions for procurement.

The phased review of the project manual should also include coordination with the drawings. Consistent terminology, elimination of duplicate information, the inclusion of all products, and other concerns should be checked. If the specifier discovers errors or omissions in the drawings, comments should be referenced to the drawings for corrections.

2.4 Project Manual Coordination within the Project Team

Taking the right initiatives at the right time is paramount. It is always essential to gather project requirements at the earliest possible time, analyze them, and resolve conflicts. Communicating with the project team effectively and in a timely manner ensures that the project manual can also be developed effectively, efficiently, and timely.

By planning and setting goals, maintaining a set of the latest documents, and obtaining approvals from applicable stakeholders, the specifier can ensure that the project manual addresses all project requirements. Communication is the most crucial task in coordinating the project manual. At the beginning of the project, a well-informed project team makes the specifier's direct specifying activities easier to perform later on and ensures that the project manual is done on time.

2.4.1 A/E Coordination

The prime A/E on a project may use a specifier within the firm or an independent specifier to prepare the project manual. In either case, the specifier must work with the prime A/E's design team to ensure the design's quality is adequately covered in the specifications. This effort may require regular reviews with the design team to discuss the project manual preparation, such as checking on the status of product decisions, reviewing details of product decisions, and coordinating the terminology used on the drawing and in the specifications, to name a few.

Cloud-based collaboration tools that allow the design team to access project specifications as they are being developed ensure timely and accurate feedback for the specifier, which minimizes time-consuming meetings to review the specifications section by section.

It is essential to establish a method of communicating specification-related information between the design team and the specifier. One method is to create a protocol that all product information relayed to the specifier comes from a specific individual or individuals, such as the project manager, project A/E, or both. Cloud-based collaboration tools, where conveyed information is visible to all team members, allow conflicts to be identified and corrected.

2.4.2 Consultant Coordination

Consultants may write some sections of the project manual. This is often the case for the mechanical, electrical, structural, landscape architect, and civil engineering sections because these disciplines may have different professional requirements for sealing their documents. Other sections may also be written by specialists, such as sections for roofing and waterproofing, door hardware, commercial kitchen (food service) equipment, theatre equipment, pool and water features, acoustics, vertical transportation, materials handling, laboratory equipment, and lighting. Such situations require special coordination among team members to ensure that the specifications are complete, compatible, consistent, and without duplications or omissions.

The prime A/E should assume responsibility for the overall coordination of the specifications. Information regarding the type of project, contract, specifications formats, general conditions, and especially Division 01 requirements should be made available to consultants before they prepare any sections. Input from them for Division 01 sections should be requested at the same time. The consultants must resist listing general notes on their drawings regarding administrative matters and terms and conditions more appropriate for Division 01 and other contract documents. In this manner, the consultants can avoid writing separate general requirements for their disciplines, reducing the likelihood of conflicting requirements. Coordination with sustainability consultants may cross all disciplines and should be coordinated by the prime A/E.

DOMAIN 1
Planning,
Development,
& Organization

DOMAIN 2
Coordination

DOMAIN 3
Procurement,
Contracting,
& General
Requirements

DOMAIN 4
Research

DOMAIN 5
Analysis
& Evaluation

DOMAIN 6
Production

2.4.3 Owner Coordination

Verify if the owner already has a contract with a selected contractor and ask to review both the contract and any conditions of the contract. Also verify if the contractor or owner is preparing the procurement requirements. It may be necessary to revise some Division 01 sections to conform to the requirements in these documents.

Even though the owner may use standard agreement forms published by professional societies and other organizations, the A/E should avoid including the agreement form by reference only. It is more appropriate to include the actual agreement forms in the project manual. The possibility of referencing an incorrect or out-of-date form is also eliminated if the forms are bound into the project manual.

Owners are typically responsible for providing a geotechnical report for the project's location. This information is essential for the A/E, its consultants, and the contractor, and should be included or referenced in Division 00 of the project manual as Available Project Information.

In addition to the A/E's consultants, the owner may have consultants of their own for the project. Examples of consultants regularly hired by owners include commissioning agents, security advisers, and construction managers (i.e., CM as advisor; see Section 10.4). Sometimes the owner's consultants have responsibilities that involve interaction with the contractor during construction. In that case, the project specifications should address the contractor's responsibilities in working with the owner's consultants.

Some owners may have developed a design manual that covers many specification-related items. The requirements in these design manuals might be performance-based or prescriptive. Some may even be structured using UniFormat® or MasterFormat® to ease the process of finding specific requirements. The owner may have a process for approving materials and products that are not directly prescribed, which must be followed to prevent costly problems later.

2.4.4 Contractor Coordination

For traditional construction projects, the owner selects consultants to design the project.

A contractor is then selected to execute the construction; this is typical of the design-bid-build project delivery method. Early contractor involvement, such as that provided by the construction manager at risk (CMAR) and integrated project delivery (IPD) project delivery methods, utilizes the contractor's skills early in project design to bring constructability and cost efficiencies to the design phase.

If the project involves the contractor in the early stages of design, the contractor should be included in the project manual coordinating group. If multiple work packages are used for a fast-track project, then it would be prudent to work with the contractor to determine how the project manual might be best issued. In some cases, subcontractors may be included in a design-assist role to offer the design team their expertise in a particular design element. For example, a curtain wall installer may provide calculations to determine framing and glazing sizes, installation details, and specification information to help develop the construction documents.

2.4.5 Product Representative Coordination

In most situations, the use of a specific type of product or assembly is necessary. Product representatives are a source of information that assists in preparing the project manual relative to the products they represent. During design, coordination with a product representative provides valuable assistance to the design team in identifying cost savings in design and construction. They do this by soliciting or proposing alternative design or construction technology to reduce costs without sacrificing quality or performance.

Product representatives can review draft specification sections for their products to ensure all necessary components are specified. They may also help identify comparable products from their competitors to ensure equitable specification sections are prepared. When product representatives provide their assistance to the design team on a particular product, the product is often included in the specifications as a *basis-of-design product*. If used, a definition for basis-of-design products should be included in Division 01 and how comparable products, if permitted, would be accepted.

2.5 Coordination of the Specifications

Regular reviews of the specifications by the project staff endeavor to provide ongoing coordination between the specifications and the drawings. Sharing design and product decisions with project team members must begin at the earliest phases of the project. The A/E should assume the responsibility for coordinating the flow and documentation of project information.

Design changes, errors, and omissions as a group are the primary cause of rework in construction. Identifying strategic activities and potential delays, (while ensuring all work timeliness), is the most important coordination step in construction.

Specifications complement, but should not repeat, the information shown on the drawings, nor should the drawings duplicate information in the specifications. If a requirement on the drawings or specifications is duplicated, an opportunity arises for discrepancies between them. An addendum covering a design change may correct the item in one location but potentially overlook it in the other. Last-minute changes are most likely to create discrepancies of this sort. Such discrepancies may cause bidders/proposers to make different interpretations of the requirements, often resulting in change orders and extra costs. Properly prepared drawings and specifications should dovetail like a jigsaw puzzle, without overlaps or gaps.

To facilitate coordination, especially on complex projects with many different materials, components, and trades, design teams should adhere to the Construction Specifications Institute (CSI) principle established for locating information properly within the contract documents using CSI formats, often referred to as "say it once and in the right place."

For projects issued in multiple packages, coordination between packages is critical to the execution of the project. Modifications issued in early packages must be incorporated into later packages. If a change occurs in a later package, it must be *back-coordinated* with earlier packages for consistent documentation.

2.5.1 Product and Material Coordination

The specifier should be the default coordinator of products and materials. This role does not mean the specifier is the sole decision-maker on which products are specified or not. The specifier is the last line of defense to ensure products and materials are being used as intended and are compatible with adjacent products and materials.

Although specifiers might be included with the design team to make the day-to-day product decisions, the specifier is often given the products and materials to specify after designers selected them. However, there may be situations where one design team member selected one product that may not have been coordinated with another product selected by another design team member, and the two products interface with each other in the building. There may be no problem with this situation. But if these two products are not compatible and that is not discovered before construction, then a latent defect could be integrated into the building. For example, a self-adhering air barrier required to tie into a polyvinyl chloride (PVC) roofing membrane may have an acrylic pressure-sensitive adhesive that does not maintain a bond with the PVC roof membrane and may likely fail over time.

Another type of product and material coordination involves selecting products approved as part of a tested assembly or required to comply with a prescriptive code requirement. For example, fire-resistance-rated wall construction relies on tested assemblies consisting of specifically listed products and materials. Deviations from the approved product and material lists are generally not permitted. Therefore, the specifier should ensure the products requested coordinate with the indicated tested assemblies.

2.5.2 Alternates Coordination

Many projects include alternates to maximize the owner's construction budget or ensure that an acceptable bid/proposal is received within its budget. Alternates provide challenges since they may include products and materials not already specified for use as base bid products and materials. In these cases,

the specifier must prepare sections for products and materials that may never be accepted for the project.

Alternates need to be coordinated with Section 01 23 00 — Alternates, which lists all alternates proposed for a project. The list of alternates should clearly describe for each alternate what the base bid includes and what the alternate includes. Further, these descriptions should reference applicable specifications and drawings relevant to the base bid and each alternate. Each specification section affected by an alternate should include a paragraph

stating such and reference Section 01 23 00. This coordination should be done for all sections affected by alternates, including those prepared by consultants.

Finally, each alternate should be identified by a designation (e.g., Alternate No. 1) and a title (e.g., Shell Space Lobby Finishes). These designations and titles (and what they include) should be distributed to all design team members to ensure that references to alternates in the construction documents are consistent.

DOMAIN 3:
PROCUREMENT, CONTRACTING,
& GENERAL REQUIREMENTS

Chapter 3

GENERAL
REQUIREMENTS

3.1 Division 01 — General Requirements

The sections in Division 01, which are collectively referred to as the General Requirements, specify administrative requirements, procedural requirements, temporary facilities and controls, performance requirements, and life cycle activities. Administrative and procedural requirements are related to the process of contract administration and the assignment of contractual responsibilities, including submittal procedures and the methods of communicating, controlling, and assuring quality. Temporary facilities and controls are put into place for use by the contractor only during the construction period and are removed when no longer required for construction operations. Performance requirements are related to facility and system performance. Life cycle activities are related to commissioning, facility operation, facility maintenance, and facility decommissioning.

Division 01 sections expand on specific administrative and procedural provisions in the conditions of the contract and apply broadly to work specified in other sections of the specifications. Administrative and procedural requirements unique to a specific section should be covered in the affected section. Division 01 sections cover general requirements for the work execution and should be written in language broad enough to apply to sections in Divisions 02 through 49. Without Division 01, these requirements would need to be repeated throughout the specifications, increasing the possibility of conflicts and omissions. This Division 01 concept adheres to the Construction Specifications Institute (CSI) principle of stating information only once and in the right place. Figure 3.1 illustrates the relationships between Division 01 and each of the other construction documents.

3.2 Organizational Basis for Division 01

The administrative sections of Division 01 parallel the succession of titles in MasterFormat® and the procedural sequence of PART 1, PART 2, and PART 3 in SectionFormat® to lay out a consistent and logical organization of titles.

DOMAIN 1
Planning,
Development,
& Organization

DOMAIN 2
Coordination

DOMAIN 3
Procurement,
Contracting,
& General
Requirements

DOMAIN 4
Research

DOMAIN 5
Analysis
& Evaluation

DOMAIN 6
Production

Figure 3.1
Division 01
Relationship to
Other Documents

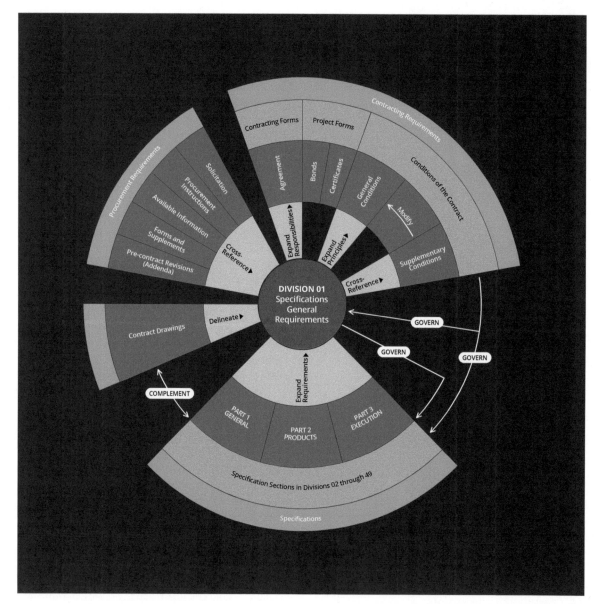

3.2.1 Division 01 and MasterFormat®

MasterFormat® provides the section numbers and titles for Division 01. When applying MasterFormat® to Division 01, consider the following:

- Some numbers and titles in MasterFormat® may never appear in a project manual for a construction project, such as Section 01 93 00 — Facility Maintenance.

- Some numbers and titles in MasterFormat® have particular relevance to project manuals because they deal specifically with construction activities. Two examples of this are Section 01 14 00 — Work Restrictions and Section 01 50 00 — Temporary Facilities and Controls.

- Because construction specifications are created for the construction stage of a facility's life cycle, some numbers and titles in MasterFormat® would be more likely to appear in a stage other than construction, such as facility management.

3.2.2 Division 01 and SectionFormat®

Division 01 specifies procedural requirements common to many specification sections and the project as a whole. Most of these requirements are related to the project's administrative activities, while others govern products and execution requirements. Accordingly, the numbers and titles of Division 01 in MasterFormat® have been arranged to approximate the sequence of information in SectionFormat®.

The following Division 01 sections align with PART 1 — GENERAL:

- Summary
- Price and Payment Procedures
- Administrative Requirements
- Quality Assurance
- Temporary Facilities and Controls

The following Division 01 sections align with PART 2 — PRODUCTS:

- Product Requirements
- Performance Requirements
- Quality Control (Source)

The following Division 01 sections align with PART 3 — EXECUTION:

- Quality Control (Field)
- Execution and Closeout Requirements
- Life Cycle Activities

The relationship between Division 01 and SectionFormat® defines an organizing principle. This organization's logic provides flexibility by combining procedural requirements into a few sections or dividing them into many as dictated by the project's complexity.

3.3 Division 01 Relation to Other Documents

Each of the contract documents complements one another and should not duplicate specific information. The provisions of the conditions of the contract and the agreement apply broadly to the work of the project, and Division 01 expands on these provisions, giving just enough detail to apply broadly to the other specification sections. The specifications and drawings further expand on Division 01 and provide detailed requirements for specific portions of the work.

DOMAIN 1
Planning,
Development,
& Organization

DOMAIN 2
Coordination

DOMAIN 3
Procurement,
Contracting,
& General
Requirements

DOMAIN 4
Research

DOMAIN 5
Analysis
& Evaluation

DOMAIN 6
Production

There is often confusion among owners and architects/engineers (A/Es) regarding who is responsible for preparing Division 00 documents and Division 01 sections. Often, non-practitioners in writing specifications characterize these non-technical divisions as "front end" documents; this term should be avoided in favor of faithful adherence to "Division 00" and "Division 01." Under no circumstances should the specifier begin preparing Division 00 documents or Division 01 sections without careful review of the construction contract's proposed owner-provided conditions of the contract and owner-contractor agreement.

3.3.1 Procurement Requirements

By definition, in the American Institute of Architects' (AIA), Engineers Joint Contract Documents Committee's (EJCDC), and ConsensusDocs Coalition's general conditions, procurement requirements are not a part of the contract documents. Provisions that are stated only in procurement requirements are not enforceable during the administration of the construction contract.

The procurement requirements should not repeat Division 01 provisions but should instead refer to the appropriate Division 01 sections, by number and title, to direct the bidder/proposer to relevant information.

Provisions applicable only during the procurement stage — such as document acquisition and cost, bid security requirements, and bid opening dates — should be stated in the procurement requirements rather than in Division 01.

3.3.2 Owner-Contractor Agreement

The owner-contractor agreement includes by reference all other contract documents. Some provisions of the owner-contractor agreement are supplemented by the provisions of Division 01 sections that define the parties' responsibilities in greater detail.

For example, Section 01 10 00 — Summary specifies administrative details and the responsibilities of the owner and the contractor, including a summary of the work, identification of other contracts, work restrictions such as limitations on access and use of the site, and the need to accommodate the owner's occupancy during construction.

Similarly, Section 01 20 00 — Price and Payment Procedures expands on the related provisions stated in the agreement, such as allowances, alternates, and unit prices.

3.3.3 General Conditions

The contract's general conditions govern the work's execution and apply broadly to all sections of the specifications, including those in Division 01. The topics usually covered are property surveys, temporary utilities and services, warranties, progress schedules, record documents, submittals, cutting and patching, cleaning, schedule of values, applications for payment, and closeout procedures. As these topics are covered only in very broad terms, they must be specified in further detail in Division 01 to tailor requirements to a specific project. Although the topics are addressed in two locations, the Construction Specifications Institute's (CSI's) principle of "say it once and in the right place" is not violated because the requirements are stated in two different levels of detail, without duplication or conflict.

For example, the general conditions broadly state that the owner may employ separate contractors and provide coordination. If separate contractors are employed, Division 01 could specify this in Section 01 12 00 — Multiple Contract Summary and further identify the contracts, the scope of work in each, and the responsibilities of the owner, the A/E, and each contractor in the coordination process.

3.3.4 Supplementary Conditions

Supplementary conditions should not repeat information in the General Conditions or encroach on topics that belong more appropriately in Division 01. Proper coordination between Division 01 and supplementary conditions avoids conflicts, omissions, and duplications.

Other than a statement establishing the authority of Division 01, the supplementary conditions should not contain general references to Division 01. Statements in the supplementary conditions referring to specific sections in Division 01 are unnecessary but may help the user.

For example, a statement may be added to the supplementary conditions stating that shop drawings, product data, samples, and other submittals shall be prepared and submitted according to the requirements of specification Section 01 33 00 — Submittal Procedures.

3.3.5 Other Specification Sections

Specification sections are subject to the administrative and procedural requirements of the conditions of the contract and Division 01. Project requirements become more specific for each successive level of a three-tier hierarchy:

- The general conditions state provisions in broad terms.

- Division 01 — General Requirements elaborate on the broad provisions of the conditions of the contract, but it is still written broadly enough to apply to the work of all specification sections.

- PART 1 — GENERAL in a specification section becomes very specific in project requirements for that section only.

Refer to Figure 3.2 for illustration of this hierarchy. For example, the general conditions establish the fact that testing may be required. Division 01 specifies the broad administrative and procedural requirements for testing laboratory services such as who selects the laboratory, who pays for which services, qualifications of the testing laboratory, submittal of reports, and the contractor's responsibilities for cooperation. The individual specification sections state further requirements of particular tests to be performed, the number of tests required, and other details applicable only to the work or products in that section. As another example, although routine submittal procedures are covered in Division 01, the specific items for which shop drawings or samples must be submitted are unique to individual specification sections, and specific requirements must be identified in those sections. Figure 3.3 gives examples of the levels of detail of general

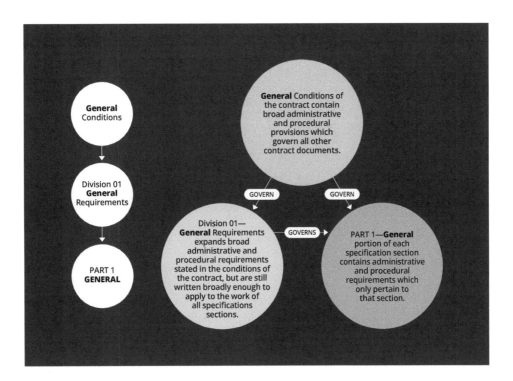

Figure 3.2
Hierarchy of General Administrative and Procedural Requirements

DOMAIN 1
Planning,
Development,
& Organization

DOMAIN 2
Coordination

DOMAIN 3
Procurement,
Contracting,
& General
Requirements

DOMAIN 4
Research

DOMAIN 5
Analysis
& Evaluation

DOMAIN 6
Production

Figure 3.3
Comparison
of the Level of
Detail between
AIA Document
A201®, Division
01 Sections, and
Related Technical
Sections

AIA DOCUMENT A201, GENERAL CONDITIONS OF THE CONTRACT FOR CONSTRUCTION

3.12 SHOP DRAWINGS, PRODUCT DATA AND SAMPLES

3.12.1 Shop Drawings are drawings, diagrams, schedules and other data specially prepared for the Work by the Contractor or a Subcontractor, Sub-subcontractor, manufacturer, supplier or distributor to illustrate some portion of the Work.

3.12.2 Product Data are illustrations, standard schedules, performance charts, instructions, brochures, diagrams and other information furnished by the Contractor to illustrate materials or equipment for some portion of the Work. materials or equipment for some portion of the Work.

3.12.3 Sample are physical examples that illustrate materials, equipment or workmanship and establish standards by which the Work will be judged.

3.12.4 Shop Drawings, Product Data, Samples and similar submittals are not Contract Documents. Their purpose is to demonstrate the way by which the Contractor proposes to conform to the information given and the design concept expressed in the Contract Documents for those portions of the Work for which the Contract Documents require submittals. Review by the Architect is subject to the limitations of Section 4.2.7. Informational submittals upon which the Architect is not expected to take responsive which the Architect is not expected to take responsive action may be so identified in the Contract Documents. Submittals that are not required by the Contract Documents may be returned by the Architect without action.

3.123 The Contractor shall review for compliance with the Contract Documents, approve and submit to the Architect Shop Drawings, Product Data, Samples and similar submittals required by the Contract Documents in accordance with the submittal schedule approved by the Architect or in the absence of an approved submittal schedule, with reasonable promptness and in such sequence as to cause no delay in the Work or in the activities of the Owner or of Separate Contractors.

3.12.6 By submitting Shop Drawings, Product Data, Samples and similar submittals, the Contractor represents to the Owner and Architect that the Contractor has (1) reviewed and approved them, (2) determined and verified materials, field measurements and field construction criteria related thereto, or will do so and (3) checked and coordinated the information contained within such submittals with the requirements of the Work and of the Contract Documents.

3.12.7 The Contractor shall perform no portion of the Work for which the Contract Documents require submittal and review of Shop Drawings, Product Data, Samples or similar submittals until the respective submittal has been approved by the Architect

3.12.8 The Work shall be in accordance with approved submittals except that the Contractor shall not be relieved of responsibility of deviations from requirements of responsibility of deviations from requirements of the Contract Documents by the Architect's approval of Shop Drawings, Product Data, Samples or similar submittals unless the Contractor has specifically informed the Architect in writing of such deviation at the time of submittal and (1) the Architect has given written approval to the specific deviation as a minor change in the Work, or (2) a Change Order or Construction Change Directive has been issued authorizing the deviation. The Contractor shall not be relieved of responsibility for errors or omissions in Shop Drawings, Product Data, Samples or similar submittals by the Architect's approval thereof.

3.12.9 The Contractor shall direct specific attention, in writing or on resubmitted Shop Drawings, Product Data, Samples or similar submittals, to revisions other than those requested by the Architect on previous submittals. In the absence of such written notice, the Architect's approval of a resubmission shall not apply to such revisions.

3.12.10 The Contractor shall not be required to provide professional services that constitute the practice of architecture or engineering unless such services are specifically required by the Contract Documents for a portion

of the Work or unless the Contractor needs to provide such services in order to carry out the Contractor's responsibilities for construction means, methods, techniques, sequences and procedures. The Contractor shall not be required to provide professional services in violation of applicable law.

3.12.10.1 If professional design services or certifications by a design professional related to systems, materials or equipment are specifi cally required of the Contractor by the Contract Documents, the Owner and the Architect will specify all performance and design criteria that such services must satisfy. The Contractor shall be entitled to rely upon the adequacy and accuracy of the performance and design criteria provided in the Contract Documents. The Contractor shall cause such services or certifications to be provided by an appropriately licensed design professional, whose signature and seal shall appear on all drawings, calculations, specifications, certifications, Shop Drawings and other submittals prepared by such professional. Shop Drawings and other submittals related to the Work designed or certified by such professional, if prepared by others, shall bear such professional's written approval when submitted to the Architect. The Owner and the Architect shall be entitled to rely upon the adequacy, accuracy of the services, certifications and approvals performed or provided by such design professionals, providedthe Owner and Architect have specifiedto the Contractor the performance and design criteria that such services must satisfy. Pursuant to this Section 3.12.10, the Architect will review and approve or take other appropriate action on submittals only for the limited purpose of checking for conformance with information given and the design concept expressed in the Contract Documents.

3.12.10.2 If the Contract Documents require the Contractor's design professional to certify that the Work has been performed in accordance with the design criteria, the Contractor shall furnish such certification to the Architect at the time and in the form specified by the Architect.

administrative and procedural requirements found in various construction documents.

Although Division 01 requirements are generally arranged in the order of the three parts of SectionFormat®, PART 1 — GENERAL should, in most cases, contain the bulk of these provisions.

PART 2 — PRODUCTS and PART 3 — EXECUTION may include some items related to administrative and procedural requirements. For example, quality control requirements covered in Division 01 may include general erection and approval procedures for the use of mock-ups as quality standards.

SUPPLEMENTARY CONDITIONS

3. In Paragraph 3.12.5 add the following: "Prepare and submit Shop Drawings, Samples and other data in accordance with Section 01 33 00—Submittal Procedures."

SECTION 01 33 00- SUBMITTAL PROCEDURES, PART 1-GENERAL

1.03 SUBMITTAL PROCEDURES

A. Transmit each submittal with AIA Document G810.

B. Sequentially number transmittal forms. Resubmittals to have original number with an alphabetic suffix.

C. Identify Project, Contractor, Subcontractor, or supplier pertinent Drawing sheet and detail number and specification Section number as appropriate.

D. Affix Contractor's stamp, signed or initialed certifying that review verification or product's required field dimensions, adjacent construction Work, and coordination of information, is in accordance with the requirements of the Work and Contract Documents.

E. Schedule submittals to expedite the Work and deliver to Architect/Engineer at business address. Coordinate submittal of related items.

F. Identify deviations from Contract Documents and limitations of product or system which may be detrimental to successful performance of the completed Work.

G. Provide space for Contractor and Architect/Engineer review stamps.

H. Revise and resubmit submittals as required. Identify all changes made since previous submittal.

I. Distribute copies of reviewed submittals to concerned parties. Instruct parties to promptly report any inability to comply with provisions.

SECTION 05 42 00—COLD-FORMED METAL JOIST FRAMING

1.05 SUBMITTALS

A. Submit shop drawings and product data.

B. Indicate on shop drawings component details, framed openings, welds, type and location of fasteners, and accessories or items required of other related work.

SECTION 09 60 00—ACCESS FLOORING

1.09 SUBMITTALS

A. Submit shop drawings and product data.

B. Indicate flooring layout, interruptions to grid, special sized panels required, panels drilled or cut-out for services, appurtenances or interruptions, edge details, elevation differences, grilles, and registers.

PART 1 — GENERAL of the section on glazed curtain walls may stipulate that a mock-up is tested for air and water infiltration according to the referenced ASTM International (ASTM) requirements or Fenestration and Glazing Industry Alliance (FGIA) standards.

PART 2 — PRODUCTS may require the manufacturer to perform the tests as part of a source quality control program under the owner's testing laboratory consultants' supervision.

PART 3 — EXECUTION might require the manufacturer to provide factory representatives

DOMAIN 1
Planning,
Development,
& Organization

DOMAIN 2
Coordination

DOMAIN 3
Procurement,
Contracting,
& General
Requirements

DOMAIN 4
Research

DOMAIN 5
Analysis
& Evaluation

DOMAIN 6
Production

to ensure that field erection and quality control procedures conform to those used in the approved mock-up. Although the Division 01 role in governing the work has been accepted in practice for many years, this authority is not explicitly stated in either the AIA or EJCDC general conditions. Until that change is made, the authority should be established by a provision in the supplementary conditions as follows:

> Sections of Division 01 — General Requirements govern the work of all sections of the specifications.

Include a similar statement in the project manuals' supplementary conditions for projects using federal, state, city, or county documents that do not already grant such authority.

3.3.6 Drawings

Drawings graphically define particular Division 01 subject matter, such as the extent of work, and may define related work that may or may not be part of the contract.

Purely procedural sections of Division 01, such as submittals, quality requirements, and closeout procedures, need no coordination with the drawings.

Other sections, such as those covering the site's use, phased construction, and multiple prime contracts, usually require extensive delineation on the drawings and close coordination between the drawings and Division 01.

3.4 Writing Division 01 Sections

Division 01 sections are organized and written in the same outline style and three-part SectionFormat® as sections in Divisions 02 through 49. Section 01 57 00 — Temporary Controls, for example, might include not only the PART 1 administrative and procedural provisions for surface water control but also PART 2 requirements for containment devices and PART 3 requirements for their installation and subsequent removal. However, many of the Division 01 sections may have no PART 2 — PRODUCTS or PART 3 — EXECUTION when limited to

administrative and procedural requirements. Whenever this is the case, the unused parts are listed but noted as "Not Used" (e.g., PART 2 — PRODUCTS — Not Used).

3.4.1 Coordination of Division 01 — General Requirements

Many articles in the conditions of the contract are usually expanded in Division 01 — General Requirements to accommodate specific administrative and procedural requirements of a project. Articles in the conditions of the contract on allowances, progress schedules, record documents, shop drawings, product data and samples, schedules of values, and closeout procedures and submittals are commonly developed in greater detail in Division 01. General and supplementary conditions are written in a paragraph style, while Division 01 is written in the three-part SectionFormat®.

Proper use of Division 01 avoids mixing conditions of the contract with the specifications' administrative and procedural details. A comparison of conditions of the contract and Division 01 — General Requirements is shown in Figure 3.4. Coordination is necessary between each section of Division 01 and the sections of Divisions 02 through 49, and among the sections of Division 01 that cover interrelated administrative and procedural requirements. For example, Section 01 14 00 — Work Restrictions contains restrictions on the contractor's operations within a building occupied by the owner. At the same time, Section 01 35 00 — Special Procedures may establish similar restrictions based on the type of activity or project type. The specifier should verify that each requirement is in one location, offering the basis for imposing the requirement.

Division 01 sections on allowances and alternates require careful coordination with the sections in other divisions that specify the affected products (refer to Figure 3.5). Division 01 sections that cover cash allowances for materials should include procedural details for the selection of specific products, identify the allowance items by item number and title, along with the type of product and the dollar amount to be allowed, and cross-reference the affected sections in Divisions 02

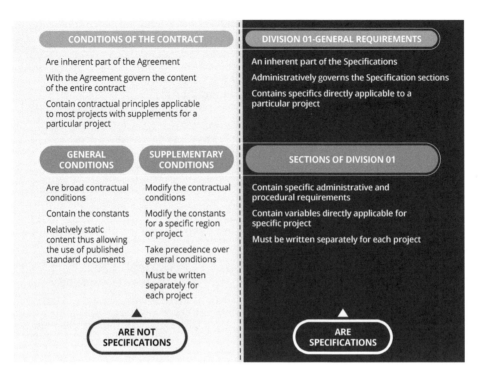

Figure 3.4
Conditions of the
Contract versus
Division 01 —
General
Requirements

through 49. In turn, the sections specifying the installation of products that are purchased under a cash allowance should cross-reference the Division 01 section specifying the dollar amounts without repeating the Division 01 administrative and procedural requirements.

Section 01 23 00 — Alternates should identify the alternates by number, give the procedures for bidding/proposing and considering, and describe how alternates are accepted. It should also describe the changes to other work required by accepting each alternate and list the sections affected by each. Sections specifying products affected by an alternate should cross-reference Section 01 23 00 — Alternates. Work involving rehabilitation, owner-occupied projects, hazardous materials, phased and fast-track techniques, construction management, multiple-prime contracts, purchasing, and overall performance requirements requires special attention to Division 01 to carefully describe the administrative and procedural responsibilities of each of the participants involved in the construction process.

Since the owner requires many of the contractual relationships and responsibilities described in Division 01 sections for any project, the A/E should obtain instructions for preparing the affected

sections. The individuals involved in preparing a project manual represent various professional disciplines and may be members of the same firm or consultants under contract to the A/E. The A/E should establish the team members' primary responsibilities for preparing the Division 01 requirements and for overall coordination of the specifications. This process closely coordinates Division 01 provisions early in producing the contract documents to avoid conflicts, duplications, and omissions in the project manual. The coordination effort should include the following:

- Distributing a draft of Division 01 to the contributors to the specifications early in project development

- Preparing a list of requirements solicited from the consultants and other contributors on administrative, procedural, and temporary facility and control requirements for specific sections or divisions

- Comparing this list of requirements with the draft of Division 01

- Determining which of these requirements should be covered in Division 01 and which are specific only to individual specification sections

DOMAIN 1
Planning,
Development,
& Organization

DOMAIN 2
Coordination

DOMAIN 3
Procurement,
Contracting,
& General
Requirements

DOMAIN 4
Research

DOMAIN 5
Analysis
& Evaluation

DOMAIN 6
Production

Figure 3.5
Sample Use of
Allowances

CONDITIONS OF THE CONTRACT
Supplementary Conditions

Delete Paragraph 11.8—Cash Allowances, and substitute the following:

11.8—Allowances: Include in the Contract Sum all allowances stated in the Contract Documents. Allowances include specific monetary sums and quantities of work for certain scheduled items. Refer to Section 01 21 13—Cash Allowances and Section 01 21 19—Quantity Allowances for allowance descriptions and requirements.

SPECIFICATIONS
Division 01—General Requirements

SECTION 01 21 13
CASH ALLOWANCES

1.06 SCHEDULE OF CASH ALLOWANCES

    A.   Section 04 20 00—Unit Mansonry: Include the unit price of $350.00 per thousand for purchase and delivery of facing brick. Stipulate the estimated quantity on the Bid Form. Include Installation costs in Contract Sum.

Division 04—Masonry

    SECTION 04 20 00
    UNIT MASONRY

1.05 ALLOWANCES

    A.   Provide selected facing brick under cash allowances specified in Section 01 21 13—Cash Allowances.

SECTION 01 21 19
QUANTITY ALLOWANCES

1.06 SCHEDULE OF QUANTITY ALLOWANCES

    A.   Section 09 68 00—Carpeting: Provide 200 SY, including purchase, delivery, and installation of Type "A" Sheet Carpet.

    B.   Section 09 68 00—Carpeting: Provide 400 SY, including purchase, delivery, and installation of Type "B" Sheet Tile.

Division 09—Finishes

    SECTION 09 68 00
    CARPETING

1.05 ALLOWANCES

    A.   Provide carpet quantities specified under Section 01 21 19—Quantity Allowances.

- Resolving overlapping requirements, omissions, and conflicts

- Revising the Division 01 draft for review by specification contributors

Multiple sections within an individual division have administrative and procedural requirements unique to that division. However, the common requirements should be specified in Division 01. Often, some sections or divisions are written by different professional disciplines. To ensure proper coordination, the general requirements common to sections or divisions should be in their proper location in Division 01. This task can be accomplished by distributing drafts of the applicable Division 01 sections to each team member for markup or developing a checklist to allow the team members to note their requirements.

Administrative and procedural requirements unique to an individual section should be covered in the affected sections.

The practice of including Basic Requirements or Special Provisions sections in individual divisions is not recommended and may result in conflicts with Division 01.

3.4.2 Cautions about Specifying Division 01 Sections

Division 01 administrative and procedural requirements and temporary facilities and controls involve both direct and indirect costs. Overspecifying in Division 01 may increase construction costs unnecessarily and may create excessive obligations for the entity administering the construction contract.

3.5 Commonly Used Division 01 Sections

Several of the more commonly used Division 01 sections are listed in the following paragraphs, with some guidelines for the general types of information that might be included in each. For detailed examples of these sections, refer to master guide specification systems such as the American Institute of Architect's MASTERSPEC® (published by Deltek), Deltek's

SPECTEXT, Building Systems Design's (BSD) SpecLink, or DoD/NASA's Unified Facilities Guide Specifications.

3.5.1 Section 01 10 00 — Summary

Section 01 11 00 — Summary of Work. Use this section to describe the work if the scope required by the project manual and drawings is accomplished under one contract. If the section includes a description of the project, specify the type of contract used, and fully and accurately define its extent. To further define the scope of the section, include owner-furnished material and equipment installed by the contractor. The A/E should identify work under other contracts and specify required work sequences if the work's phasing is critical.

Section 01 12 00 — Multiple Contract Summary. Use this section if the work described in the project manual and drawings is to be accomplished by more than one contract. The situation of multiple contracts may arise from techniques including multiple-prime contracts, construction management, and, in some cases, design-build. If the section includes a description of the project, specify the type of contract used, and fully and accurately define its extent. To further define the section's scope, include owner-furnished material and equipment to be installed and by which contractor.

Section 01 14 00 — Work Restrictions. Specify owner requirements for early partial occupancy of new construction or occupancy of existing buildings. Carefully define restrictions on the contractor's use of the premises, especially if the project area is occupied during construction. Limit this section to restrictions on the contractor's use of the premises. Specify protection for the owner's occupancy in Section 01 56 00 — Temporary Barriers and Enclosures, and place requirements to provide access in Section 01 53 00 — Temporary Construction and Section 01 55 00 — Vehicular Access and Parking. The following is a general list of things to consider:

- Obtain and include occupancy and access requirements from the owner.

- Determine the number of days of prior notice required for work in occupied areas.

- Specify work areas and access routes to be used by the contractor.

- Provide work and utility outage schedules per the owner's occupancy of affected areas.

- Provide owner-required working hours for the contractor's operations.

3.5.2 Section 01 20 00—Price and Payment Procedures

Section 01 21 00—Allowances. Allowances may be used when individual design decisions have not been made and when quantities or unknowns cannot be determined before starting work. Allowances are typically cash allowances or quantity allowances. Include these only if directed by the owner or as agreed upon by the project team. The amount or quantity indicated should be determined by the owner or as agreed upon by the project team.

Section 01 22 00—Unit Prices. Include the procedures regarding unit prices and measurement for payment. Define who is responsible for the actual measurement of unit price quantities, including administration and coordination procedures. There should also be a reference to the unit price schedule as incorporated into the agreement. The preferred practice includes listing unit price items showing the item number, a designation of the item, unit of measurement, and measurement method in the unit price schedule incorporated into the agreement. A detailed discussion of aspects of the work associated with each unit price item should be included in the relevant specification sections.

Section 01 23 00—Alternates. Obtain in writing from each team member a list of alternates included in their work and the effect of other alternates on their work. Clearly define the limits of each alternate's work and the procedure used for evaluation and acceptance. Refer to each specification section that contains technical requirements for alternate products or systems or their installation. Where possible, refer to other sections covering work that is significantly affected by alternates. Refer to drawings when alternates affect the extent of work.

Section 01 24 00—Value Analysis. Specify general requirements and procedures for conducting value analysis, including descriptions of participants, schedule, costs, evaluation, and reports. Indicate the method of acceptance and the implementation of results.

Section 01 25 00—Substitution Procedures. Specify basic requirements for consideration of the contractor's proposals for substitution of products, including general rules and procedures for determining whether products are equivalent. If substitutions are allowed during procurement and after the contract is awarded, the procedures may serve both time frames. However, the procurement requirements need to refer to this section as the basis for the procurement process. Specify requirements and procedures for substitution of a specified installer.

Section 01 26 00—Contract Modification Procedures. Provide a method to allow the contractor or the owner to request clarification about an item of work insufficiently described or detailed in the contract documents. The method should allow the A/E to respond with a clarification that does not require a change to the contract sum or time.

A standardized request for information (RFI) form with space for requesting an interpretation and space for a response aids the A/E in answering questions. A copy of the form should be placed in the project manual and distributed to the contractor for use. Refer to Appendix B for a sample RFI form.

Specify the modification procedures to be followed and the data required to process contract modifications and substantiate claims for extra time and costs. Stipulate the required types of forms to be used by the contractor and A/E for requesting contract modifications and for issuing accepted contract modifications.

Section 01 29 00—Payment Procedures. Specify related requirements for the contractor's submittal of a schedule of values and applications for payment, including specific steps for each process. Identify forms, templates, or software applications to be used, how they are to be executed, how many copies are needed (if printed copies are required), and when the applications need to be submitted.

DOMAIN 1
Planning,
Development,
& Organization

DOMAIN 2
Coordination

DOMAIN 3
Procurement,
Contracting,
& General
Requirements

DOMAIN 4
Research

DOMAIN 5
Analysis
& Evaluation

DOMAIN 6
Production

3.5.3 Section 01 30 00 — Administrative Requirements

Section 01 31 00 — Project Management and Coordination. Specify requirements and procedures for project coordination, project meetings, and project/site administration. Specify requirements for coordination drawings. If multiple-prime contracts are being used, assign coordination responsibilities to the appropriate contractor. Specify requirements for supervisory personnel. Regardless of the prime contract arrangement, use this section to specify requirements regarding the administration of subcontractors and coordination with other contractors and the owner. When applicable, address requirements for pre-construction meetings, pre-installation meetings, coordination meetings, and progress meetings. If the project is constructed under multiple-prime contracts, determine responsibility for project meetings, whether one of the contractors or the construction manager. Specify the frequency and location of meetings.

Section 01 32 00 — Construction Progress Documentation. Specify requirements for the contractor's submittal of construction progress schedule, including the type of schedule and time allowed for submittal. Specify requirements for daily construction reports. Specify the type of photographic documentation, whether printed images, digital images, or video.

Section 01 33 00 — Submittal Procedures. Specify requirements for a schedule of submittals. Specify requirements for shop drawings, product data, samples, and sustainable design reporting, including reports and data to be processed as a basis before accepting the product or activity. Specify the shop drawing format (i.e., prints, reproducible, or electronic deliverables), the required number of copies to be submitted, and the required number of copies to be retained for the owner's use.

Section 01 35 00 — Special Procedures. Specify procedures for projects requiring exceptional or unusual workmanship, such as restorations, preservations, historic restorations, alterations, and hazardous material abatement. Specify procedures for specific facility types, including airports, detention facilities, hospitals, shopping centers, and nuclear facilities.

For projects seeking specific points through a sustainability rating system, such as the US Green Building Council's (USGBC) Leadership in Energy and Environmental Design (LEED) Green Building Rating System, use this section or one or more of the Level 3 numbers (i.e., Section 01 35 63 — Sustainability Certification Project Requirements and Section 01 35 66 — Sustainability Certification Project Procedures). If a project's sustainability goal is to achieve a particular rating and the means and methods to achieve it are left to the contractor, use Section 01 81 13 — Sustainable Design Requirements.

3.5.4 Section 01 40 00 — Quality Requirements

Specify the procedures to manage, measure, and report the contractor's construction and performance quality. Specify the construction, review, and use of mock-ups and field samples applied or assembled at the site to be used as quality standards for installed work. Specify qualifications of testing laboratories, limitations of authority, contractor cooperation requirements, responsibilities for payment, and reference to required tests.

3.5.5 Section 01 50 00 — Temporary Facilities and Controls

All team members should review this section and any subordinate sections. If the project is constructed under multiple-prime contracts, assign responsibilities for temporary facilities to the appropriate contractors. In renovation work, rehabilitation projects, or additions to existing facilities, specify whether existing utilities, services, or facilities are available for construction use and whether existing elevators and toilets may be used by construction personnel.

Section 01 51 00 — Temporary Utilities. Include temporary water, fire protection, electric service, lighting, telephone, heating, cooling, and ventilating. Specify responsibility for installation and usage costs. Provide for equipment having special requirements.

Section 01 52 00 — Construction Facilities. For field offices and sanitation facilities, identify the contractor responsible for installation and costs. Specify requirements and limitations for location.

Section 01 53 00 — Temporary Construction. Specify requirements for temporary structures required to accommodate access to the construction or accommodate the owner's operations. Limit the specifications in this section to the structural components. Facilities for temporary access and parking are located in Section 01 55 00 — Vehicular Access and Parking.

Section 01 54 00 — Construction Aids. Specify requirements for temporary elevators, hoists, cranes, scaffolding and platforms, and swing staging. Include requirements for using tools and equipment during construction. Indicate requirements for sharing construction aids when multiple contracts are used.

Section 01 55 00 — Vehicular Access and Parking. Specify requirements for temporary facilities needed or to accommodate access and parking for the construction or accommodate the owner's operations. Specify the procedures related to maintaining and controlling traffic and access to the construction. Limit these specifications to maintaining and controlling access; special restrictions on the contractor's access are specified in Section 01 14 00—Work Restrictions.

Section 01 56 00 — Temporary Barriers and Enclosures. Include requirements for facilities and procedures for protecting facility users and existing spaces during construction. Specify requirements for fences, noise barriers, and dust barriers.

Section 01 57 00 — Temporary Controls. Include administrative and procedural provisions for surface water control and containment devices and their installation and subsequent removal. Specify erosion and sediment control. Include pest control requirements.

Section 01 58 00 — Project Identification. Specify requirements and limitations for project identification and temporary signs.

3.5.6 Section 01 60 00 — Product Requirements

Section 01 62 00 — Product Options. Specify the basic requirements for contractors' options in selecting products, including general rules and procedures for determining whether products are equivalent.

Section 01 64 00 — Owner-Furnished Products. This section may be used to define the administrative requirements for owner-furnished products. If appropriate, state the essential characteristics of products furnished by the owner for installation by the contractor. Specify basic requirements and procedures for coordinating, scheduling, and receiving products to ensure that the products' condition is acceptable at the time of delivery. Extraordinary precautions beyond the requirements of Section 01 65 00 — Product Delivery Requirements may also be included. If this section is used, the list of owner-furnished products should be located here and cross-referenced in Section 01 10 00 — Summary.

Section 01 65 00 — Product Delivery Requirements. Specify the basic requirements for packing, shipping, delivery, and acceptance of products at the site.

Section 01 66 00 — Product Storage and Handling Requirements. Specify the basic requirements for handling and storage of products at the site.

3.5.7 Section 01 70 00 — Execution and Closeout Requirements

Section 01 71 00 — Examination and Preparation. Specify unique requirements for preparing for construction, including initial construction layout, protection of adjacent construction, and surveying. Specify the basic requirements for preparing to install, erect, or apply products.

Section 01 73 00 — Execution. Specify the basic requirements for installing, applying, or erecting new and pre-purchased products. Specify the basic requirements for installing owner-furnished products, but refer to Section 01 64 00 — Owner-Furnished Products for the product characteristics. Specify procedures for dealing with existing material and equipment, making distinctions among the following possibilities:

- Material and equipment to be salvaged (removal, repair, and storage) and reinstalled in the work

DOMAIN 1
Planning,
Development,
& Organization

DOMAIN 2
Coordination

DOMAIN 3
Procurement,
Contracting,
& General
Requirements

DOMAIN 4
Research

DOMAIN 5
Analysis
& Evaluation

DOMAIN 6
Production

- Material and equipment to be salvaged and retained by the contractor with the salvage value accruing to the owner

- Material and equipment to be salvaged and delivered to the owner

Section 01 74 00 — Cleaning and Waste Management. Specify requirements for cleaning during construction and final cleaning. Include requirements for recycling materials.

Section 01 75 00 — Starting and Adjusting. Specify the schedule for starting and adjusting equipment and systems. Describe requirements for starting, adjusting, and servicing equipment. Include requirements for seasonal operation. Include the method for reporting compliance with specified requirements.

Section 01 76 00 — Protecting Installed Construction. Include basic requirements and procedures for protecting finished work and existing finishes, if applicable, while continuing construction. Describe remedial and replacement requirements.

Section 01 77 00 — Closeout Procedures. Specify administrative procedures for substantial completion and final completion of the work. Describe the procedures required to identify, correct, and complete punch-list items.

Section 01 78 00 — Closeout Submittals. Specify requirements for closeout submittals such as record documents, warranties, spare parts, and maintenance and operation data. Specify the number and form of data to be submitted, such as manuals.

Section 01 79 00 — Demonstration and Training. Specify requirements and procedures to demonstrate the products and systems used in the facility, including training of the owner's operations and maintenance staff.

3.5.8 Section 01 80 00 — Performance Requirements

Section 01 81 00 — Facility Performance Requirements. Specify general performance applicable to the entire facility, such as sustainability, energy, and environmental design requirements. For projects that must achieve specific points

for a particular rating system, use Section 01 35 00 — Special Requirements or its Level 3 section numbers and titles.

Other sustainable design goals and systems for buildings that are performance-based would also be included in these sections.

Sections 01 82 00 through 01 89 00. Specify the facility's overall performance requirements that include materials, products, and systems included in multiple specification sections, including substructure, superstructure, interiors conveying equipment services, equipment and furnishings, site, and other project-specific locations. Use these sections when the performance involves work results across multiple sections that must perform together to achieve a minimum performance level. It is the contractor's responsibility to develop the means and methods to achieve that minimum performance.

3.5.9 Section 01 90 00 — Life Cycle Activities

Section 01 91 00 — Commissioning. Specify general requirements for commissioning the facility and its systems, including the specific responsibilities of the commissioning agent and other contractors. Specify requirements for the evaluation of the system performance. Specify procedures for testing, adjusting, and balancing facility systems as part of the commissioning process. Coordinate this section with Section 01 75 00, which addresses the starting and adjusting equipment before the commissioning process.

Section 01 92 00 — Facility Operation. Describe requirements and procedures for operating the facility as a part of a contract.

Section 01 93 00 — Facility Maintenance. Describe requirements and procedures for maintenance of the facilities, including provisions for maintenance records and logbooks. Specify procedures for recycling programs.

Section 01 94 00 — Facility Decommissioning. Specify basic requirements for deactivating or removing a facility or its systems or equipment from operation, including protecting deactivated facilities, deconstruction/demolition, and removal. Specify procedures related to abatement, removal, and disposal of hazardous materials.

3.6 Specifying Allowances

The use of allowances in a construction project requires written provisions in several procurement documents that must be carefully coordinated. Typically, allowance requirements appear in the procurement requirements, conditions of the contract, Division 01 — General Requirements, and the individual specification sections for the items covered by the allowances. These documents must state the following:

- Precisely what is included under the allowance

- Who is to authorize items covered by allowances

- How costs are adjusted if the actual price, quantity, or time varies from the amount stated

3.6.1 Conditions of the Contract

Both the AIA and EJCDC publish standard general conditions containing articles about cash allowances summarized in the following paragraphs.

The *Allowances* articles in AIA Document A201™, *General Conditions of the Contract for Construction*, and *ConsensusDocs 200, Standard Agreement and General Conditions Between Owner and Constructor (Lump Sum),* provide cash allowances included in the contract sum. However, the provisions limit the cash allowance to the materials and equipment delivered to the site, including taxes. Items may be furnished by persons designated by the owner; however, the contractor may refuse to contract with them if the contractor provides a reasonable objection. The contractor's labor costs, unloading and handling at the site, installation, overhead, profit, and other expenses are included in the contract sum unless otherwise provided in the contract documents. The article also states that the contract sum will be (may be, per ConsenusDocs) adjusted by a change order to reflect the allowance's cost difference.

DOMAIN 1
Planning,
Development,
& Organization

DOMAIN 2
Coordination

DOMAIN 3
Procurement,
Contracting,
& General
Requirements

DOMAIN 4
Research

DOMAIN 5
Analysis
& Evaluation

DOMAIN 6
Production

The *Cost of the Work; Allowances; Unit Price of Work* article in EJCDC® C-700, *Standard General Conditions of the Construction Contract*, provides for cash allowances included in the contract sum. The article's provisions limit the cash allowances to materials and equipment delivered to the site, including taxes. Work must be done by subcontractors and suppliers acceptable to the owner and engineer. The article also states that before final payment, an appropriate change order will be issued to reflect the actual cost and adjustment of the contract price. There may be situations where requirements stated in the general conditions need to be modified to include other items, such as installation, quantities, or time. In that case, the appropriate provisions in the general conditions should be deleted via the supplementary conditions and the modified or expanded allowance requirements stated in Division 01.

3.6.2 Specifications

Section 01 21 00 — Allowances or the subordinate sections should specify the dollar amount or quantities, as well as administrative and procedural matters relating to handling allowances. Specific items covered by each allowance should be identified and may include the product's cost, delivery to site, installation (if applicable), and taxes. Cost items not covered by the allowance should also be identified to ensure they are included in the contract sum. Specific items not covered by an allowance may include delivery, storage and handling at the site, installation of the product (if applicable), overhead and profit, and other expenses necessary for a complete installation. These sections should contain appropriate cross-references to sections in Divisions 02 through 49 in which the allowance items are specified.

Sections in Divisions 02 through 49 affected by allowances should contain an article in PART 1 — GENERAL calling attention to allowances' provisions. The items covered by an allowance should be cross-referenced to an allowance amount stated in the applicable Division 01 section. Additionally, the A/E must provide enough information in PART 2 and PART 3 of each section so that bidders know precisely what is covered by the allowance. Both the products and their installation should be specified as completely as possible.

Figures 3.5 and 3.6 show how allowances are covered and coordinated in the various contract documents. In this example, both cash and quantity allowances are used.

3.7 Specifying Alternates

Most master guide specifications and standard documents do not contain extensive provisions for alternates, as they are generally unique to each project. If alternates are to be used, special provisions must be incorporated in the documents to make them useful. Figure 3.7 illustrates how an alternate for adding television sets to a hospital project might be stated in the various procurement documents.

Procurement Requirements. The solicitation, such as the invitation for bids, should inform bidders or proposers of the request for alternate prices. Solicitation instructions may contain guidance for preparing alternate bids or proposals and state considerations for evaluation and contract award. Bid or proposal forms should clearly identify alternates with spaces for the respective prices.

Agreement and Conditions of the Contract. The executed agreement must indicate, as part of the work description, which alternates have been selected by the owner. The contract sum must accurately reflect those decisions. Modifications of standard general conditions are generally not required because alternates listed in the agreement form become part of the work.

Specifications. Section 01 23 00 — Alternates should identify each alternate and describe the work changes included in each. Where possible, refer to individual specification sections affected by the alternates. If not shown on the drawings, certain areas or portions of the work may be described to clarify the locations of changes necessitated by the incorporation of alternates. The sections in Divisions 02 through 49 affected by the alternates should contain a coordinating or clarifying statement calling attention to the provisions for alternates. Statements should be included in PART 1 — GENERAL under the *Summary* article.

Figure 3.6
Partial Bid
Form and
Corresponding
Division 01
Schedule
of Quantity
Allowances

BID FORM

If quantities for the following allowance items vary from the amounts specified in Section 01 21 29—Quantity Allowances, the Contract Sum will be adjusted in accordance with the following unit prices:

ITEM DESIGNATION	UNIT OF MEASURE	UNIT PRICE
1. Tenant Corridor Entrance	Each	$ _____
2. Corridor Partition	LF	$ _____

SECTION 01 21 29—QUANTITY ALLOWANCES

1.06   SCHEDULE OF QUANTITY ALLOWANCES

A.   Item No.1 - Tenant Corridor Entrance: Allow a quantity of 55 installed entrances, each to include:

1.   Fire-rated hollow-metal frames, Section 08 11 00—Metal Doors and Frames.

2.   1-1/2 hour fire-rated wood doors, 3 feet by 7 feet, Section 08 14 00—Wood Doors, and Section 08 15 00—Plastic Doors.

3.   Hardware Set No. 3, Section 08 70 00—Hardware.

4.   Doors sign, Section 10 14 00—Identification Specialties.

B.   Item No.2 - Corridor Partition: Allow a quantity of 250 linear feet of installed 8-foot high partition include:

1.   3-5/8-inch, 0.0179-inch-thick steel studs spaced 24 inches on center, with two layers of 5/8-inch Type X gypsum board screw attached to each side, Section 09 21 16—Gypsum Board Assemblies.

2.   Tenant side finish: One coat of primer and two coats eggshell latex paint, Section 09 90 00—Painting and Coating.

3.   Corridor side finish: Type A vinyl wall covering, Section 09 72 00—Wall Coverings.

DOMAIN 1
Planning,
Development,
& Organization

DOMAIN 2
Coordination

DOMAIN 3
Procurement,
Contracting,
& General
Requirements

DOMAIN 4
Research

DOMAIN 5
Analysis
& Evaluation

DOMAIN 6
Production

Figure 3.7
Sample Use of
Alternates

PROCEDURE REQUIREMENTS

Invitation to Bid

Type of Bids: Bids shall be on a stipulated-sum basis of the base contract, and include a separate price for each alternate.

Instructions to Bidders

Each alternate is described is described in the Specifications and is provided for in the Bid Form.

The price of the Bid for each alternate will be the amount to be added to or deducted from the price of the Base Bid if the Owner selects the alternate.

The Owner may accept alternates in any order, regardless of how they are listed, and determine the lowest responsible bidder on the basis of the sum of the base bid plus any selected alternates.

Bid Form

Alternate No.1—Patient Room Televisions:

Add _____ Dollars ($ _____)

                       (In Words)   (In Numerals)

CONTRACTING REQUIREMENTS

Agreement

The Contractor shall perform all work required by the Contract Documents for TLC Nursing Home at 123 Primrose Lane, Anywhere, USA, including Alternates No. 1, 2, 3 as described in Section 01 23 00—Alternates, of the Specifications.

SPECIFICATIONS
SECTION 01 23 00

1.06 ALTERNATIVE NO. 1—PATIENT ROOM TELEVISIONS

    A.   Provide 72 bedside bracket-mounted television sets on the first floor of "A-Wing" as Specified in Section 27 41 19—Portable Audio-Video Equipment.

SECTION 26 61 50
1.04 ALTERNATES

    A.   Refer to Section 01 23 00—Alternates, for description of work under this Section affected by alternates.

3.8 Specifying Unit Prices

Whether a project is based on a stipulated sum contract with a few unit prices listed for minor variables or is based entirely on unit prices, the requirements and procedures for handling unit prices must be defined in the procurement documents. These requirements involve the bid or proposal form and carefully written Division 01 sections, both of which must be coordinated with the applicable sections in Divisions 02 through 49.

3.8.1 Conditions of the Contract

Specified unit price requirements must be coordinated with statements in the conditions of the contract to avoid conflicts, duplication of information, or omission of essential requirements. Most standard general conditions address unit prices. Typically, these requirements need to be expanded in Division 01.

AIA Document A201® and related documents from the Engineers Joint Contract Documents Committee (EJCDC), Design-Build Institute of America (DBIA), and the ConsensusDocs Coalition include the following paragraphs relating to changes in the work and unit prices:

- AIA Document A201® covers unit price adjustments caused by changes in quantities of magnitude that become a substantial inequity to the owner or contractor and includes determining the cost or credit to the owner resulting from a change in the work.

- EJCDC® C-700 defines the contract documents as including the contractor's bid when listed and attached as an exhibit to the agreement. This document also:

  - establishes authority for the engineer to determine actual quantities and classifications of unit price work;

  - establishes the contract price for unit price work as the sum of each estimated quantity multiplied by its unit price;

  - points out that estimated quantities are not guaranteed but are for the purpose of comparing bids;

  - stipulates that unit price bids include the contractor's overhead and profit. It also covers contract price changes because of significant differences between estimated and actual quantities paid by unit price; and

  - provides for claims for additional costs.

Review the related general conditions from the DBIA, Construction Management Association of America (CMAA), or ConsensusDocs Coalition to determine the stipulated requirements if any of those documents apply to the project.

In situations where the owner has provided their own documents, including the general conditions, the documents must be reviewed closely. Any coordination with other project requirements needs to be confirmed with the owner.

3.8.2 Specifications

Section 01 27 00 — Unit Prices is generally the place for establishing procedural requirements for unit prices. The section covers methods of determining actual quantities for both progress and final payments. The section must be coordinated with the general conditions, as it may either establish or expand upon the following requirements:

- Unit prices include all necessary material, labor, equipment, overhead, profit, and applicable taxes.

- The substantiated measurements of quantities are included with payment applications.

- Quantities outlined in the bid form are estimates based on the work shown on the drawings. They are the basis on which bids are compared and the contract sum determined. Payment is made for work actually performed and measured. The owner reserves the right to increase or decrease the quantities shown on the drawings by a stated maximum amount.

- The final contract sum is adjusted by change order to reflect actual quantities for unit price items. Section 01 27 00 — Unit Prices must define who is responsible for measuring unit

DOMAIN 1
Planning,
Development,
& Organization

DOMAIN 2
Coordination

DOMAIN 3
Procurement,
Contracting,
& General
Requirements

DOMAIN 4
Research

DOMAIN 5
Analysis
& Evaluation

DOMAIN 6
Production

price quantities. If it is the owner or the owner's representative, procedures must be defined for administration and coordination. If the contractor is responsible for measurement, the methods for controlling and verifying by the owner must be specified.

The section may include a listing of unit price items showing the item number, designation, unit of measurement, and measurement method. Estimated quantities are not required in this section because these are stated on the bid or proposal form.

Describing unit price items in this section simplifies the bid or proposal form, as only the item designation and number are required on the bid or proposal form. Figure 3.8 illustrates a schedule of prices for the bid form and a schedule of unit price items in Division 01 for a civil engineering project. Other Division 01 sections may need to contain requirements for, or references to, unit prices depending on the project.

If the project contains quantity allowances used in conjunction with unit prices, then either the Level 2 Section 01 21 00 — Allowances or the Level 3 Section 01 21 29 — Quantity Allowances may contain the following unit price requirement:

> *Quantities stated for allowances are estimates for the purpose of equitable bidding and establishing an estimated quantity of work. The owner reserves the right to increase or decrease quantities by a maximum stated amount. The requested unit prices are used to adjust the contract sum to reflect actual quantities.*

Figure 3.8 is a sample partial bid form and the corresponding Division 01 schedule of quantity allowances for tenant corridor entrances and corridor partitions. When alternates are specified, they may be based on the stated quantities and the unit prices requested. In this instance, Section 01 23 00 — Alternates would also need to reference

unit prices. It may be necessary to designate which quantities and unit prices are included in alternates. Matching alternates with applicable quantities may become complicated and must be defined as clearly and accurately as possible. Again, as with the use of allowances, it is advisable to limit the use of alternates.

Specification sections in Divisions 02 through 49 should contain a cross-reference to the applicable section in Division 01 dealing with unit prices. The Division 01 sections should describe how specific unit price items are measured. These requirements would be in PART 1 under the *Unit Prices* article. Care must be used in defining the payment for unit price items. There must be a careful correlation with typical details for unit price items shown on the drawings. The method of measurement to be employed must also be clearly stated.

Ordinarily, some items are measured directly, and others are treated as subsidiary obligations, such as pipe and associated fittings. It is best if the measured quantities relate directly to the way the work is performed. However, this is not always practical because of the effort required to measure some work items.

For example, in an earthwork project, the contractor may excavate, stockpile, and eventually place the soil in the finished location. Three unit prices would accurately reflect the work done. However, much more measurement effort is required when three unit prices are used rather than a single unit price for earth fill measured in place. The extra measurement effort for three unit prices reduces the risk that the contractor may be overpaid, but the owner must pay for the additional measurement effort. Therefore, earthwork is usually measured in place, either in the finished work or from the borrow pit. Truckload and loose volume measurements should be avoided whenever possible.

BID FORM

SCHEDULE OF PRICES

ITEM NO	DESIGNATION	UNIT OF MEASURE	UNIT OF PRICE	ESTIMATED QUANTITY	TOTAL PRICE
	Refer to Section 01 22 00 - Unit Prices		Dollars/ Cts		Dollars/ Cts
1	Earthwork for Utilities	CY	$_____	563	$_____
2	10-inch Ductile Iron Pipe	LF	$_____	62	$_____
3	30-inch Steel Pipe	LF	$_____	234	$_____
4	30-inch Prestressed Concrete Cycliner Pipe	LF	$_____	115	$_____
5	30-inch Valve and Vault	EA	$_____	2	$_____

TOTAL PRICE: _____ ($ _____)

        (In Words)   (In Numerals)

SECTION 01 22 00—UNIT PRICES

1.04 SCHEDULE OF UNIT PRICE ITEMS

    A.   Item No. 1 Earthwork Utilities
        1. Trench Excavation, select granular backfill, and compaction in accordance with Section 31 23 00—Excavation and Fill.
        2. Unit Measure: Cubic yards of backfill compacted in place.

    B.   Item No. 2 10-inch Ductile Iron Pipe
        1. Pipe and fittings including pressure-testing in accordance with Section 33 10 00—Water Utilities.
        2. Unit Measure: Linear feet of pipe installed.

    C.   Item No. 3 30-inch Steel Pipe
        1. Pipe and fittings including pressure-testing in accordance with Section 33 10 00—Water. Utilities.
        2. Unit Measure: Linear feet of pipe installed.

    D.   Item No. 4 30-inch Pre-stressed Concrete Cylinder Pipe
        1. Pipe and fittings including pressure-testing in accordance with Section 33 10 00—Water. Utilities.
        2. Unit Measure: Linear feet of pipe installed.

    E.   Item No. 5 30-inch Valve and Vault
        1. Valve, vault, roadway box, frames, and covers in accordance with DPW Standard No. 890.01 and Section 33 10 00—Water Utilities.
        2. Unit Measure: Each valve with vault installed.

DOMAIN 3:
PROCUREMENT, CONTRACTING,
& GENERAL REQUIREMENTS

Chapter 4

MODIFICATIONS

4.1 Procurement and Contract Document Modifications

The architect/engineer (A/E) helps the owner develop an overall procurement strategy for the construction project. The plan considers local practices, local labor market, and chances of unfavorable site conditions to evaluate the use of a general contractor, multiple contractors, and project delivery methods. There is no substitute for clear, concise, correct, complete, and carefully coordinated contract documents. Despite best efforts and planning, situations requiring changes do develop. The A/E, owner, and contractor must have adequate means for dealing with such changes. Addenda and change orders may be employed to modify procurement and contract documents, but reliance on them to correct poorly prepared drawings and project manuals should be avoided. Addenda are modifications issued either before receipt of bids and proposals or, in some cases, before the time the agreement is executed. Change orders are modifications issued after the agreement is executed.

Although many public agencies have established forms and procedures for addenda and change orders that may differ slightly from suggestions offered in this chapter, the differences are procedural and do not affect stated principles.

4.2 General Criteria

Written construction document modifications are the means for communicating changes to the bidders or proposers during procurement and to the contractor during construction. Most changes are best expressed in words and augmented by drawings where necessary. However, it is sometimes difficult, if not impossible, to change intricate drawings by written statements alone. Oral instructions or changes should be avoided, even where it is intended for an addendum or change order to be prepared later to cover the change. Instead of giving an oral interpretation, the A/E should state that an addendum or change order will be issued promptly to clarify the items in question. Most instructions to bidders or proposers state that oral interpretations

DOMAIN 1
Planning,
Development,
& Organization

DOMAIN 2
Coordination

DOMAIN 3
Procurement,
Contracting,
& General
Requirements

DOMAIN 4
Research

DOMAIN 5
Analysis
& Evaluation

DOMAIN 6
Production

are not binding, and the general conditions usually require all contract modifications to be in writing. As discussed in Chapter 1, there are two basic methods for preparing written changes to procurement and contract documents: the narrative method and the revised page method. In addition to managing the changes within the specifications, these methods are also used for all other procurement and contract documents.

4.3 Procurement Documents Modifications

Addenda are written or graphic instruments issued to clarify, revise, add to, or delete information in the procurement documents or previous addenda. Typically, addenda are issued before the opening of bids/proposals. Addenda must be sent with sufficient time to allow bidders/proposers to evaluate and incorporate changes into their bids or proposals.

The general conditions of the American Institute of Architects (AIA) and the Engineers Joint Contract Documents Committee (EJCDC) general conditions differ slightly in their addenda approach. AIA Document A201®, *General Conditions of the Construction Contract*, states that addenda are instruments issued before the agreement's execution. This approach allows for negotiated adjustments of a bid/proposal by the issuance of an addendum. In contrast, EJCDC® C-700, *Standard General Conditions of the Construction Contract*, define addenda as instruments issued before receipt of bids.

The AIA Document A201® definition reflects the perspective of the private-sector owner who is not bound by public policy and can negotiate and issue addenda right up to the agreement's time of execution. However, the addendum's primary purpose is to make changes to the procurement documents before opening bids/proposals. ConsensusDocs 200, *Standard Agreement and General Conditions Between Owner and Constructor (Lump Sum)*, addresses addenda similar to AIA's document.

The EJCDC® C-700 definition reflects the view of the public works projects that may preclude modification of procurement documents between bid opening and

execution of the agreement. Some jurisdictions allow negotiation with the lowest responsible bidder. Refer to Figure 4.1 for an illustration of this concept.

4.3.1 Purpose

Since the primary purpose of addenda is to make changes to the procurement documents, these changes, in many cases, are the result of questions raised by bidders or proposers. Other changes include adding new requirements, including the extent of work, and correcting errors or omissions in procurement documents. Addenda are used when it is necessary to change the procurement documents in any way. Examples include the following:

- To change the date, time, or location of receipt of bids or proposals

- To add to, delete from, or revise procurement documents

- To include additional qualified products or approved substitutions

References to addenda, the method of issue, and other pertinent facts concerning addenda are included in the instructions for procurement, the bid/proposal form, the agreement, and the conditions of the contract.

When issued, addenda become part of the procurement documents, and those portions of addenda that affect the contract documents become part of the contract documents once the agreement is executed.

4.3.2 Procedures

The value of the work should determine whether a change should be made. It may sometimes be advantageous not to issue addenda for non-critical changes that do not affect cost or time and defer them until the agreement is executed. Numerous minor changes can be covered with simple statements.

Addenda should be numbered consecutively. Where separate contracts are to be awarded, a separate series of addenda numbers for each contract should be used. Where feasible, a simple numbering system for items within an addendum helps future cross-referencing.

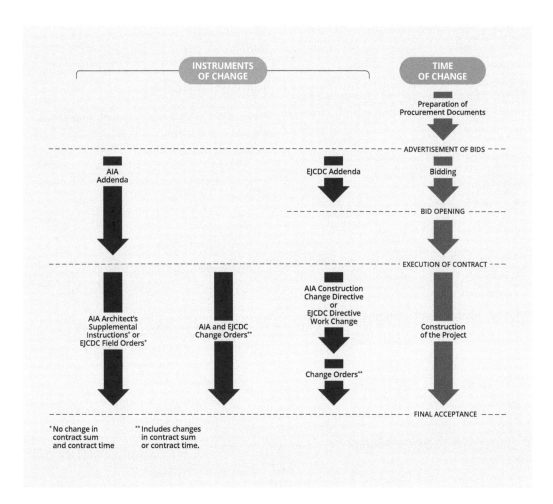

Figure 4.1
Changes in
Procurement
and Contract
Documents

In the procurement process, addenda should be issued to bidders/proposers with sufficient time to prepare prices. If an unforeseen but critical question arises, it may be wise to issue an addendum, even if it means delaying the bid/proposal opening. A minor addendum may sometimes be issued as late as four days before the bid/proposal due date without imposing hardship on the bidders/proposers.

However, standard instructions to bidders usually establish time limits within which the bidder may submit questions or request substitutions.

- AIA Document A701™, *Instructions to Bidders*, stipulates at least seven days before the date of receipt of bids.

- EJCDC® C-200, *Suggested Instructions to Bidders for Construction Contracts*, recommends submitting questions at least 10 days before the bid opening date.

There are no standard instructions to proposers; therefore, if proposals are the procurement method, the instructions to bidders may be used as a template. Attempts to make significant last-minute changes by issuing a few simple inadequate statements in a hastily prepared addendum should be avoided. If it is imperative that a last-minute addendum describing a significant change be issued, the owner should be advised and, if possible, the bid opening date should be postponed. Addenda issued in a proposal process should follow the same guidelines.

Bidders and proposers often need to forward copies of addenda to sub-bidders; therefore, addenda should be easily reproducible or in electronic form. If addenda are to be issued electronically, they should be produced in an electronic format that prevents modification, such as a portable document format (PDF).

DOMAIN 1
Planning,
Development,
& Organization

DOMAIN 2
Coordination

DOMAIN 3
Procurement,
Contracting,
& General
Requirements

DOMAIN 4
Research

DOMAIN 5
Analysis
& Evaluation

DOMAIN 6
Production

4.3.3 Addenda Format

Drawings may accompany written addenda.
Addenda items should be arranged in the same
sequence as the project manual and drawings. Basic
components of addenda and the order in which they
should appear are as follows:

A. Addenda number and date of addendum

B. Project identification

C. Name and address of A/E

D. To whom addendum is issued

E. Opening remarks and notice to
    bidders or proposers

F. Changes to prior addenda

G. Changes to procurement requirements

H. Changes to contracting requirements

I. Changes to specifications, in sequence,
    including approved substitutions

J. Changes to drawings, in sequence

4.3.4 Sample Addendum

The items shown on the left side of Figure 4.2
correspond to the 10 basic components of an
addendum format, as listed previously. This
sample has been limited to one page, although
an actual addendum may require many pages.
Each item should be numbered consecutively for
ease of reference.

4.4 Contract Documents Modifications

The respective AIA, EJCDC, ConsensusDocs
Coalition, and Design-Build Institute of America
(DBIA) conditions of the contract expressly set
forth procedures for the A/E or owner to issue
interpretations of contract documents and order
minor modifications of the work consistent with
these interpretations. Provisions and procedures
are also included for the contractor and owner to
claim changes in the contract sum or contract time

if the contractor or owner believes such changes are
justifiable based on the A/E's written interpretation.

4.4.1 Purpose

When you modify a contract, you change the
original contract in some way. This modification can
include adding, deleting, or correcting portions of
the contract documents. The contract modification
does not replace the entire contract but often
substitutes a part of it.

Frequent reasons for issuing modifications
include the following:

- Incorporation of changes in the owner's
  requirements, including additions or deletions

- Unforeseen field conditions that
  necessitate changes

- Changes in regulatory code provisions or other
  requirements of authorities having jurisdiction,
  which require changes in work

- Changes in market conditions (e.g., specified
  products are not available, new products are
  considered that offer price advantages or other
  benefits, or new information is made available
  that affects specified products)

- Correction of contract documents to eliminate
  errors, omissions, or discrepancies

4.4.2 Procedures

Contract document modifications should be
issued in a timely and orderly fashion to minimize
delays and added costs. A change initiated early in
the construction process allows time to consider
proposals and alternatives and determine a mutually
acceptable change without affecting progress.

Contract document modifications can usually be
kept concise by referring to attachments that describe
changes and cost breakdowns in detail.

Procedural requirements for initiating and
processing modifications should be specified
in Division 01, Section 01 26 00 — Contract
Modification Procedures and closely coordinated
with the conditions of the contract and the
agreement. The method used to describe contract

Figure 4.2
Sample Addendum

Number and Date	**ADDENDUM NO. 2, MAY 1, 2019**
Project Identification	<u>RE:</u> First National Bank of Brownsville project No. 11863

Name and Address of A/E	<u>FROM:</u> ONES and SMITH, Architects and Engineers
	          John Doe Building Washington, D.C.
	          (202) 555-8888

To Whom Addendum is issued	<u>TO:</u> Prospective Bidders
Opening Remark and Notice to Bidders	This Addendum forms a part of the Contract Documents and modifies the original Procurement Documents dated April 15, 2019, and Addendum No. 1 dated April 19, 2019, as noted below. Acknowledge receipt of this Addendum in the space provided on the Bid Form. **Failure to do so may subject Bidder to disqualification.** This Addendum consists of one page and the attached drawing, Sheet S-9-A, with the revised date of April 19, 2019.
Changes to Prior Agenda	CHANGES TO PRIOR ADDENDA: 1. Addendum No. 1, item No. 13, Page AD-1-1, change the number of the reference drawing from "G-1" to "G-7."
Changes to Bidding Requirements	CHANGES TO PROCUREMENT REQUIREMENTS: 2. Instructions to Bidders, Page 00 21 13-2, Item 15, replace first sentence with "Proposed substitutions must be submitted in writing at least 15 days before the date for opening bids."
Changes to Contracting Requirements	CHANGES TO CONTRACTING REQUIREMENTS: 3. Supplementary Conditions Item No. 12, Page 00 73 00-3, change limit of public liability from "$100,000/$500,000" to "$300,000/$500,000."

Changes to Specifications	CHANGES TO SPECIFICATIONS:
	
	4. Section 09 21 16—Gypsum Board Assemblies, subparagraph 2.01 C.3, add the following: "3. Smooth shank nail:
	       a. ASTM C 514.
	       b. Length: 1-3/8 inches (35mm)."
	
	5. Section 23 61 00—Refrigerant Compressors subparagraph 2.03 B. 2, change total square feet (square meters) of surface from "298 (27.68)" to "316 (29.36)."

Changes to Drawings	CHANGES TO DRAWING: 6. Delete sheet S-9-Beam Schedule and replace with attached Sheet S 9-A. 7. Sheet M-1-Mechanical Plan, at Room 602, change "12 x 6" exhaust duct, to "12 x 18".
	END OF ADDENDUM

document modifications may be similar to the method used for an addendum.

4.4.3 Methods of Modification—AIA Documents

There are three recognized ways to modify contract documents when using AIA Document A201®:

- Change order
- Construction change directive
- Minor changes in the work

4.4.3.1 Change Order

A *change order* is a written instruction to the contractor issued after execution of the agreement that authorizes an addition, deletion, or revision in the work that includes an adjustment in the contract sum or the contract time. The contract sum or time can be adjusted only by written change order. The standard form for a change order is AIA Document G701™, *Change Order*.

According to AIA Document A201®, a change order is a written instrument prepared by the architect and

DOMAIN 1
Planning,
Development,
& Organization

DOMAIN 2
Coordination

DOMAIN 3
Procurement,
Contracting,
& General
Requirements

DOMAIN 4
Research

DOMAIN 5
Analysis
& Evaluation

DOMAIN 6
Production

signed by the owner, contractor, and architect, stating their agreement on all of the following:

- A change in the work

- Amount of the adjustment, if any, in the contract sum

- The extent of the adjustment, if any, in the contract time

4.4.3.2 Construction Change Directive

A *construction change directive* is an instrument of ordering changes in the work when the owner and contractor have not agreed on the proposed changes in contract sum or time. The standard form is AIA Document G714™, *Construction Change Directive.*

According to AIA Document A201®, a construction change directive is a written order prepared by the architect and signed by the owner and architect, directing a change in the work before agreement on adjustment and stating a proposed basis for adjustment, if any, in the contract sum or contract time, or both. With a construction change directive, the owner may, without invalidating the contract, order changes in the work within the contract's general scope consisting of additions, deletions, or other revisions. The contract sum, time, or both are to be adjusted accordingly per the proposed method.

A construction change directive is used in the absence of total agreement on the terms of a change order. Upon receipt of a construction change directive, the contractor is required to perform the changes and advise the owner and architect of agreement or disagreement with the proposed method for adjusting contract sum or time.

If the contractor agrees with the proposed method for adjusting the contract sum or time by signing the construction change directive, the agreement should be recorded as a change order.

If the contractor disagrees with the proposed method for adjusting the contract sum or time, the work must still be performed. The architect is usually required to determine the method and amount of adjustment based on reasonable expenditures with an allowance for overhead and profit.

4.4.3.3 Minor Changes in the Work

Minor changes in the work are defined as instructions or interpretations not involving adjustment to the contract sum or time. Such changes direct the contractor to make stated modifications. A minor change does not require the owner's signature. The standard form is AIA Document G710™, *Architect's Supplemental Instructions*; however, if the architect decides to use another document for issuing minor changes, this document should be indicated in the specifications in Section 01 26 00 — Contract Modification Procedures.

According to AIA Document A201®, the architect has the authority to order minor changes in the work that do not involve an adjustment in the contract sum or extension of the contract time and are consistent with the contract documents' intent. Such changes must be effected by written order and are binding on the owner and contractor. The contractor is required to carry out such written orders promptly. For architects working on projects with a construction manager, refer to AIA Document G701/CMa™, *Change Order — Construction Manager-Adviser Edition*, for use with AIA Document A232™, *General Conditions of the Contract for Construction, Construction Manager as Adviser Edition.*

4.4.4 Methods of Modification — EJCDC Documents

There are four recognized ways to change contract documents when using EJCDC® C-700:

- Change order

- Work change directive

- Field order

- Written interpretation or clarification

4.4.4.1 Change Order

Change orders must be signed by the engineer recommending the change, the owner authorizing the change, and the contractor accepting the change. The contract price or time can be adjusted only by written change order. The standard form for a change order is EJCDC® C-941, *Change Order*.

EJCDC® C-700 defines a change order as a document recommended by the engineer, signed by the contractor and the owner, and authorizing an addition, deletion, or revision in the work or an adjustment in the contract price or the contract time, issued on or after the effective date of the agreement.

4.4.4.2 Work Change Directive

The *work change directive* may or may not affect the contract price or time but is evidence that the changes will be incorporated in a change order once the work's value is established. The standard form is EJCDC® C-940, *Work Change Directive*.

EJCDC® C-700 defines a work change directive as a written directive statement to the contractor issued on or after the agreement's effective date and is signed by the owner. A work change directive is used to order additions, deletions, or revisions in the work or respond to differing or unforeseen subsurface or physical conditions under which the work is to be performed. It may also be used to address emergencies.

A work change directive does change the contract price or the contract times. However, it is evidence that the parties expect that the change directed, ordered, or documented by a work change directive will be incorporated in a subsequently issued change order following negotiations by the parties as to its effect, if any, on the contract price or contract times.

4.4.4.3 Field Order

Under EJCDC® C-700, a *field order* is a written order issued by the engineer that orders minor changes in the work that does not involve a change in the contract price or contract times. These orders must be in writing but do not require an executed change order or the owner's signature. EJCDC does not have a standard form for field orders.

4.4.5 Methods of Modification—ConsensusDocs

ConsensusDocs® 200 recognizes three methods of changing the contract documents:

- Change order
- Interim directive
- Written amendment

4.4.5.1 Change Order

The change order is used to formalize changes in the work and adjust contract time and price. The change order is also used to accept substitutions. The standard form for a change order is ConsensusDocs® 202, *Change Order*. The ConsensusDocs change order only requires the signature of the owner and the contractor.

4.4.5.2 Interim Directive

The *interim directive* is a written order directing the contractor to perform work before agreeing on an adjustment to the contract time or price. The owner also uses the interim directive to direct work that the owner believes is not a change. The standard form for an interim directive is ConsensusDocs® 203, *Interim Directive*. Only the owner is required to sign the interim directive.

4.4.5.3 Written Amendment

The written amendment is not a formal change document specifically mentioned in ConsensusDocs® 200 but is only mentioned at the end where the general conditions describe the order of precedence. Written amendments are listed along with change orders. ConsensusDocs does not have a standard form for written amendments.

4.4.6 Methods of Modification—DBIA Documents

DBIA Document No. 535, *Standard Form of General Conditions of a Contract Between Owner and Design-Builder*, recognizes three ways to change the contract documents:

- Change order
- Work change directive
- Minor changes

DOMAIN 1
Planning,
Development,
& Organization

DOMAIN 2
Coordination

DOMAIN 3
Procurement,
Contracting,
& General
Requirements

DOMAIN 4
Research

DOMAIN 5
Analysis
& Evaluation

DOMAIN 6
Production

4.4.6.1 Change Order

The owner and design-builder sign change orders to document changes in the scope of the work, amount of adjustments to the contract price, and extent of adjustment to contract time. The standard form for a change order is DBIA Document No. 500D2, *Design-Build Change Order Form*. The DBIA change order requires the signature of the owner and design-builder.

4.4.6.2 Work Change Directive

A written order is prepared and signed by the owner, directing a change in the work before an agreement on the adjustment in the contract price or contract time. The general conditions require both parties to negotiate in good faith on reaching an agreement. The final agreement on cost and time is documented in a written change order. The standard form for a change order is DBIA Document No. 500D5, *Design-Build Work Change Directive Form*. The DBIA work change directive requires the signature of the owner and the signature of the design-builder upon acceptance.

4.4.6.3 Minor Changes

DBIA general conditions allow the design-builder to make minor changes in the work as long as the changes do not materially or adversely affect the design, quality, performance, and workmanship required by the contract documents. Minor changes must be consistent with the contract documents' intent, and the design-builder must promptly inform the owner in writing.

4.4.7 Methods of Modification — Other

Other entities produce general condition contract documents such as the General Services Administration (GSA), the US Department of Defense (DOD), state and other public works, and so on. In situations where a standard contract document is not being used, care must be given to confirm the method, procedures, supporting documents, and forms applicable to manage modifications.

Pay close attention to any special requirements that may also apply to any modifications to the documents before final bidding or negotiating the contract for these non-standard contract documents.

4.4.8 Change Orders

An axiom of AIA, EJCDC, ConsensusDocs Coalition, and DBIA is that only the owner has the authority to execute a change order. *Execute* may be defined as authorizing the change order.

The A/E signs the change order recommending the change, and the contractor signs the change order indicating acceptance of the change. Change orders may originate either by issuing an AIA construction change directive, an EJCDC work change directive, a ConsensusDocs interim change directive, a DBIA work change directive, or a *change order proposal request*.

The A/E can initiate a change order proposal request by issuing an AIA Document G709™, *Work Changes Proposal Request,* or similar document. A change order proposal request describes proposed changes, supplemented by additional or revised drawings and specifications if necessary. It solicits a proposal from the contractor for an adjustment of the contract sum, contract time, or both. A change order proposal request is for information only and is not an instruction to execute the proposed changes or stop the work in progress. The contractor then responds to the change order proposal request with a proposed adjustment of the contract sum, contract time, or both. Upon agreement of terms, the A/E writes the change order, which is signed by the owner, co-signed by the A/E (if applicable), and then signed by the contractor indicating acceptance of the agreed-upon change.

**DOMAIN 3:
PROCUREMENT, CONTRACTING,
& GENERAL REQUIREMENTS**

Chapter 5

SPECIFYING FOR PURCHASE OF GOODS

5.1 Introduction to Specifying for the Purchase of Goods

Purchasing is the direct acquisition of materials and equipment by an owner for the owner's use or installation in the owner's project. The term *goods* is used in purchasing specifications to designate the materials or equipment to be purchased. This term is also used in the *Uniform Commercial Code* (UCC), which governs most purchasing contracts, so the terminology is consistent between the specifications and applicable law.

The goods, which may range from office supplies to furniture, fixtures, and equipment (FF&E), are purchased from a manufacturer, fabricator, dealer, supplier, or other vendors. The purchasing of goods necessitates a contract or agreement, so the vendor is called the goods contractor.

Unlike the construction contractor, the goods contractor is involved in little or no on-site activity, such as construction, installation, or erection. This lack of on-site activity is one of the distinguishing factors of a purchasing contract. The owner may purchase goods under a purchasing contract for installation by the construction contractor. However, if the goods contractor is required to participate in the actual construction, the goods would be furnished and installed under a subcontract agreement. This agreement is between the goods contractor and the construction contractor rather than under a purchasing contract. Equipment, furniture, or other items requiring only assembly and placement but that are not built into the construction may still be purchased under a separate purchasing contract. The goods contractor may also perform special services such as providing technical assistance during installation of the goods by others, testing the goods after installation, conducting start-up procedures, and training the owner's personnel.

The purchased goods might be for the owner's use, such as for maintenance or a manufacturing process. The goods may also be incorporated into the owner's construction project by another contractor. Figure 5.1 illustrates the case in which the goods' delivery and disposition are made to the construction contractor for installation in the project. In the

Construction
Specifications
Practice Guide

DOMAIN 1
Planning,
Development,
& Organization

DOMAIN 2
Coordination

DOMAIN 3
Procurement,
Contracting,
& General
Requirements

DOMAIN 4
Research

DOMAIN 5
Analysis
& Evaluation

DOMAIN 6
Production

illustration, an architect/engineer (A/E) has been contracted by the owner to produce both the purchasing and the construction documents. An A/E should prepare purchasing documents that consist of a project manual and drawings in a manner similar to the preparation of construction documents.

5.1.1 Procurement/Supply Chain Management

The concept of supply chain management as a natural, evolutionary managerial advancement over the traditional purchasing function is much more prevalent and commonly accepted than in the past and has become the norm. Traditional supply chain management theory holds that an organization can reduce procurement costs, reduce procurement cycle time, and add value to the procurement process by taking actions such as the following:

Reducing the number of suppliers used. Many organizations have found that maintaining many suppliers for the same or similar products or services and managing that supplier base is more expensive than the savings potentially realized from extensive competition among fewer suppliers for orders. Having many suppliers also introduces quality and consistent performance issues that are more difficult to manage.

Negotiating long-term contracts with the few preferred suppliers. Cost savings can be realized by making significant commitments to a few suppliers instead of making only short-term commitments to many suppliers.

Conducting more rigorous and detailed timelines and quality tracking of the preferred supplier base. The significant purchase commitments made to a few suppliers are coupled with increased requirements for quality and performance.

Figure 5.1
Purchasing
Contract

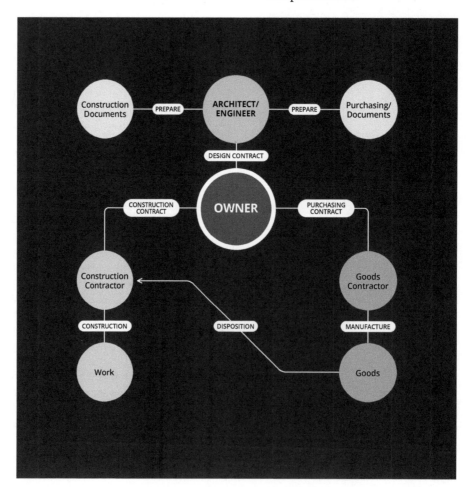

Supply chain management concepts recognize that the acquisition function does not operate in a reactive vacuum. Instead, it is a component in a more extensive management system that provides value and profitability by merging customer needs and supplier capabilities with the organization's value-added processes.

5.1.2 Typical Procurement Steps

The usual procurement steps in a project are as follows:

1. **Solicitation, Request for Bids, or Request for Proposals.** These may also be called the Advertisement or Notice to Bidders.

2. **Bidding or Accepting Proposals.** In this stage, the bidders/proposers receive a complete set of the procurement documents, also known as the project manual. The project manual typically includes a copy of the solicitation, instructions-to-bidders/proposers, bid/proposal forms, certifications and representations, general provisions, contract conditions, a copy of the contract, project drawings, technical specifications, and related project documents.

3. **Bid/Proposal Evaluation.** The period when the buyer tabulates and reviews all bids/proposals for responsiveness and responsibility.

4. **Award.** The point when the buyer formally awards the contract to the successful bidder/proposer.

5. **Execution of Contract.** The point when the buyer formally enters into a legally binding agreement with the goods contractor to perform services or provide goods.

5.2 Use of Purchasing

Purchasing documents may be prepared to cover several activities by the goods contractor:

- To manufacture, fabricate, or supply and transfer to the owner or the owner's representative at the goods contractor's plant

- To manufacture, fabricate, or supply and deliver to a designated location

- To perform additional special services, which may include the preparation of shop drawings, the compilation of operation and maintenance data, technical assistance or guidance during on-site construction or installation of the goods by others, field checking or testing of the goods after installation or erection by others, start-up procedures, and training of the owner's personnel

Each of these activities has particular requirements that must be carefully considered and coordinated throughout the project manual. Note that these activities all stop short of actual on-site construction or installation by the goods contractor. Properly employed purchasing procedures are of appreciable benefit. The uses of purchasing documents to purchase goods in advance of construction or installation include the following:

- To aid in establishing a project budget, as costs of the purchased goods are known in advance

- To gain lead time on goods that require long manufacturing or fabrication periods, and thereby avoid construction delays

- To anticipate shortages of either materials or manufacturing capability

- To take advantage of present favorable cost or to protect against inflation

- To provide information for the design of facilities required to accommodate the specific goods purchased

- To permit the acquisition of goods to fulfill the cash allowances of a construction contract by assignment of the purchasing contract to the construction contractor

- To obtain uniformity of function, appearance, or operation and for ease of maintenance, repair, and replacement

- To provide for the proprietary or single-source acquisition of goods

- To permit the acquisition of goods for which an owner may be entitled to tax exemptions not available to a construction contractor

DOMAIN 1
Planning,
Development,
& Organization

DOMAIN 2
Coordination

DOMAIN 3
Procurement,
Contracting,
& General
Requirements

DOMAIN 4
Research

DOMAIN 5
Analysis
& Evaluation

DOMAIN 6
Production

- To permit the acquisition of goods in situations where a construction contractor would not have the necessary technical expertise or the necessary financial or administrative resources

- To reduce the amount of a construction contract, to reduce bonding requirements, or to enable small construction contractors to bid

- To permit the A/E to procure the goods in conjunction with a design construction contract or the purchasing agency to acquire the goods for an industrial/process engineering organization

- To serve as an adjunct to fast-track construction

- To establish an inventory of goods for later use or installation by the owner

Conversely, the acquisition of goods through purchasing contracts may not always be advantageous. The following precautions should be considered:

- The owner's financial investment may be significant before the use of the goods.

- The goods may become obsolete before use because of the subsequent production of improved goods.

- The owner and the A/E might invest appreciable administrative time that the construction contractor would usually provide if the goods were provided as part of a construction contract.

- A burden may be imposed on the construction contractor due to purchased goods being stored on the site.

- The owner may become responsible for the time of delivery, handling, storage, maintenance, the condition of the goods at the time of turnover, the suitability of items furnished, and the completeness of items specified. The owner may therefore be liable to claims by the construction contractor for late or incomplete delivery. This possibility should be considered in establishing liquidated damages in the purchasing contract.

- A particular type and extensive level of expertise are required to develop the purchasing documents.

- The A/E assumes additional responsibilities for coordination of the purchasing and construction.

- The owner or A/E must prepare documents and negotiate and administer more than one contract.

- The construction contractor may object to installing goods that have been purchased separately and may not provide the same warranty as for the items supplied under the construction contract.

- Problems may arise over the assignment of responsibility for performance failures because the goods were acquired under one contract and installed under another.

- Provisions for equipment warranties become more complex and must be carefully addressed to suit specific project needs.

- Certain proprietary goods may be available only from specific dealers and could limit competition and pricing.

5.3 Purchasing Contract and Construction Contract Differences

One of the purchase-specifying principles is that the goods contractor's on-site activities are limited, and no construction or installation is usually involved. The solicitation, procurement instructions, bid or proposal forms, agreement, conditions of the contract, and Division 01 — General Requirements used in purchasing contracts differ from those used in construction documents. Most of these differences are readily apparent. The more subtle differences occur in the conditions of the contract. The following subjects should be carefully considered.

5.3.1 Procurement Challenges in Construction Contracts

All products used on a construction project are procured in some manner, whether provided by the contractor, subcontractor, or owner. However, through a construction project, the product

procurement process involves more than just giving a specification to a contractor or the owner supplying the product.

The challenges contractors and subcontractors face in procuring products tend to be more schedule related. The procurement process typically begins early enough so that the products arrive well before the time they are needed for installation. However, for some project sites, this could be a logistics problem. Project sites with limited space cannot afford the space to store products and materials well before their scheduled installation date. Thus, either an arrangement must be made to store the products off-site, or the products must be scheduled to ensure just-in-time (JIT) delivery. For off-site storage, the contract documents should establish the conditions that must be met for this option to be used, especially if the owner is asked to pay for the stored products and materials before they are brought onto the project site.

Once a delivery date is determined, then it is a matter of setting the start date of the procurement process based on the combined duration of all activities that must occur before delivery. These activities typically include preparing submittals, reviewing and approving submittals, preparing shop drawings (including reviewing and approving if required),

fabricating or manufacturing (if made to order), and finally shipping. Any delay in this process may likely impact the project schedule. Since submittals play an essential role in this process, Section 01 33 00—Submittal Procedures should provide the contractor with the minimum review times that the A/E must be given to review submittals. This review time should include the first submittal and one resubmittal.

Owners may procure products for the project and furnish them to the contractor for installation. Products provided in this manner are referred to as *owner furnished-contractor installed* (OFCI) products and are frequently used in construction projects. If the owner plans to furnish products to the contractor, these should be identified in the construction documents. Either Section 01 10 00—Summary or Section 01 64 00—Owner-Furnished Products may be used to list the OFCI products. The section used should also state the responsibilities of the owner and contractor regarding the OFCI products.

Less frequently used in construction contracts are *contractor furnished-owner installed* (CFOI) and *owner furnished-owner installed* (OFOI) products. For CFOI products, the procurement process is the same as for products purchased and installed by the contractor or subcontractor except for the

DOMAIN 1
Planning,
Development,
& Organization

DOMAIN 2
Coordination

DOMAIN 3
Procurement,
Contracting,
& General
Requirements

DOMAIN 4
Research

DOMAIN 5
Analysis
& Evaluation

DOMAIN 6
Production

installation part. Once received by the contractor, the products are turned over to the owner to install at their convenience unless the CFOI products must be in place before the contractor's subsequent work. OFOI products may include those products that the contractor needs only to provide supporting construction or utility services, such as water, power, and gas. If asked by the contractor, the owner should provide any information about the products so construction and services can be precisely located. Section 01 10 00 — Summary can be used to provide and list CFOI and OFOI products and state the owner and contractor's responsibilities regarding those products.

In some cases, the contractor may be required to procure products through the owner's established purchase contracts. Through this process, the contractor purchases and installs the selected products. If using the owner's purchase contract, the contractor is not relieved of its responsibilities applicable to products purchased by the contractor through other sources.

No matter how the products are procured, there are some common challenges involved when it comes to construction contracts:

Risk mitigation. Supply risk is always a significant challenge in the procurement process. Market risks, potential frauds, cost, quality, and delivery risks constitute the most common type of risks.

Long process cycle. Occasionally, products and services are procured with a sense of urgency at the last minute. As a result, the actual lead times and the procurement cycle tend to be considerably longer than anticipated or scheduled. Here are some common reasons for delays in the procurement process:

- Delays in preparing submittals, shop drawings, or scopes of work

- Extended review times for submittals and shop drawings

- Overlooking the procurement schedule, such as required lead times

Setbacks in contract negotiation. The parties may fail to thoroughly prepare to negotiate.

If the negotiating parties do not understand each other's needs, it can hinder reaching a mutual agreement.

Inaccurate data. To make sound procurement decisions, buyers need accurate and reliable data. Making purchases based on inaccurate procurement data can lead to receiving the wrong items or incorrect quantities.

Supplier-related issues. One of the most significant challenges in procurement is supplier management. From identifying the right supplier to keeping track of vendor performance and ensuring a stable supply of quality products, the whole process is filled with complications.

Strategic procurement. As the procurement process becomes more strategic and collaborative, organizations are starting to realize the benefits of having a solid procurement strategy. However, understanding every step's strategic implications and figuring out a way to implement it across all construction areas is a distinct challenge.

5.3.2 Definitions

The definitions commonly found in construction documents — particularly those related to on-site construction or installation activities — are not always applicable to purchasing documents. Inapplicable definitions must be avoided. It is possible for both a purchasing contract and a construction contract (which includes installing the purchased goods) to be in place simultaneously for the same products. Although definitions of the same word or term may appear in the documents for both contracts, there may be a slight difference between them. It is imperative that the various definitions not conflict with one another.

5.3.3 Bonds

Depending on the type of goods to be purchased and their intended disposition, a performance bond should usually be required. The bond provides recourse for the owner in the event of non-performance in the manufacture, supply, or delivery of goods.

5.3.4 Insurance

The types of insurance needed for purchasing contracts depend entirely on the goods contractor's specific activities. Manufacture or fabrication is generally at the goods contractor's plant and so will not usually be subject to direct control or supervision by the owner. Liability insurance coverage should be part of the goods contractor's regular business operation. Stipulations are therefore generally inappropriate, except that property insurance should be required, at the owner's request, to protect the owner's interest in undelivered goods for which payment has been made and for goods that have been delayed in shipment.

When the purchasing contract includes delivery by the goods contractor to a designated location, the documents should require the goods contractor to provide transit insurance to cover the goods during shipment, especially if any payment has been made. Receipt by the owner or construction contractor at the point of delivery generally involves the transfer of responsibility. Insurance after delivery is usually the responsibility of the owner.

Technical assistance during on-site construction or installation, field checking or testing after installation, conducting start-up procedures, or training the owner's personnel are on-site activities that may directly involve the goods contractor. Although the goods contractor's exposure to insurable risk under the purchasing contract may be limited compared to a construction contract, the exposure still exists. The documents for such purchasing contracts should require the goods contractor to provide liability insurance during on-site activities similar to the insurance provided under construction contracts. Coverage should include workers' compensation, general liability, and automobile liability coverage. All decisions concerning types and amounts of required insurance should be made by the owner in consultation with legal counsel and insurance advisers.

5.3.5 Goods Contractor's Responsibilities

Generally, the goods contractor should not be charged with responsibilities directly related to on-site construction. The goods contractor should not be required to visit the site or conduct on-site investigations unless field measurements are required, existing field conditions may affect the production of the goods, or technical assistance is specified. Matters such as construction permits, licenses, construction equipment, temporary facilities, and safety should be the construction contractor's responsibility.

Unless the goods to be purchased are exceptionally expensive or complicated, subcontractors are usually not involved in a purchasing contract. Therefore, most purchasing documents do not include stipulations concerning subcontractors, such as relationships between contractor and subcontractors, or owner and subcontractor.

Except when unique codes or laws govern—as in the case of purchasing nuclear components, pressure vessels, or fire protection systems—it should not be necessary to stipulate the goods contractor's compliance with laws and regulations about manufacturing processes or to specify provisions for safety and protection. However, it is appropriate to require compliance with applicable standards, such as those from the ASTM International (ASTM), American National Standards Institute (ANSI), American Society of Mechanical Engineers (ASME), or National Electrical Manufacturers Association (NEMA). Manufacturing or fabrication remains solely the goods contractor's responsibility as part of normal business operations.

5.3.6 A/E Responsibilities

If the A/E is involved in preparing construction documents under which the goods are to be installed, the A/E must coordinate the construction contract's purchasing provisions. Proper relationships must exist between the contracts, and suitable provisions must be stipulated in each so that pertinent items are neither omitted nor duplicated. Receipt and handling of the goods, utility connections, start-up procedures, training of the owner's personnel, and similar items must be clearly stipulated.

The responsibilities of the A/E for a purchasing contract vary according to project requirements and the owner's desires. Responsibilities must be carefully established and thoroughly understood by both the owner and the A/E.

DOMAIN 1
Planning,
Development,
& Organization

DOMAIN 2
Coordination

DOMAIN 3
Procurement,
Contracting,
& General
Requirements

DOMAIN 4
Research

DOMAIN 5
Analysis
& Evaluation

DOMAIN 6
Production

The A/E may or may not be obligated to visit the goods contractor's plant or conduct or witness shop tests. The A/E may or may not become involved in the observation or verification of the goods at the delivery time. These items materially affect the purchasing contract provisions and the A/E agreement for professional services and must be clarified with the owner in advance.

5.3.7 Shop Drawings, Product Data, and Samples

The A/E typically manages the review and approval of submittals. Stipulations covering the submittal of shop drawings and product data are similar to the requirements generally found in construction contracts. A greater-than-usual number of approved submittals may be acquired for records and for transmittal to the construction contractor or other end users of the purchased goods. It may also be advantageous to make these submittals available during solicitation on the construction contract.

5.3.8 Operation and Maintenance Manuals

Documents for traditional construction contracts frequently include a requirement for operation and maintenance manuals, particularly for complex equipment or systems. These manuals might be even more critical under a purchasing contract. There may be little direct contact between the goods contractor and the eventual installer or erector; therefore, the information supplied by operation and maintenance manuals may be of critical importance.

5.3.9 Payment, Completion, and Acceptance

Payment procedures depend primarily on the nature of the goods being purchased. Items may be such that partial deliveries and corresponding progress payments are necessary. For some complex equipment, progress payments may sometimes occur during manufacturing or fabrication. In most instances, however, procedures are based on making a payment at each of three stages:

- Approval of submittals

- Delivery to the designated location

- Final acceptance

Suppose progress payments are to be made while the goods are being manufactured and remain under the goods contractor's control. In that case, provisions should be included for protecting the owner's interest in the partially completed goods. Appropriate contract language for this purpose should be obtained from the owner's legal counsel.

As the A/E may be involved in observation or verification of the goods delivered, the corresponding obligations should be considered in establishing procedures for acceptance and payment. The A/E should not assume unnecessary responsibilities or risk undue exposure on matters with which they have no direct knowledge or control.

Procedures for final acceptance and final payment also depend on the nature of the goods. Some items are complete and entirely acceptable at the delivery time, and final payment is made accordingly. For other items such as equipment, final acceptance is reserved until the item has been installed or placed in service and proven acceptable. However, in fairness to the goods contractor, some reasonable time limit should be set between the delivery time and the installation time, after which final payment should be made regardless of whether the item has been installed and tested. In any case, the procedures to be followed must be clearly specified.

Although goods delivered to the site are usually covered by property insurance, measures may need to be taken to prevent theft or damage.

5.4 Uniform Commercial Code

The primary source of commercial contract law is the *Uniform Commercial Code* (UCC). The UCC, as a uniform law, must be adopted as law by each state separately. As a result, there are differences in the UCC from state to state.

The current law governing contracts for the transaction of any *goods* between buyers and sellers is Article 2 of the UCC. It has been adopted in 49 states (Louisiana is the exception) and in some US territories and Native American nations. Article 2 presents some general principles of contract law. It covers contract formation, contractual obligations of the seller and the buyer, rules for performing on a contract, what constitutes a breach of contract, and remedies for breach of contract.

The written contract must contain sufficient detail to indicate that a contract for sale has been made between the parties and signed by the party against whom enforcement is sought or by their authorized agent or broker. Article 2 contains three requirements of the written contract:

- It must provide evidence that there was a contract for the sale of goods.

- It must be signed by the party to be charged.

- It must specify a quantity.

A contract is enforceable as long as these three requirements are included.

The A/E should be aware of the basic provisions of the UCC, which become effective in the absence of (or may sometimes actually override) written contract provisions. Each of the using states publishes the UCC as a part of its state statutes.

The UCC comprises articles that govern a wide variety of frequently recurring business transactions, including the sale of goods, negotiable instruments, and financial transactions involving security interests. Article 2, dealing with sales, has the most significant effect on purchasing contracts. Its coverage is limited to sales of movable goods, so contracts primarily for services are excluded. The term *services* includes activities by the goods contractor such as technical assistance or an installation check.

The following sections cover the four basic areas of contract law addressed by Article 2 of the UCC.

5.4.1 Contract Enforceability and Formation

Contracts for the sale of goods costing more than $500 must be in writing to be enforceable. Generally, a written contract without ambiguities is construed

DOMAIN 1
Planning,
Development,
& Organization

DOMAIN 2
Coordination

DOMAIN 3
Procurement,
Contracting,
& General
Requirements

DOMAIN 4
Research

DOMAIN 5
Analysis
& Evaluation

DOMAIN 6
Production

as the total agreement between the parties and may not be contradicted by a prior agreement or a concurrent oral agreement. The strict common-law contract rules relating to offer and acceptance and the formation of a contract are somewhat relaxed under the UCC. The thrust of Article 2 is to establish a contract with various terms and conditions, even though there was never an actual meeting of the minds in the contract-law sense. The legal test is whether the parties intended to make a contract. Contract terms, including price, may be left open to be determined at a later date.

5.4.2 Warranties

The UCC attaches certain warranties, expressed and implied, to sales transactions and governs warranties provided by the seller. Generally, a seller warrants the transfer of a clear title, free of any security interest of which the buyer is unaware. (See Section 9.5.9.)

5.4.3 Contract Interpretation

The UCC acknowledges the common commercial practice by which the contracting parties leave specific terms to be agreed upon at a later date or based on reasonable commercial practices. Quantity must generally be agreed upon; however, the UCC may supply details of payment, delivery, and even price if the written contract does not cover them. Unless otherwise agreed, the UCC allocates risk of loss or damage to the goods between the buyer and the seller, depending on the extent to which the agreement has been performed. FOB (free on board), CIF (costs, insurance, and freight), and similar shorthand mercantile terms that place responsibility for transportation costs, insurance, and risk of loss are defined in the UCC.

A requirement binds the parties to an agreement governed by the UCC that they act in good faith, as unfair or unconscionable contracts are not enforceable.

5.4.4 Remedies

The UCC provides remedies for the seller if the buyer becomes insolvent or breaches the contract by wrongfully rejecting the goods, refusing to pay, or revoking acceptance. The seller may elect to

stop delivery, reclaim the goods, recover the price, or recover damages. Conversely, if the seller is at fault for failing to deliver the goods as specified, the buyer may cancel the contract, purchase a substitute, and recover damages. The UCC provides alternative bases for computing actual damages and allows the recovery of incidental and consequential damages if appropriate. A liquidated damages clause is enforceable if the amount is reasonable and verifiable; however, if the amount is excessive and unsubstantiated, the clause is unenforceable.

5.5 Format

Assuming the goods are to be competitively bid, MasterFormat®, SectionFormat®, PageFormat®, and other organizational tools offered by the Construction Specifications Institute (CSI) may be greatly beneficial. The organization, concepts, locations of subject matter, and language established by CSI can be adapted to purchasing documents. The use of documents similar to those already accepted and familiar to goods contractors and suppliers in the construction industry helps avoid confusion. Usually, a purchasing contract for goods and a construction contract that includes installation of those goods can be in force simultaneously, in which case the two project manuals should be similar and must be carefully coordinated.

5.5.1 Procurement and Contracting Requirements

A purchasing project manual customarily contains procurement requirements, contracting forms, conditions of the contract, and specifications. These documents are similar to those used for construction projects but reflect the differences previously discussed.

The procurement requirements might include pre-bid information, instructions to bidders, information available to bidders, bid forms, and bid security forms. An agreement form, performance bond, general conditions, and supplementary conditions should also be elements of the purchasing project manual. Standard documents available for purchase projects are discussed at the end of this chapter.

5.5.2 Division 01 — General Requirements

Division 01 specifications are as crucial for purchase projects as they are for construction projects. These sections should expand the general conditions' provisions and provide general procedural requirements that govern the other specification sections. The Level 2 and Level 3 sections listed in MasterFormat® fall into three categories concerning purchasing contracts.

The first category includes those sections that are generally applicable to all purchasing contracts:

> Section 01 10 00 — Summary

> Section 01 30 00 — Administrative Requirements

> Section 01 40 00 — Quality Requirements

> Section 01 60 00 — Product Requirements

The second category includes those sections that are sometimes applicable to purchasing contracts, the determining factors being the level of activity required of the goods contractor and the particular aspects of the project:

> Section 01 20 00 — Price and
> Payment Procedures

> Section 01 70 00 — Execution and
> Closeout Requirements

> Section 01 80 00 — Performance Requirements

The third category includes those sections that are generally not applicable to purchasing contracts because they relate to on-site activities:

> Section 01 50 00 — Temporary
> Facilities and Controls

> Section 01 92 00 — Facility Operation

> Section 01 94 00 — Facility Decommissioning

5.5.3 Divisions 02 through 49

Use of the appropriate divisions and sections of the technical specifications are determined by the project requirements, just as they are in construction contracts. Depending on the goods to be purchased, the project manual may contain one or more specification sections. Many of the MasterFormat® titles deal exclusively with construction and would not be appropriate for purchasing, but others pertaining essentially to FF&E or materials may be used. SectionFormat® presents a format for organizing a specification section that readily lends itself to a purchase project's specific requirements.

DOMAIN 1
Planning,
Development,
& Organization

DOMAIN 2
Coordination

DOMAIN 3
Procurement,
Contracting,
& General
Requirements

DOMAIN 4
Research

DOMAIN 5
Analysis
& Evaluation

DOMAIN 6
Production

Of the three parts of SectionFormat®, PART 3 — EXECUTION deals with on-site activities and is the least used in purchasing. Items related to the disposition of goods and special services required of the goods contractor would typically be stated in PART 3. However, if there are no requirements to be stated in PART 3, one can simply note "Not Used." Development of individual articles under each of the three parts is determined by the following:

- The basic purchasing procedures

- The nature of the goods

- Whether the section is written as a proprietary, descriptive, reference standard, or performance specification

- The required level of contractor activity

- The eventual disposition of the purchased goods

5.5.4 Disposition of Goods

Preparation of purchasing documents must include consideration of the purchased goods' eventual disposition, as each of the methods of disposition has its effect on various document sections. Three basic methods should be considered:

Retention by Owner for Own Use and Installation. This form is the simplest method of disposition, with the owner establishing a stockpile or inventory of goods for future use. The owner purchases the goods, with or without delivery by the goods contractor, and after that assumes full responsibility for them. After completion and final payment, the A/E and the goods contractor should no longer be involved, except for the goods contractor's warranty responsibility.

Furnished by Owner for Installation by Others. In this case, the owner is involved in a construction contract, and the purchased goods are to be furnished for installation as part of the construction project. The owner is usually involved in the receipt, storage, and maintenance of the goods and possibly delivering them to the construction contractor. The owner is responsible to the construction contractor for the suitability, completeness, and condition of the goods at the time of transfer.

The construction contractor, after that, becomes responsible for the storage and handling of the goods and their installation. The construction contractor includes in the construction contract the cost of storage, handling, and installation of the goods, and must therefore be provided with all pertinent information. Transfer of any warranties for the goods to the construction contractor might be doubtful, and the owner, as the original purchaser, may be required to retain and enforce the warranties.

Assignment of Purchasing Contract to Construction Contractor. Under this arrangement, the construction contractor accepts the purchasing contract, similar to a purchase order, and assumes all responsibilities for the receipt, payment, administration, and installation. The construction contractor again must be provided with all pertinent information before determining contract cost. The owner may lose a part of any cost advantage that may have been gained through purchasing but retains other inherent advantages.

In any case, the method of disposition must be clearly stipulated in the purchasing documents. If a construction contract is also involved, the method of disposition must be stipulated in the construction contract as well, and the procedures definitively established with both the goods contractor and the construction contractor. The documents must state which items, appurtenances, accessories, or other parts are to be furnished under each contract and must establish responsibilities for the remainder. These procedures require particularly close study and coordination by the A/E.

5.6 AIA Purchasing Documents

The American Institute of Architects (AIA) Document A151™, *Standard Form of Agreement Between Owner and Vendor for Furniture, Furnishings, and Equipment (FF&E)*, provides the agreement and conditions for the provision of FF&E for a project. AIA also publishes AIA Document A751™, *Invitation and Instructions to Vendors for Quotations for Furniture, Furnishings, and Equipment (FF&E)*, for the procurement of vendors to provide

DOMAIN 1
Planning,
Development,
& Organization

DOMAIN 2
Coordination

DOMAIN 3
Procurement,
Contracting,
& General
Requirements

DOMAIN 4
Research

DOMAIN 5
Analysis
& Evaluation

DOMAIN 6
Production

FF&E for a project. AIA Document A151™ includes references to the UCC but states that if there are any conflicts between the agreement and the UCC, the agreement takes precedence. Both documents contain requirements for the vendor to inspect the premises and to assemble or install the FF&E.

When the work only requires the purchase of FF&E without assembly or installation, then AIA Document A152™, *Purchase Order*, should be used along with its companion document AIA Document A152™ Exhibit A, *Terms and Conditions*. Like AIA Document A151™, AIA Document A152™ references the UCC; however, it does not stipulate that the terms and conditions have precedence should there be a conflict between the two.

5.7 EJCDC Procurement Documents

The Engineers Joint Contract Documents Committee (EJCDC) uses the term procurement instead of purchasing or sale of goods as used by CSI and AIA. The following paragraphs are excerpted and paraphrased from EJCDC® P-001, *Commentary on the 2019 EJCDC Procurement Documents*, and are updated to reflect the more recent editions of published documents.

These EJCDC documents are used when an owner purchases *Goods* (also generically referred to as "engineered materials and equipment" in EJCDC® P-001) directly from the provider for use on engineer-designed projects. These purchasing documents are an alternative to accepting standard purchase order forms provided by manufacturers and suppliers, and they avoid the inadequacies of such forms and the difficulties of adapting them to adequately address the owner's needs and the project's requirements. There are four primary EJCDC purchasing documents:

EJCDC® P-200, *Instructions to Bidders, Procurement Contracts*

EJCDC® P-520, *Agreement Between Buyer and Seller for Procurement*

EJCDC® P-700, *Standard General Conditions for Procurement Contracts*

EJCDC® P-800, *Guide to the Preparation of Procurement Supplementary Conditions*

5.7.1 General Considerations

Purchasing documents are closely integrated, and the terms used in all four primary purchasing documents are defined in the general conditions. A change in any one of these documents may require a change in the others. Anyone using the EJCDC purchasing documents would do well to read those parts of EJCDC® C-001, *Commentary on the 2018 Construction Series Documents*, which pertain to the comparable forms for construction contracts. EJCDC® P-400, *Bid Form for Procurement*, is used in conjunction with EJCDC's other procurement documents. In preparing the purchasing documents, EJCDC paid close attention to the suggested locations of subject matter as outlined in EJCDC® N-122, *Uniform Location of Subject Matter*.

5.7.2 Intended Use

The purchasing documents are not intended for use where the manufacturer or supplier of the goods must participate in the installation at the project site. However, the EJCDC documents address *special services* provided by the seller, but this is limited to assisting the installing entity (See Section 5.7.3). The EJCDC documents assume that the owner's personnel, a construction contractor, or a subcontractor at the site installs the furnished goods. When the contractor is required to include installation, the project is more like a traditional construction contract. The standard forms for construction contracts should be used, or the primary purchasing documents should be modified to include installation. If the purchasing documents are to be used in cases where there are multiple deliveries of the same item, changes to the primary procurement documents should be made using supplementary conditions.

5.7.3 Definitions

In the interest of uniformity, many terms used in the EJCDC documents for construction contracts are defined in the purchasing documents as having the same or similar meanings. Accordingly, the manufacturer or vendor furnishing the goods is referred to as the *Seller* who has entered into an agreement with the owner, or *Buyer*. A person or entity referred to in the documents as a manufacturer, supplier, fabricator, distributor, or vendor would be a party having a subcontract with one of the prime construction contractors or a sub-subcontract with one of the subcontractors performing work at the project site.

Frequently, the seller is required to be present at the project site during installation, testing, or starting of the goods and may instruct the owner's personnel or provide other consulting or advisory services. Such construction site services are referred to as *special services*. Special services are not intended to cover installation services by the goods contractor because the purchasing documents are not intended to apply to a furnish, deliver, and install relationship. The various categories of special services to be furnished are generally described in Article 1 of the agreement and particularized in the supplementary conditions or the specifications. The term *work*, defined in construction contract documents, is not used in the purchasing documents.

5.8 ConsensusDocs Purchasing Documents

The ConsensusDocs family includes three standard documents used for the purchase of goods. These documents are as follows:

ConsensusDocs® 702, *Standard Purchase Order for Commodity Goods*

ConsensusDocs® 702.1, *Terms and Conditions for Purchase Order for Commodity Goods*

ConsensusDocs® 703, *Standard Purchase Agreement for Non-commodity Goods by a Contractor*

The ConsensusDocs purchasing documents use terminology identical to that used in the EJCDC documents. The items purchased are *Goods*, the owner is the *Buyer*, and the party offering the Goods for purchase is the *Seller*. However, unlike EJCDC and AIA documents, the ConsensusDocs documents do not directly reference the UCC. Instead, ConsensusDocs® 702.1 and 703 both state that the laws in effect at the project's location govern the agreements. If the location is within a state that has adopted the UCC, then the UCC would govern by default.

ConsensusDocs® 703 is intended for the use in the purchasing of complex goods. Similar to AIA Document A151™, ConsensusDocs® 703 provides for the purchase of goods, including the installation. On the other hand, ConsensusDocs® 702 is used along with ConsensusDocs® 702.1 to purchase goods that do not require any installation. Both documents are very similar in their organization; however, since ConsensusDocs® 703 also includes installation, it provides additional insurance, safety, and indemnity provisions.

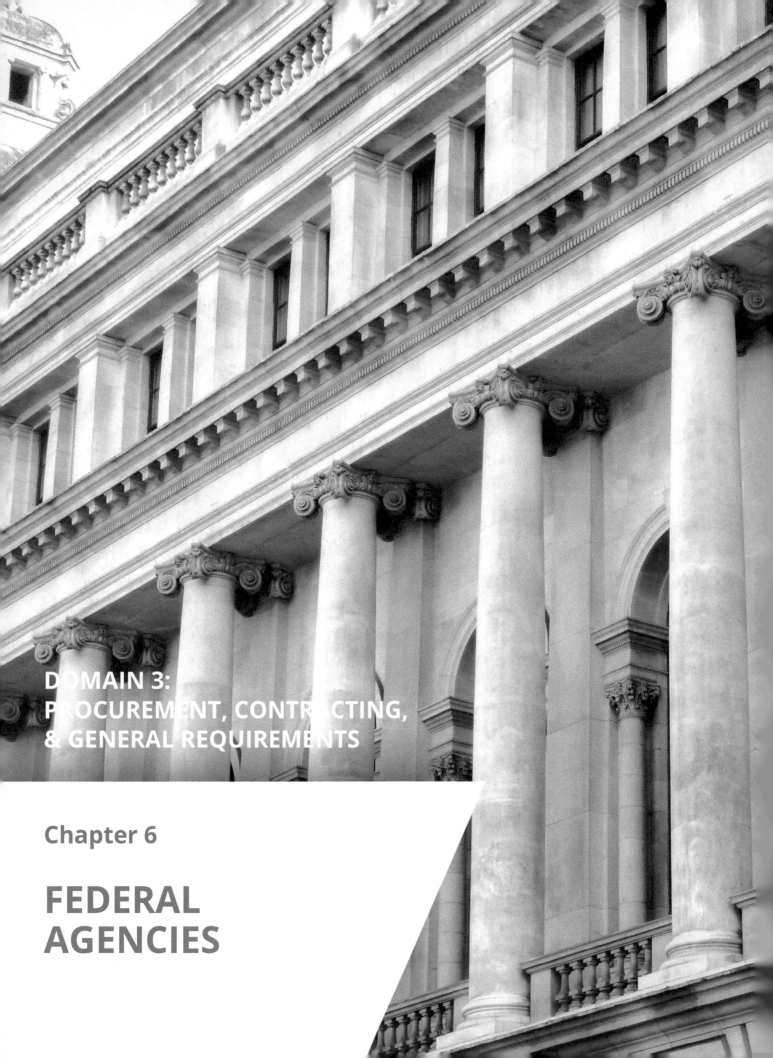

DOMAIN 3:
PROCUREMENT, CONTRACTING,
& GENERAL REQUIREMENTS

Chapter 6

FEDERAL
AGENCIES

6.1 The Federal Acquisition Regulation (FAR)

The Federal Acquisition Regulation (FAR) provides uniform policies and procedures for acquisition by all executive agencies. The Federal Acquisition Regulations System consists of the FAR—the primary document—and acquisition regulations developed by federal agencies that implement or supplement the FAR.

6.1.1 Vision

The Federal Acquisition Regulations System's vision is to deliver the best value product or service to the customer on a timely basis while maintaining the public's trust and fulfilling public policy objectives. Participants in the acquisition process should work together as a team and be empowered to make decisions within their responsibility area.

6.1.2 Guiding Principles

The Federal Acquisition Regulations System will do the following:

- Satisfy the customer in terms of cost, quality, and timeliness of the delivered product or service (e.g., maximizing the use of commercial products and services, using contractors who have a track record of successful past performance, using contractors who demonstrate a current superior ability to perform, and promoting competition)

- Minimize administrative operating costs

- Conduct business with integrity, fairness, and openness

- Fulfill public policy objectives

6.1.3 Authority

The FAR is prepared, issued, and maintained jointly by the Secretary of Defense, the General Services Administration (GSA) administrators, and the National Aeronautics and Space Administration (NASA).

DOMAIN 1
Planning,
Development,
& Organization

DOMAIN 2
Coordination

DOMAIN 3
Procurement,
Contracting,
& General
Requirements

DOMAIN 4
Research

DOMAIN 5
Analysis
& Evaluation

DOMAIN 6
Production

6.1.4 Responsibilities

The Federal Acquisition Regulations System includes government personnel assigned to manage and administer the federal contracting functions. Each position has a defined responsibility described in the FAR. These positions include the following:

6.1.4.1 Acquisition Team

The acquisition team consists of all government acquisition participants, including representatives of the technical, supply, and procurement communities; the customers they serve; and the contractors who provide the products and services.

6.1.4.2 Head of the Contracting Activity

The head of the contracting activity (HCA) is the official responsible for managing the contracting activity. HCAs are contracting officers by virtue of their position.

6.1.4.3 Contracting Officers

Only contracting officers may enter into contracts and sign them on behalf of the United States government. Contracting officers have the authority to enter into, administer, or terminate contracts and make related determinations and findings. These individuals may bind the government only to the extent of the authority delegated to them. They receive clear written instructions from the appointing authority regarding the limits of their authority. Information on the limits of the contracting officer's authority is readily available to the public and agency personnel.

No contract shall be executed unless the contracting officer ensures that all requirements of the law, executive orders, regulations, and all other applicable procedures, including clearances and approvals, have been met.

Contracting officers are responsible for ensuring the performance of all necessary actions for effective contracting, ensuring compliance with the terms of the contract, and safeguarding the interests of the US in its contractual relationships. To perform these responsibilities, contracting officers should be allowed wide latitude to exercise business judgment.

6.1.5 Construction Contracts

Construction contracts are subject to requirements in other parts of the FAR (FAR Part 36) and must be followed when applicable. When a requirement in this part is inconsistent with a requirement in another part of this regulation, Part 36 takes precedence if construction acquisition is involved. A contract for construction and supplies or services must include clauses applicable to the work's predominant part. If the contract is divided into several parts, the clauses apply to each portion.

6.1.5.1 Special Aspects of Contracting for Construction

Contracting officers acquire construction contracts using sealed bid procedures. An independent government estimate of construction cost is prepared and furnished to the contracting officer for each proposed contract and contract modifications anticipated to exceed the simplified acquisition threshold. In general, no contract for constructing a project shall be awarded to the firm that designed the project or its subsidiaries or affiliates. Also, it is generally prohibited to have cost-reimbursement contracts operating concurrently with fixed-price contracts on the same site. Agencies are required to implement high-performance, sustainable building principles for design, construction, renovation, repair, commissioning, operation and maintenance, management, and demolition of federal buildings.

6.1.5.2 Contract Modifications (FAR Part 43)

Only contracting officers acting within the scope of their authority are empowered to execute contract modifications on behalf of the government. Other government personnel cannot execute modifications, act in such a manner as to cause the contractor to believe that they have authority to bind the government, or direct or encourage the contractor to perform work that should be the subject of a contract modification.

Contract modifications can be either of the following:

- *Bilateral*, to make negotiated, equitable adjustments resulting from a change order, definitize letter contracts, and reflect other agreements modifying the terms and conditions

- *Unilateral*, to make administrative changes, issue change orders, make changes authorized by clauses other than the *Changes* clause, and issue termination notices

Generally, government contracts contain a *Changes* clause (FAR 52.243–4) permitting the contracting officer to make unilateral changes in designated areas within the contract's scope.

Upon receipt of a change order, the contractor may not cease work but must rather comply with the change (i.e., the contractor has an obligation to proceed), except that in cost-reimbursement or incrementally funded contracts, the contractor is not obligated beyond the limits of the *Limitation of Cost* clause (FAR 52.232–20) or *Limitation of Funds* clause (FAR 52.232–22). If the contractor and the government cannot agree on an equitable adjustment amount, the contractor may consider initiating a claim.

6.1.5.3 Quality Assurance (FAR Part 46)

Federal agencies are required to ensure the following:

- Contracts include inspection and other quality requirements (including warranty clauses when appropriate) that are necessary to protect the government's interest.

- Supplies or services tendered by contractors meet contract requirements.

- Government contract quality assurance is conducted before acceptance (except as otherwise provided in this part) by or under the direction of government personnel.

- No contract precludes the government from performing inspections.

- Other agencies' quality assurance and acceptance services are used when this is effective, economical, or otherwise in the government's interest.

6.1.5.4 Warranties (FAR 46.7)

The principal purpose of a warranty in a government contract is to delineate the rights and obligations of the contractor and the government regarding

DOMAIN 1
Planning,
Development,
& Organization

DOMAIN 2
Coordination

DOMAIN 3
Procurement,
Contracting,
& General
Requirements

DOMAIN 4
Research

DOMAIN 5
Analysis
& Evaluation

DOMAIN 6
Production

defective items and services, and to foster quality performance. Generally, a warranty should provide a contractual right for the correction of defects notwithstanding any other requirement of the contract about acceptance of the supplies or services by the government and a stated period of time or use, or the occurrence of a specified event, after acceptance by the government to assert a contractual right for the correction of defects.

The benefits to be derived from a warranty must be commensurate with the cost of the warranty to the government. The use of a warranty is not mandatory.

Warranty clauses cannot limit the government's rights under an inspection clause concerning latent defects, fraud, or gross mistakes that amount to fraud. Except for warranty clauses in construction contracts, warranty clauses must provide that the warranty applies notwithstanding inspection and acceptance or other clauses or terms of the contract.

6.1.5.5 Termination of Contracts (FAR Part 49)

The government exercises termination for convenience or default when it is in its best interests. Terminations are generally settled by one of the following methods: negotiated

agreement, termination contracting officer (TCO) determination, costing out under Standard Form (SF) 1034, or a combination of these methods. When possible, the TCO should negotiate a fair and prompt settlement with the contractor. There are two types of termination:

Termination for Default (FAR 49.4) is generally the exercise of the government's contractual right to wholly or partially terminate a contract because of the contractor's actual or anticipated failure to perform its contractual obligations. Under a termination for default, the government is not liable for the contractor's costs on undelivered work and is entitled to repayment of any advance and progress payments applicable to that work.

Termination for Convenience (FAR 49.502) allows the government to terminate the performance of work under a contract, either in whole or in part, if the contracting officer determines that termination is in the government's best interest. The contracting officer terminates the contract by delivering a Notice of Termination to the contractor. The notice describes the extent of the termination and the effective date. The government is only

liable for payment for services rendered up to the effective date of termination.

6.1.5.6 Access to Records and Reports (FAR 970.5232–3)

The contractor must maintain an acceptable cost accounting system. The contractor agrees to provide the owner, the federal agencies, the Comptroller General of the United States, or any of their duly authorized representatives access to any books, documents, papers, and records of the contractor directly pertinent to the specific contract. This access is required so the government can audit, examine, excerpt, and transcribe the information. The contractor agrees to maintain all books, records, and reports required under this contract for not less than three years after final payment and all pending matters are closed.

6.1.5.7 Buy American— Construction Materials (FAR 25.2)

The contractor agrees to comply with 41 USC Chapter 83 — Buy American, which restricts the purchase of construction materials to those produced domestically. To comply with this FAR, a material must pass a two-part test:

1. The material must be manufactured in the United States.

2. The cost of domestic components must exceed 55 percent of the cost of all components for materials that are not wholly or predominantly of iron or steel. For construction materials that are wholly or predominantly of iron, steel, or a combination thereof, foreign iron and steel must be less than 5 percent of the material's cost.

An exception to the preceding requirement is the provision for *commercially available off-the-shelf* (COTS) items. To be considered a COTS item, the material must be sold in substantial quantities in the commercial marketplace and is available to the government without modification in the same form in which it is sold commercially. Contractors are permitted

to submit a request to use foreign material, and then the government reviews the request to make a determination.

6.2 Specifying for Federal Agencies

Many federal agencies administer construction programs, and each has different construction document preparation requirements. This section identifies some of the unique requirements involved in preparing contract documents for federal agency projects. Many of the principles discussed here also apply when the client is a city, county, or state government agency or a school district with specific requirements for their construction documents' form and content.

MasterFormat® is often the common link between the federal government and private-sector specifications. Most government agencies use MasterFormat® to organize their guide specifications. However, their section numbers and titles may sometimes differ from those in the current edition. Also, federal agencies sometimes intentionally deviate from MasterFormat® to accommodate their unique requirements.

Most government guide specifications conform to SectionFormat®. However, the method of numbering paragraphs may not always follow the preferred alphanumeric arrangement in PageFormat®. Some agencies number their paragraphs and subparagraphs in a legal style using an Arabic numeral format (e.g., 1.1, 1.1.1, 1.1.2, 1.1.2.1). Some agencies also require the specification of procedural matters for maintenance information and shop drawings to be included in each technical specification section.

6.3 Procurement and Contracting Requirements

Federal agencies usually do not require the architect/ engineer (A/E) to prepare all the components of a document package used to solicit bids for a construction contract. In some cases, the A/E

DOMAIN 1
Planning,
Development,
& Organization

DOMAIN 2
Coordination

DOMAIN 3
Procurement,
Contracting,
& General
Requirements

DOMAIN 4
Research

DOMAIN 5
Analysis
& Evaluation

DOMAIN 6
Production

prepares the general requirements and technical specifications, and the agency prepares the procurement and contracting requirements. The A/E must be familiar with these client-agency procedures before preparing the specifications. When using agency-prepared documents, the content of Division 01 may vary significantly from a Division 01 prepared for use in the private sector.

The first difference regarding the contract conditions for a federal project is the title given to the document. Unlike the AIA Document A201®, *General Conditions of the Contract for Construction*; EJCDC® C-700, *Standard General Conditions of the Construction Contract*; or ConsensusDocs® 200, *Standard Agreement and General Conditions Between Owner and Constructor (Lump Sum)*, the federal documents might be titled "General Provisions," "General Standards," "Special Provisions," or "Contract Clauses." Regardless of how they are titled, they are all based on the FAR.

There are other significant ways in which federal general conditions differ from their private-sector counterparts:

- A contracting officer, rather than the A/E, is responsible for administering the contract's procurement and construction phases. The contracting officer is either a military officer or a civilian employee of the government. Consequently, the A/E does not exercise the same authority on federal projects that it ordinarily would on projects in the private sector.

- The federal government is both the owner and the primary regulating authority.

- Local building code authorities do not have jurisdiction on federal property, although other federal agencies may have authority. Local authorities having jurisdiction (AHJs) do, however, have jurisdiction on private property leased by federal agencies. Federal guide specifications may include requirements that take exception to or exceed local building codes.

- The federal government is self-insuring and does not procure commercial insurance for its buildings or their contents. Federal guide specifications may contain more stringent requirements for fire protection, safety, security,

and component and construction durability than those in the private sector.

- The methods used to settle contract disputes are different from the methods encountered in the private sector. Although the methods used usually do not directly affect the specifications, they significantly impact the contract administration.

6.4 Social Value Regulations

Federal government contracts may include certain "social value" regulations designed to assist particular industries and other special interest groups. Some examples are wage rates, environmental regulations, preference for American shipping, affirmative action, utilization of small businesses, utilization of businesses owned by women and minorities, labor standards, and accessibility standards. The Buy American Act is another such provision (see Section 6.1.5.7).

6.5 Use of Manufacturers' Names

In almost all situations, federal agencies prohibit the use of brand names, manufacturers' names, or other proprietary or restrictive requirements for products. The intention is to encourage unlimited competition consistent with the work's type and requirements, and maximize the use of standard products and current models to meet the project's functional requirements. Specifications for acquisitions should state only the government's actual minimum requirements and describe the supplies or services in a manner that encourages maximum practicable competition. The use of brand names in federal government specifications is acceptable only under the following exceptions:

- When there is no other feasible way to describe the essential functional or physical characteristics (such as to describe the color of paint, the appearance of stone, or the performance of a high-technology product).

- When an agency is extending or connecting to an existing system, the new portion or components must match the existing system. In this situation, the agency would prepare a justification and approval document to procure the one brand. When a specific brand name is required, the A/E may be required to provide technical input to prepare the justification for approval as part of the specifications preparation effort.

- When specifications include a statement explaining that brand names are included only to establish the minimum salient characteristics of a product (such as color, pattern, and operational characteristics), other products having equal or better characteristics are permitted.

- When specifications provide a minimum of three acceptable products, they specifically state that other acceptable products from other manufacturers are permitted.

When brand-name descriptions are necessary, the specifications must clearly identify and describe the particular physical, functional, or other characteristics of the brand-name items that are considered essential to satisfying the requirement.

The justification for using a brand-name specification and the posting of the justification should take place when the requirement for the brand-name item is determined. This condition may result in different timing between multiple-award contracts from single-award contracts (i.e., requirements contracts). By definition, a *requirements contract* is with a single source contract. Therefore, the requirement for the source's brand-name item is determined before the award of the primary contract, and the justification for purchasing a brand-name item should be completed before the award of the requirements contract. On the other hand, a multiple-award contract offers buyers products from various sources, some of which may offer particular brand-name products. The existence of a brand-name item on a multiple-award contract does not imply that it is the only such item available for purchase. In this case, the requirement for a single manufacturer's brand-name item is determined at the time of the order, not when the multiple-award contract is placed. Therefore, the justification for the brand-name item would be required when placing the order.

To eliminate any chance that the use of brand names in specifications might limit competition, the listing of the brand name plus the "or equal" phrase should be included by the agency's contracting authority whenever brand names are used, as previously described.

In some cases, it is necessary to limit the contractor to use a single product for a particular function and identify that product by brand name and model number. These proprietary specifications are the exception to the generic specifications typically used in federal specifications and should be used only when no other product can accomplish the given task. The A/E is required to provide a technical justification to support this proprietary requirement. The agency reviews the justification and approves or disapproves of the proprietary specification's inclusion in the project specifications.

6.6 Reference Standards

There are four classifications of reference standards used for specifying government construction. Listed in the order of preferred usage, they are private-sector standards, commercial item descriptions (CIDs), federal specifications, and military specifications.

CIDs are defined in 41 CFR 101–28 as "an indexed, simplified product description that describes by function or performance characteristics of available, acceptable commercial products that will satisfy the Government's needs." The GSA issues and controls CID documents.

Federal Specifications (abbreviated "FED") and *Federal Standards* (abbreviated "FED-STD") were initially established to meet a vital need, and many of them also have set standards for the industry. However, current government policy encourages the development and use of non-government standards to replace federal specifications and standards. Private-sector organizations such as the ASTM International (ASTM), the National Fire Protection Association (NFPA), and the American National Standards Institute (ANSI) are now more active in developing standards for construction products. Federal specifications and standards are

DOMAIN 1
Planning,
Development,
& Organization

DOMAIN 2
Coordination

DOMAIN 3
Procurement,
Contracting,
& General
Requirements

DOMAIN 4
Research

DOMAIN 5
Analysis
& Evaluation

DOMAIN 6
Production

being replaced by these standards, or by CIDs, which include references to ASTM, ANSI, and other industry standards. Government policy currently favors using such private-sector standards when they exist and when they meet the agency's needs. Many federal specifications have not been updated and, providing the owner has no objections, should not be used when more current standards are available.

Federal specifications and standards are documents issued by the GSA Federal Supply Service and cover a wide variety of items used by the federal government, including some construction products. Federal specifications and standards generally appear as a reference within PART 2 — PRODUCTS of a specification section.

Most federal specifications are classification documents that include requirement levels of the product described and grade the product per its physical and functional characteristics. When referencing a federal specification, it is usually necessary to state the particular class or grade of the specified product.

Military specifications (abbreviated "MIL-SPEC"), like CIDs and federal specifications and standards, describe the physical and operational characteristics of a product used for military needs and are issued by the US Department of Defense (DOD). These may consist of products unique to the military or commercial products modified for military purposes. Military specifications are organized using various classifications of type and quality. The current DOD policy is to convert military specifications to private-sector standards or federal specifications when used in non-military construction.

6.7 Specification Items for Consideration during A/E Contract Fee Negotiation

Preparing specifications for a federal agency may take more time than specifications for a private-sector owner, including the time required to read agency manuals and other documents containing the project's requirements. Consider the following items when negotiating the contract fee:

- What is the form of the available master guide specifications (e.g., printed copies, electronic files that might require special software, or text files that might not be compatible with the A/E's software)?

- Who develops or provides specification sections not included in the agency-furnished specifications?

- How many reviews are required by the agency?

- In what form are the specifications to be presented for each review?

- How many copies are required for each review submittal?

- Will the agency provide the front-end documents, or will the A/E be required to write them?

- What effect will this have on the preparation of the remainder of the contract documents?

- What is the timeframe for reviewing submittals and for the agency's review?

- Will the agency's specification page format require additional work?

- Will the agency require all sections to be produced in the same typeface? (A mixture of printing developed by separate disciplines may not be accepted, for example.)

- Will reference documents need to be acquired and, if so, will the agency provide copies or reimburse their acquisition cost?

6.8 Federal Government Agencies' Construction Documents Policies

Each agency involved in construction has its own policies and procedures for administering construction programs. Each agency also publishes its own procurement and contracting documents and forms, or they are combined with other federal agencies to publish common documents. In Divisions 01 through 49, the

A/E tailors the federal guide specifications to the specific project. The agency later incorporates the procurement requirements and contracting requirements into the construction documents before issuing the project for procurement. Figure 6.1 illustrates policies followed by several federal agencies issuing documents to A/E firms for use in construction contracts.

6.9 Federal Government Guide Specification Program

Some federal agencies involved in construction have developed master guide specifications independently to meet their own particular needs. Various groups and individuals have recommended uniform specifications development to minimize duplication of effort and make it easier and less costly for contractors, A/Es, manufacturers, and others that do business with the federal government. Since the

Figure 6.1
Chart Illustrating the Policies Followed by Several Federal Agencies in Issuing Documents to A/E Firms for Use in Construction Contracts

Agency Name	Procurement and Contracting Requirements		Divisions 01–49			
	Agency Supplies	Agency Supplements	A/E Supplies	Agency Supplies Guide Specifications	Agency Approves A/E Specifications	Agency Supplements A/E Specifications
COE	✕			✕		
EPA		✕				✕
FmHA	✕				✕	
FAA		✕			✕	
FBOP	✕		✕	✕		
FHWA			✕			✕
FHA	✕			✕		
FS	✕			✕		
GSA	✕					
HUD		✕			✕	
NASA	✕			✕		
NAVFAC	✕			✕		
NIH		✕			✕	
NPS	✕				✕	
SCS	✕				✕	✕
USPS	✕		✕	✕		
VA	✕			✕		

Acronyms for the definition of abbreviations used in this figure.

COE	Department of the Army, Corps of Engineers	**FS**	Forest Service	**NIH**	National Institutes of Health
EPA	Environmental Protection Agency	**GSA**	General Services Administration	**NPS**	National Park Service (agency of the Dept. of Interior)
FmHA	Farmers Home Administration	**HUD**	Department of Housing and Urban Development	**SCS**	Soil Conservation Service
FAA	Federal Aviation Administration			**USPS**	United States Postal Service
FBOP	Federal Bureau of Prisons	**NASA**	National Aeronautics and Space Administration	**VA**	Veterans Administration
FHWA	Federal Highway Administration	**NAVFAC**	Naval Facilities Engineering Command		
FHA	Federal Housing Authority				

*GSA uses a commercially available master guide specification system.

advent of the National Institute of Building Sciences (NIBS) and the Whole Building Design Guide (WBDG) Federal Facility Criteria, most government agency specifications are available online.

6.9.1 WBDG Federal Facility Criteria

The WBDG Federal Facility Criteria, which started as the Construction Criteria Base (CCB), grew out of a study of problems experienced in publishing federal master guide specifications for construction.

The system was developed to disseminate electronic information such as master guide specifications, technical manuals, standards, and other documents. Its objective is to put information at the user's fingertips as quickly and cost-effectively as possible. The purpose of the WBDG Federal Facility Criteria is to improve the quality of construction, decrease overlap and conflicts among criteria, speed introduction of new technology into the construction process, and improve the dissemination of master guide specifications and other design and construction documents. Information on the WBDG Federal Facility Criteria is updated regularly and is easily downloadable.

The WBDG Federal Facility Criteria includes the combined Unified Facilities Guide Specifications (UFGS) published through a joint effort of the US Army Corps of Engineers (USACE), the Naval Facilities Engineering Command (NAVFAC), the Air Force Civil Engineer Center (AFCEC), and the National Aeronautics and Space Administration (NASA). The system includes specifications processing software called SpecsIntact (see Section 6.9.2).

The WBDG Federal Facility Criteria also provides access to documents for several departments and agencies, including the following:

- Department of Defense (DOD) — Unified Facilities Criteria (UFC), Unified Design Guidance, manuals, and handbooks

- US Access Board — Guidelines and standards

- Environmental Protection Agency (EPA) — Federal Green Construction Guide for Specifiers, EPA criteria, and Energy Star manuals

- National Institute of Standards and Technology (NIST) — Voluntary product standards and NIST criteria

- National Park Service (NPS) — Standards for the Treatment of Historic Properties and Standards for Rehabilitation, and Illustrated Guidelines on Sustainability for Rehabilitating Historic Buildings

- Department of Homeland Security (DHS) — Federal Emergency Management Agency (FEMA) design guides and documents

6.9.2 SpecsIntact

SpecsIntact, meaning "specifications kept intact," is an automated system that NASA created for developing construction project specifications. UFGS and NASA specifications are formatted to allow editing within the SpecsIntact system. SpecsIntact features include the following:

- Verification that references listed in the front of each section are cited in the document

- Submittal verification

- Generation of submittal lists

- Paragraph renumbering

- Note deletion

- Testing requirement report generation

- Page numbering options

- Creation of tables of contents

- Section reference verification

- Use of multiple specification sources

- Online help

Once the appropriate specifications have been located and listed, the user can access SpecsIntact, which processes a specification section tailored to the project requirements. SpecsIntact embeds notes into the body of the specification section. The software includes a feature that deletes the notes during the printing process. SpecsIntact is a free download from the NASA Kennedy Space Center website (https://specsintact.ksc.nasa.gov/software/software.shtml).

DOMAIN 1
Planning,
Development,
& Organization

DOMAIN 2
Coordination

DOMAIN 3
Procurement,
Contracting,
& General
Requirements

DOMAIN 4
Research

DOMAIN 5
Analysis
& Evaluation

DOMAIN 6
Production

6.10 Using Federal Government Master Guide Specifications

Before entering into a design contract with a federal agency, the A/E should determine whether the agency has master guide specifications, if their use is required, and if editable copies are provided free of charge. The time required to produce project specifications from agency guide specifications is subject to many variables. Chief among these is the A/E's degree of familiarity with the required methods of specifying products and systems within the agency's guide specifications (e.g., extensive use of reference standards and general descriptions in place of manufacturers' names and model numbers). The greater the differences between the agency's documents and the A/E's office master guide specifications, the more time that is required. Difficulties may be compounded if the agency's master guide specifications do not conform to Construction Specifications Institute (CSI) principles and practices, such as section numbers and titles that differ considerably from the current edition of MasterFormat®. If differences exist between the agency's specifications and MasterFormat®, the A/E is usually expected to use the numbers and titles defined by the agency.

6.10.1 Editing Master Guide Specifications

The agency's master guide specifications are just that—guides—and must be edited to suit each project. Guide specifications are usually written for new construction and may require considerable modification for repair or rehabilitation projects. Where coverage is lacking, the A/E must provide the needed material in an agency-approved form. Individual guide specification sections may often be much more detailed than those to which the A/E is accustomed. For example, some guide specification sections might be over 100 pages long. If help is needed to interpret master guide specifications, most agencies provide assistance. Several guidelines should be followed when editing agency master guide specifications:

- The sections should be tailored to suit the project, not merely copied in their entirety.

- Identification markings should be deleted on the master (such as headers or footers with the section number or revision number and revision notations within the section's text). If the UFGS or NASA specifications are used, the SpecsIntact software is capable of doing this electronically.

- The sections should be edited to avoid conflicts related to products occurring in more than one section.

- Additional information should be added as necessary.

- Paragraphs should not be selected by title alone.

- The entire section, not just the bracketed text, should be read and edited.

- All required selections should be made and all blanks edited.

- Applicable requirements from the editing notes should be incorporated.

- The A/E should coordinate requirements in the editing notes. If SpecsIntact is used, the software is capable of deleting editing notes electronically.

- The references listed at the beginning of the section should be edited to include only the standards remaining within the edited specification. If SpecsIntact is used, the software is capable of doing this electronically.

- Each reference listed should indicate the current issue or revision date unless there is a specific reason to reference an older standard or unless the agency directs otherwise.

- The agency's written instructions should be carefully followed for page format, layout, and placement of the agency's contract number. Most agencies are very explicit concerning these details.

- All specifications should be proofread; do not depend on agency reviewers to find errors and discrepancies.

- The index in the front of each section should be deleted after the editing process is complete unless the agency requires otherwise. If SpecsIntact is used, the software is capable of producing an index electronically.

- If the agency requires submittal of the marked-up section:

  - A readable copy of the original should be used so that it can be reproduced for the submittal.

  - Use of a highlighter on a review copy should be avoided, as some highlighting photocopies solid black.

  - Handwritten additions and deletions should be dark enough so that notations scan clearly. If permitted by the agency, make insertions and deletions electronically using the editing application's comment features.

  - Some agencies require redlining on the electronic media rather than markups of hard-copy originals. Agency requirements should be followed in this regard.

If the agency does not have a guide specification for a required section, the A/E must prepare the section using other resources. The new section must conform to the agency standards for format and numbering and avoid proprietary or restrictive product requirements. The specifications should permit unlimited competition consistent with the type and quality of work. The new sections should be prepared based on standard products and current equipment models that meet the facility's functional requirements.

6.11 The Review Process

Depending on the agency and the project's size and extent, the submittal and review process can either be brief or extend over a couple of years before a project is ready to be advertised for bids. This timeframe should be clearly described in the A/E contract with the government agency. The A/E should review submittal requirements with the agency before starting a new phase of the work. During the design phase, the agency often wants reviews at the 30 percent, 50 percent, 90 percent, and final completion milestones. An A/E working with an agency for the first time may have a submittal rejected or found inadequate if procedures are not followed, and a resubmittal may be required. The following list outlines what the A/E may expect at each of the design reviews.

30 Percent Review. Provide one of the following:

- A list of specification sections intended for use on the project; the list should be generated from a master list of section titles furnished by the agency

- Outline specifications identifying products to be used

50 Percent Review. Provide one of the following:

- A manually or electronically marked-up copy of the applicable agency's guide specifications, including unnecessary specification pages marked as deleted

- A draft consisting of a manually or electronically marked-up copy of the applicable agency's guide specifications, with unnecessary paragraphs marked as deleted

- A typed rough draft

90 Percent Review. Provide one of the following:

- A resubmittal of the manually or electronically marked-up copy of the complete guide specification, including all specification pages, even though some may be deleted later

- A resubmittal of the draft consisting of a manually or electronically marked-up copy

- A resubmittal of the typed rough draft

- A processed copy in final draft form

- A single section in final form as a sample of the final product

Final review:

- Typed copy in final form in electronic format

- If the reviewers have no comments, the project is then advertised for bids by the agency

DOMAIN 1
Planning,
Development,
& Organization

DOMAIN 2
Coordination

DOMAIN 3
Procurement,
Contracting,
& General
Requirements

DOMAIN 4
Research

DOMAIN 5
Analysis
& Evaluation

DOMAIN 6
Production

6.11.1 Review Comments

Agency reviewers often require changes to the
drawings or specifications to make the documents
conform to specific government criteria. The A/E
should expect comments from the client-agency
reviewers after each of the submittals. The A/E
is expected to revise the contract documents
and incorporate the review comments before the
next submittal. There are several aspects of the
review process:

- Each of the disciplines involves a different
  reviewer (e.g., architectural; structural; fire
  protection; plumbing; heating, ventilating,
  and air conditioning [HVAC]; and electrical),
  whose comments may result in conflicting
  requirements. The agency's project manager
  should resolve conflicting requirements among
  the various reviewers.

- Each reviewer's comments must receive
  a written response, usually on a form
  provided by the agency.

- Time schedules for agency review, A/E response
  time, and subsequent resubmittals should be
  documented in writing.

- Usually, a compliance-check submittal is
  required after significant changes.

- Adequate time should be allowed in the contract
  document schedule to make revisions directed
  by the reviewers.

6.11.2 Distribution of Documents for the Review Process

Depending on the terms of the agreement between
the A/E and the agency, either the A/E or the agency
may be responsible for distributing review copies of
the contract documents, especially if printed copies
are required. This item can be important since it
affects time and expense and should be considered
when negotiating an agreement.

6.12 Regional Variations

Some federal agencies administer their construction
programs through autonomous regional or district
offices. For example, the USACE publishes its guide
specifications from its Washington, DC, office, but

the district offices often supplement and modify the specifications. Further, a local military facility may contract directly with a local A/E firm for projects not subject to USACE district jurisdiction. In such cases, the local military facility may have its own version of the guide specifications or allow the use of the A/E's office master specifications. The project funding source may also dictate the procedures to be followed when providing services under a design contract. The A/E should be aware of possible variations in procedures.

Although each federal agency has its own procedures for administering design contracts, there are some similarities among various agencies:

- The use of section numbers based on MasterFormat® is familiar to most agencies.

- The A/E is prohibited from naming manufacturers or brand names for products, except in special circumstances.

- Many agencies issue guide specifications for use by A/Es when preparing construction documents.

- Many agencies have combined their resources to publish guide specifications in a standard format, such as SpecsIntact, and have provided distribution through WBDG Federal Facility Criteria.

- Most agencies issue their own procurement requirements and contracting requirements and require their inclusion in the project manual.

- Contract documents are subject to a review process, which can be lengthy and may require extensive changes and several resubmittals by the A/E.

Preparing specifications for federal government construction for the first time can be an involved and confusing experience if the A/E does not know what to expect. These difficulties are usually the result of following the rules and procedures somewhat different from similar work in the private sector. This chapter's general guidelines may help the A/E anticipate and prepare for some of the differences likely to be encountered.

DOMAIN 3:
PROCUREMENT, CONTRACTING,
& GENERAL REQUIREMENTS

Chapter 7

CONSTRUCTION BONDS & INSURANCE

7.1 Construction Bonds and Insurance Overview

Construction bonds and insurance may appear to serve similar purposes since they both protect a party from acts and events over which the party has little to no control. However, the methods of protection employed by these services are very different.

7.2 Construction Bonds

Many construction projects today require that contractors provide bonds. Construction bonds protect the owner against non-payment, lack of performance, company default, and warranty issues. There are three basic types of bonds used in construction projects: bid bonds, performance bonds, and payment bonds. The first, if used, is a procurement requirement; the latter two are classified as contract documents. Other types of bonds may be required, such as warranty bonds or maintenance bonds, but these are generally called for by individual specification sections.

As the author and coordinator of the project manual, the architect/engineer (A/E) must be familiar with the use of bonds on construction projects. It is the owner's decision on whether to require bonds. Before the decision is made, the A/E should discuss the essential information regarding the use and form of bonds with the owner. Regardless, the A/E must recommend the owner seek bond advice from their counselor or attorney and a professional surety advisor.

Refer to Chapter 2 of the *Project Delivery Practice Guide* for definitions of terms associated with construction bonds.

7.2.1 Purpose of Bonds

A surety's obligation is analogous to the obligation of a cosigner on a note. The principal remains primarily liable to perform the bonded contract and is obligated to indemnify the surety against any loss. The surety typically has a separate indemnity agreement with the principal and, if the principal

DOMAIN 1
Planning,
Development,
& Organization

DOMAIN 2
Coordination

DOMAIN 3
Procurement,
Contracting,
& General
Requirements

DOMAIN 4
Research

DOMAIN 5
Analysis
& Evaluation

DOMAIN 6
Production

is a closely held corporation, with the individual owner, officers, or operators of the principal. Under the indemnity agreement, the principal and any indemnitors guarantee that the surety incurs no loss because of providing the bond. The principal pays a premium to the surety for providing the performance and payment bonds.

The premium is based on the amount of the contract being bonded, which is generally between 0.3 and 2 percent, depending on various factors, including the type of risk undertaken, financial strength of the principal, financial strength of any indemnitors, past claims history, and extent of the project. Bid bonds are usually offered at no cost if performance and payment bonds are required. It is important to understand the three-party relationship involved in these bonds (see Figure 7.1). Unlike insurance policies, where the insurance company accepts primary responsibility to pay claims, the surety is only secondarily liable after the principal defaults. Theoretically, the surety should not expect to make any payment out of its pocket without reimbursement from the principal or individual indemnitors. The surety should be licensed by the insurance department of the state where the project is located. Offers by a contractor to provide bonding through an individual or an unlicensed surety should generally be rejected.

Figure 7.1
Construction
Bonding

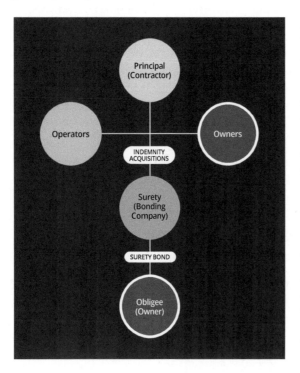

7.2.2 Rating of the Bonding Company

The AM Best Company rates insurance companies. Best's Key Rating Guide is published annually, with rating classifications that range from an A for a superior rating to a C- for a fair rating. An A- or better rating suggests that the carrier is financially excellent. Standard & Poor's, Fitch, and other companies also publish ratings of insurance companies.

The federal government has its own criteria for sureties. The US Treasury Department's Bureau of the Fiscal Service publishes an annual listing of certified surety companies acceptable for federal government projects. The Treasury's listing is published annually in the July 1 Federal Register and is available on the Treasury Department website (https://www.fiscal.treasury.gov/surety-bonds/list-certified-companies.html).

7.2.3 Obtaining Bond Information from the Owner

The A/E usually completes the project manual (which includes the procurement and contracting requirements) before issuing a project for bid or negotiation. The proper location for bid bond information is in the procurement requirements. The supplementary conditions should state the requirements for performance and payment bonds. The A/E should request bond information from the owner early enough to allow the owner to respond to the A/E in time for the A/E to incorporate the information into the project manual. When performing work for a repeat client or with an owner constructing multiple projects, the A/E should request bond information for each project.

Bond information request forms published by either the American Institute of Architects (AIA) or the Engineers Joint Contract Documents Committee (EJCDC) are recommended for documenting the bonding requirements. These forms provide the A/E with a standardized means of ensuring that the information has been appropriately requested and obtained. The AIA provides AIA Document G612™, *Owner's Instructions to the Architect*, a two-part document with Part A for the construction contract and Part B for bidding procedures. Part A requests insurance and bond requirements for the project are provided to the architect; Part B includes information regarding a bid bond. The EJCDC form is EJCDC® C-052, *Owner's Instructions Concerning Bonds and Insurance for Construction*. Additionally, EJCDC also publishes a prototype letter, EJCDC® C-051, *Letter to Owner on Bonds and Insurance for Construction*, that engineers can use for requesting the information.

7.2.4 Advantages and Costs of Bonding

There are numerous advantages of providing a fully bonded project:

- The bid bond protects the owner against the withdrawal of a favorable bid.

- The suppliers and subcontractors are protected against non-payment of amounts due to them. The owner is protected against mechanic's liens on the project.

- The owner is protected against default, breach of contract, and non-performance by the contractor.

- The owner receives additional assurance of the stability of the contractor. Most bonded contractors are financially stable, and the bond guarantees that the surety pays if the contractor fails.

- The indemnity agreement generally provides added incentive for the contractor's principals to properly perform, as they may be personally liable to the bonding company for amounts paid on a bonded project.

- Bonding satisfies statutory requirements for publicly funded projects.

There is a cost for this protection. The bond premium is included in the contractor's bid, and one of the functions of a bond requirement is to exclude contractors who cannot qualify for bonding. For residential buildings and small commercial contracts, some potential contractors may not have established relationships with sureties and may be discouraged from bidding by a bond requirement.

Whether to require bid, performance, and payment bonds is a decision that the owner should make.

However, owners often ask A/Es to provide information, input, or forms concerning bonding for a construction project. Unless the owner is expressly cautioned otherwise, the statements of the A/E may be accepted without further investigation, especially when owners do not have separate legal counsel or insurance advisers. If bonds are not required and a contractor defaults, the owner may well contend that the A/E's advice concerning bonding was insufficient. Although an A/E may provide some necessary information to an owner, the owner should always be advised to seek an attorney or surety adviser's counsel before making a final decision.

7.2.5 Bid Bond

The purpose of the bid bond is to protect the owner from losing the benefit of an accepted bid. Issuance of a bid bond commits the bidder to enter into a contract and, if required, provide performance and payment bonds. The bidder submits the bid bond with the bid at bid time. The bid bond generally provides a penal amount expressed either in dollars or as a percentage of the bid's total amount. If the selected bidder fails or refuses to enter into a contract for the bid price, the surety is obligated to pay the owner's damages up to the bid bond's penal amount. When bid bonds are required, a bidder's failure to submit a bid bond makes such bid non-responsive and results in rejection of that bid. Bid bonds are generally cost-effective for the owner, as most bonding companies do not charge separately for the bid bond if a performance bond and a payment bond are also required.

When a selected bidder finds that its bid is substantially below that of the other bidders or that a mistake has been made that is not subject to correction or modification, the accepted bidder may be reluctant to enter into the contract in that amount. Suppose the owner requests that the selected bidder sign a contract in the amount of the bid and the selected bidder refuses. In that case, the owner can go to the surety and ask for the difference between the principal's bid and that of the next lowest bidder, up to the penal amount of the bid bond. Thus, the owner gets the benefit of the low bid. Further, if the selected bidder does not sign the agreement for some reason and the owner cannot enter into a contract with the next lowest bidder—as might be if the other bidders have already withdrawn—the owner may have to

Construction
Specifications
Practice Guide

DOMAIN 1
Planning,
Development,
& Organization

DOMAIN 2
Coordination

DOMAIN 3
Procurement,
Contracting,
& General
Requirements

DOMAIN 4
Research

DOMAIN 5
Analysis
& Evaluation

DOMAIN 6
Production

rebid. In that event, the surety is not only responsible for any difference between the principal's bid and the low bid received on the reprocurement but may also be liable for the cost of the reprocurement.

The bid bond is liable only if the principal's refusal to sign the contract at the bid price is unjustified. If the principal was entitled to withdraw its bid, there is no liability under the bid bond. For example, the bid bond could be discharged if one of the following conditions exist:

- The owner did not accept the bid within the time specified in the procurement documents.

- The bidder proves a mistake that entitled it to withdraw its bid.

- The owner tries unilaterally to change the terms and conditions under which the bid was submitted.

7.2.6 Performance Bond

The *performance bond* provides the most critical protection for the owner by guaranteeing that if the contractor defaults, the surety will either complete the contract per its terms or provide sufficient funds, up to the penal amount of the bond, to fund such completion.

AIA and EJCDC performance bond forms require the owner to request that the surety attends a pre-default meeting at which an attempt can be made to prevent default. Often, financial reinforcement by the surety permits the contractor to complete the work. If there is a default and the owner makes a demand on a surety to perform under the terms of the performance bond, the surety investigates the owner's claim against the contractor. This investigation includes examining both the owner's and the contractor's positions and making an independent analysis of the situation. Once the validity of the claim has been established, the surety has some options regarding how it could fulfill the bond obligation.

If the contractor's work is satisfactory and the problems are only financial, the surety may choose to finance the contractor to complete the project. Under this option, the surety provides funds to the contractor to pay subcontractors and suppliers, buy materials, make payroll, and take other steps

necessary to complete the project. The surety only does this under careful supervision.

If the owner terminates the contract, the surety can complete the project by taking over the work itself and hiring another contractor or arranging for a completion contractor to work directly for the owner. The surety may also leave it up to the owner to finish the project and pay the difference between the balance left in the original contract and the actual cost of completion. Suppose there is a dispute concerning the contractor's default or the surety's liability. In that case, the owner may have to complete the project and then prove its claim in litigation or arbitration before receiving payment from the surety.

Whichever method of completion is used, the surety is entitled to credit for the contract balance at the time of default and is liable only for the excess costs to complete.

The performance bond protects the owner against default by the contractor, not against the owner's defaults. Suppose the owner materially breaches the contract and discharges the contractor, or the owner breaches the contract and increases the surety's risk. In that case, the surety may have a defense to any claim on the bond.

For example, if the owner pays the contractor more than the contractor is owed under the contract, or the owner materially increases the contract's scope without the surety's consent, the surety can claim a *discharge* (i.e., relief) to the difference due to overpayment or the contract sum increase over the original amount.

7.2.7 Payment Bond

The *payment bond* (sometimes referred to as a labor and materials payment bond) guarantees that subcontractors, material suppliers, and others providing labor, material, and equipment to the project will be paid. This promise benefits the owner because it protects against mechanic's liens and delays caused by unpaid subcontractors and suppliers. The payment bond generally provides payment not only to parties employed by or in a direct contractual relationship with the contractor but also to sub-subcontractors and suppliers to subcontractors. Some bonds and statutes may include even more remote claimants within the

coverage of the payment bond. Most bonds require remote claimants to give the contractor written notice that they are unpaid within 90 days of the last date they furnished labor or material to the project. This notification alleviates the unfairness of making the contractor pay remote claimants when the first-tier subcontractor was paid and did not pay its sub-subcontractors.

Payment bonds also typically require that a claimant file suit within a reasonably short time. Only labor and material on the bonded project are covered. The purchase price of capital goods or inventory available for use on multiple projects is not generally an obligation of the bond.

7.2.8 Bond Forms

In federal, state, county, and many municipal projects, the A/E may have no role in the form of the bond because the language is standard and, in some cases, required by law or statute. However, in situations where there is no standard format, the A/E should advise the owner to seek legal counsel regarding the choice of bond forms.

EJCDC has two published bid bond forms, EJCDC® C-430, *Bid Bond (Penal Sum)*, and EJCDC® C-435, *Bid Bond (Damages)*. EJCDC® C-435 follows the

traditional bid bond structure in that the owner is paid the actual amount of damages upon the selected bidder's failure to execute the agreement, up to the sum of the bond. The "damage" is the difference between the bid of the defaulting bidder and the next-lowest responsible bidder's bid. On the other hand, EJCDC® C-430 allows the owner to receive the bond's face amount if the selected bidder fails to execute the owner-contractor agreement. This method means the owner may receive an amount greater than the difference between the defaulting bidder's bid and the next-lowest bidder's bid; hence, the "penal" aspect of this bid bond form. AIA Document A310™, *Bid Bond*, and ConsensusDocs® 262, *Bid Bond*, are other traditional bid bond forms structured similarly to the EJCDC® C-435 bond form.

The AIA, The EJCDC, and the ConsensusDocs Coalition each include performance and payment bond forms in their contract documents packages. The AIA's document includes both forms in a single document, whereas the EJCDC and the ConsensusDocs Coalition provide separate forms for each type of bond. The following is a list of available bond forms:

> AIA Document A312™, *Performance and Payment Bond*

DOMAIN 1
Planning,
Development,
& Organization

DOMAIN 2
Coordination

DOMAIN 3
Procurement,
Contracting,
& General
Requirements

DOMAIN 4
Research

DOMAIN 5
Analysis
& Evaluation

DOMAIN 6
Production

EJCDC® C-610, *Performance Bond*, and EJCDC® C-615, *Payment Bond*

ConsensusDocs® 260, *Performance Bond*, and ConsensusDocs® 261, *Payment Bond*

The bond forms selected for use in a project should coordinate and comply with local jurisdictions, and any related language would reference the project documents. There are significant legal consequences in the choice of bond forms. If the procurement documents do not include a form, the bond form may become a matter for negotiation between the owner, contractor, and surety. This situation can be avoided by including the required bond forms in the procurement documents.

Evidence of authority to bind the surety is usually in the form of a power of attorney designating the agent authorized to sign on behalf of the surety. The instructions for procurement should require that a copy of a power of attorney is filed with the signed and executed bond form.

7.3 Construction Insurance

This section covers the kinds of construction insurance policies available, some of the risks involved in construction projects, and basic insurance terms. It does not address what constitutes adequate insurance coverage or insurance requirements for projects outside the United States. The owner's legal counsel and insurance advisor should be the source of all recommendations on construction insurance matters. The A/E should not act as an insurance advisor and should not determine or recommend insurance limits. However, the A/E should provide the owner with AIA Document G612™, *Owner's Instructions to the Architect*, or EJCDC® C-052, *Owner's Instructions Concerning Bonds and Insurance for Construction*. Both documents are insurance information request forms to obtain instructions for incorporating insurance requirements into the supplementary conditions.

7.3.1 Insurance for the Construction Contract

Every single construction project requires some type of construction insurance. In

many instances, it is a requirement to have some specific coverage to award a contract. Construction insurance is offered in many forms and policy types to provide coverage for material, risks, natural disasters, employees, and even your own business. There are many instances that property owners or project developers require the contractor to get some of these to be qualified to participate in their bidding process.

The owner of a construction project risks substantial assets, which exposes the owner to significant legal liability throughout the project's life. The owner also has a significant amount of money invested. The contractor performing the work also incurs risks that require insurance protection for itself, the owner, and third parties.

The owner's first line of financial defense is an adequately insured contractor. The owner's interest is protected in part by requiring the contractor to carry specific insurance coverage types within limits determined to be adequate for the circumstances. The insurance coverage required by the conditions of the contract provides most of the protection needed for both the owner and the contractor during a construction project. However, the contractor's insurance may not provide all the coverage the owner needs. Several policies are available to owners for coverage beyond the contractor's insurance protection.

7.3.2 Liability Insurance

Liability policies protect the named insured from losses arising from legal liability to others caused by the insured's activities. Liability policies do not cover damage or loss of the insured's products, machinery, or equipment. Coverage is effective only at the project site.

The AIA, the EJCDC, and the ConsensusDocs Coalition general conditions require the contractor to provide liability insurance because it is responsible for the project site's activities. Figure 7.2 shows the relationships among the different types of liability insurance.

7.3.2.1 Workers' Compensation Insurance

Construction can prove dangerous, especially when workers are handling power tools and heavy equipment. If an employee gets injured on the job, the contractor is responsible for providing workers' compensation coverage. This type of insurance pays for medical bills, lost wages, and other expenses related to an on-the-job injury. Different states impose varying laws regarding workers' compensation. Generally speaking, a contractor needs it if they have more than five workers.

Although popularly classified as liability insurance, workers' compensation insurance is more accurately described as protection given to an employee by an employer per a statutory no-fault/limited liability agreement. Under workers' compensation laws (some form of which exists in all states), employers must compensate their employees for employment-related injuries, regardless of fault. The employee, in return, cannot bring legal action against the employer for compensation above the statutory amount. Compensation includes reimbursements for medical costs, lost wages, and a specific amount for certain permanent injuries. Without workers' compensation insurance, the employer does not have the protection of the state law and may be sued by the employee for unlimited damages.

When the contractor has the workers' compensation insurance required by law, the owner is also protected against suits arising from injuries to the contractor's employees. Accordingly, it is essential that the contractor and all subcontractors must obtain and maintain workers' compensation insurance. This requirement should be stated in the supplementary conditions. Exempt contractors should be required to carry voluntary workers' compensation insurance, which has the same effect as required by the law.

Some states have enacted compensation laws that are not comprehensive for every injury or every category of recoverable damages. The resulting immunity gap is covered by a policy called *employer's liability insurance*. This term is used by AIA Document A201®, *General Conditions of the Contract for Construction;* EJCDC® C-700, *Standard General Conditions of the Construction Contract;* and ConsensusDocs® 200, *Standard Agreement and*

DOMAIN 1
Planning,
Development,
& Organization

DOMAIN 2
Coordination

DOMAIN 3
Procurement,
Contracting,
& General
Requirements

DOMAIN 4
Research

DOMAIN 5
Analysis
& Evaluation

DOMAIN 6
Production

Figure 7.2
Contractor's
Liability Insurance

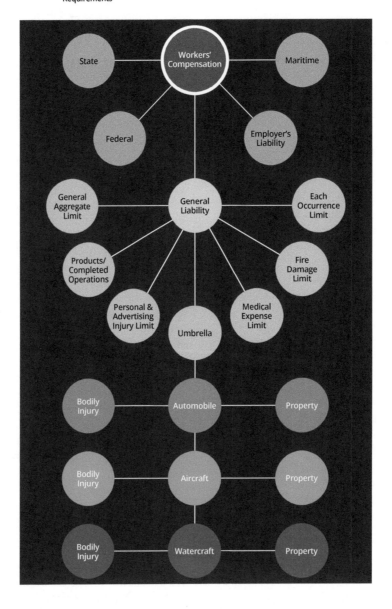

General Conditions Between Owner and Constructor. All three of these general conditions require the contractor to provide this insurance in an amount deemed prudent by the owner and the owner's insurance advisor. This coverage can also extend to third parties, such as an employee's family.

Owners should also carry workers' compensation insurance, with coverage for the statutory limits, and employer's liability insurance, for protection against suits arising from injuries to their own employees. The policy should be endorsed for coverage in all states where the owner's employees may operate. The contractor and all subcontractors must comply

with the laws in the state where the work is located. Compliance with state laws includes subassemblies fabricated in a state different from where the project is located. If a contractor performs work in more than one state, the contractor's insurance advisor should recommend insurance coverage in the states wherever the employees work. *Other states coverage* is the term used when coverage extends to all states listed in the endorsement schedule. If the project involves work related to a navigable waterway, the United States Longshoremen and Harbor Workers Act provisions apply. Other federal laws that may apply include the Federal Employees Liability Act and the Defense Base Act. Workers' compensation policies should include such special coverage by endorsement whenever it is needed.

7.3.2.2 General Liability

General liability insurance, frequently referred to as *commercial general liability* (CGL) insurance, is a class of insurance that provides liability protection to businesses in the case of bodily harm or property damage during the course of business. Insurance providers create various versions of these policies available to professionals in construction and for construction projects.

General liability insurance policies usually cover a broad range of damages, including the following:

- Faulty workmanship
- Job-related injury
- Advertising injury/defamation

Contractors or developers may be required to have a minimum level of liability insurance either by law in some states or to secure contracts that require it. Companies that complete many design-build projects should have liability insurance in case they are sued for mistakes. Also, subcontractors are frequently required to carry liability insurance to work for certain general contractors or construction management companies.

General liability policies are the most common types of insurance protection in the construction world. As the name suggests, it is a general policy covering bodily injury and property damage (each term is defined in the policy).

It is important to note that a general liability policy does not cover the costs needed to repair defective work, just the damage that results from defective work. Different policies have different exclusions, terms, and conditions.

Under a general liability policy, the insurance company agrees to pay all sums for which the insured becomes legally obligated to pay as damages. The insurance company also agrees to provide legal defense in any related suits brought against the contractor.

Most general liability policies are written on an *occurrence-basis* coverage. The occurrence-basis type of coverage means that the right to protection under the policy is fixed when the occurrence causing the damage is known. The policy must have been *in force* (i.e., active) at the time of the occurrence but need not have been in force when the claim was made. The *claims-made* policy requires that for coverage, insurance must be continuously in force from the time of the occurrence to the time of the claim. Because the contractor typically provides the liability coverage, claims-made coverage is seldom used for construction projects because of problems with keeping the policy in force long after the project is completed. With the occurrence-basis form, the coverage that was in place during the construction period remains effective after construction has been completed for any claims resulting from the construction process.

The occurrence-basis form of insurance provides better protection for the owner. Uncertainty of coverage is a risk in a claims-made policy, as claims may be made long after the event and long after the contractor has left the project. An owner has little opportunity to monitor or enforce the contractor's insurance coverage after the project is completed. Yet it is that future coverage on which the owner relies for protection when insurance is written on a claims-made basis. The occurrence-basis type of insurance is far easier to monitor and enforce because an occurrence usually arises when the contractor is under contract with the owner.

Although an occurrence usually arises during the construction stage, it could be discovered after the work is complete and give rise to a claim. For this reason, the owner should consider requiring the contractor to provide coverage for a reasonable period following completion of the contract and require certificates of insurance as proof of that coverage. The owner should consult with a qualified insurance advisor to determine the length of that period.

The ACORD Corporation provides the insurance industry's globally standard form, ACORD 25, *Certificate of Liability Insurance*, which may be used alone or with AIA Document G715™, *Supplemental Attachment for ACORD Certificate of Insurance 25*. AIA Document G715™ covers some additional subjects the ACORD form does not, such as professional liability, pollution liability, and asbestos abatement liability. EJCDC® C-700 requires the

DOMAIN 1
Planning,
Development,
& Organization

DOMAIN 2
Coordination

DOMAIN 3
Procurement,
Contracting,
& General
Requirements

DOMAIN 4
Research

DOMAIN 5
Analysis
& Evaluation

DOMAIN 6
Production

contractor to deliver to the owner certificates of insurance and other requested evidence that the required insurance coverage has been purchased. AIA Document A201® states that the contractor must obtain the required insurance. However, most insurance requirements under AIA documents are located in an exhibit to the owner-contractor agreement, AIA Document A101® Exhibit A, *Insurance and Bonds*. This exhibit requires the contractor to provide certificates of insurance before the commencement of the work. ConsensusDocs® 200 states the required insurance must be obtained before starting work and is a condition of payment, which would require the contractor to produce evidence that proper insurance coverage is provided.

When required by particular construction risks, certain vital additions to the general liability coverage are advisable. In its basic form, the commercial general liability policy has an exclusion usually called the XCU exclusion, which is short for e**X**plosion, **C**ollapse, and **U**nderground property damage. Removal of this exclusion is required to provide coverage for claims arising from blasting, the collapse of structures due to excavation or removal of shoring or support, and underground property damage caused by mechanical excavation. It is also in the owner's best interest to require the contractor to provide third-party personal injury coverage.

The commercial general liability policy combines several coverage aggregates into a single general aggregate, the maximum amount paid under the policy. The general aggregate may be modified to apply to each individual project, and the requirement for this modification should be identified in the supplementary conditions.

Six separate limits of liability are covered in commercial general liability policies. The following is an explanation for each of the six limits:

- **General Aggregate Limit.** This limit is the most that the insurance company pays in any one policy year for claims. It includes coverages for operations, personal and advertising injury, damage-to-premises-rented-to-you, and medical expenses.
- **Products and Completed Operations Aggregate Limit.** An aggregate limitation on how much an insurance company pays

due to bodily injury or property damage resulting from a product (for manufacturers) or completed operation (for contractors) hazard. This aggregate is separate from the general aggregate limit.

- **Personal and Advertising Injury Limit.** For personal injury, this covers slander, libel, invasion of privacy, and defamation of character. An advertising injury results from false advertising practices.
- **Each Occurrence Limit.** This limit is the maximum amount the insurance company pays for any single claim covered by the general aggregate limit. Each claim reduces the general aggregate limit or the products and completed operations aggregate limit, as applicable.
- **Damage-to-Premises-Rented-to-You Limit (formerly known as "Fire Damage Legal Liability").** Since standard CGL property damage cover excludes property that you rent, this limit allows claims for damage to rented or leased properties resulting from a fire only.
- **Medical Expense Limit.** This limit applies to all first aid and covered medical expenses arising from any single person's bodily injury for a single accident.

Special consideration must be given to the "general aggregate limit" in the commercial general liability policy. This limit establishes the maximum payment under the policy for all claims paid under the policy, except for claims applied to the "products and completed operations aggregate limit." Thus, if one or more claims have been paid during the policy years, the actual aggregate limits may be less than those shown on the insurance policy or the certificate of insurance provided by the insurance agent.

7.3.2.3 Commercial Automotive Insurance

The beginning of a construction project is a good time for the owner to review its automobile coverage. Ownership and operation of motor vehicles are one of the riskier business operations. The addition of a construction site to the places visited by the owner's drivers suggests the need for a coverage review.

DOMAIN 1
Planning,
Development,
& Organization

DOMAIN 2
Coordination

DOMAIN 3
Procurement,
Contracting,
& General
Requirements

DOMAIN 4
Research

DOMAIN 5
Analysis
& Evaluation

DOMAIN 6
Production

Contractors often drive large trucks and use other forms of heavy equipment. From a contractor's standpoint, the liability for the operation of owned or non-owned automobiles, including rented or hired vehicles, is generally secured through a business automobile coverage form. The contractor needs a dedicated commercial auto insurance policy to cover those vehicles. AIA, EJCDC, and ConsensusDocs documents require the *per-occurrence* (i.e., accident) type of coverage that includes coverage for bodily injury or property damage caused by a per-occurrence-basis and arising out of the use of covered vehicles.

Owned automobiles are those owned by the contractor. However, non-owned automobiles can also pose a risk of liability. For example, a contractor's employee may use a personal automobile to run an errand for the contractor. Therefore, non-owned, rented, or hired vehicle coverage should be required as part of the automobile insurance coverage. The coverage agreements and definitions in automobile liability policies uniformly exclude aircraft and powerboats exceeding a specified length and horsepower limit. When the project requires the use of aircraft or water vessels — such as using a helicopter to erect skylights or lift heavy equipment unsuitable for a crane — the owner should require appropriate liability coverage for both the owned and non-owned vehicles. Coverage should also be anticipated for all maritime projects and distant sites that may require air transport of material, equipment, or personnel.

7.3.2.4 Owner's and Contractor's Protective (OCP) Liability Insurance

The general liability insurance policy that is regularly carried by the owner for normal operations and that is required by the contract documents may not include construction risks. Therefore, the owner's insurance coverage should be evaluated to determine if there is a risk exposure due to the construction activities. It is common for the owner to be an *additional insured* on the contractor's liability insurance via the supplementary conditions, which provides better protection for the owner, but not the best. Additional coverage, called owner's and contractor's protective (OCP) insurance, may be appropriate to cover the same hazards as those

covered by the contractor's liability insurance. OCP insurance is not duplicate coverage, as a legal liability exists for the owner's role in the construction process. The contractor typically obtains the OCP insurance, which is the default in ConsensusDocs® 200 if the option is selected. The owner's interests are better served when an OCP policy is provided; however, to avoid conflicts with the owner's existing liability insurance policy, the contractor should provide the OCP insurance.

7.3.2.5 Umbrella Excess Liability Insurance

The umbrella excess liability policy provides a layer of insurance above the limits carried in the contractor's other liability coverage. Two purposes are served by specifying a relatively high-limit umbrella excess liability policy. First, this is the most economical way to secure limits above those customarily offered by general liability and automobile policies. Second, the umbrella policy can broaden the coverage provided by those policies.

AIA Document A101® Exhibit A addresses umbrella liability insurance. However, it only states that the primary and umbrella insurance's combined coverage must provide the same or greater coverage required by the stipulated primary coverages. EJCDC® C-800 addresses this by requiring a dollar amount for the general aggregate and for each occurrence in the supplementary conditions.

7.3.3 Property Insurance

Property insurance compensates the insureds for damages to covered property caused by insured perils. Builder's risk insurance is the cornerstone of the project's property insurance. The relationships of the various covered risks are shown in Figure 7.3.

7.3.3.1 Builder's Risk Insurance

Builder's risk insurance policies offer comprehensive protection against "named perils" and are specifically designed for buildings under construction. They cover the structure itself, materials, and equipment. The specific perils named in the policy can vary but typically include the following:

- Fire
- Explosion
- Theft
- Vandalism
- Lightning
- Hail
- Wind (may be limited in coastal areas)

A builder's risk policy also contains standard coverage exclusions, which are very important to understand. These exclusions most often include the following:

- Employee theft
- Flawed workmanship
- Tools and equipment
- Vehicles
- Earthquakes
- Flood damage
- Nuclear accidents

Some policies allow supplemental coverage for some of these exclusions if there is potential exposure to these kinds of risks.

The policy is designed to cover all property that has been or will be incorporated into the project. Builder's risk insurance is available in a *named peril* or an *all-risk* type of policy. The AIA, the EJCDC, and the ConsensusDocs Coalition documents require the all-risk type of policy.

The AIA, the EJCDC, and the ConsensusDocs Coalition documents state the amount of the property insurance required:

- AIA Document A101® Exhibit A: "[P]roperty insurance coverage shall be no less than the amount of the initial Contract Sum, plus the value of subsequent Modifications and labor performed and materials or equipment supplied by others."

- EJCDC® C-700: ". . . in the amount of the Work's full insurable replacement cost (subject to such deductible amounts as may be provided in the Supplementary Conditions or required by Laws and Regulations)."

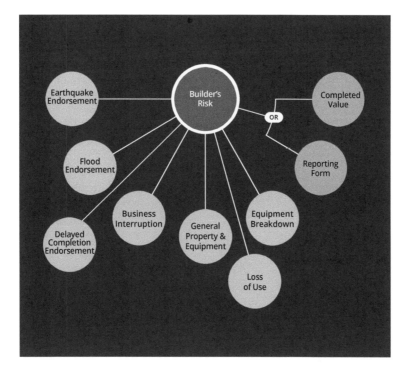

Figure 7.3
Property
Insurance

DOMAIN 1
Planning,
Development,
& Organization

DOMAIN 2
Coordination

DOMAIN 3
Procurement,
Contracting,
& General
Requirements

DOMAIN 4
Research

DOMAIN 5
Analysis
& Evaluation

DOMAIN 6
Production

- ConsensusDocs® 200: ". . . for the full cost of replacement at the time of loss, including existing structures."

Most owners prefer the all-risk form of insurance coverage, including coverage for all perils except those expressly excluded in the policy. The named peril type of coverage specifies the perils that are insured. All-risk is much more inclusive than the named peril type of policy.

When materials are installed or stored on-site and the title passes to the owner after payment, the insured interest increases to the contract sum, to the insured limit, or until the owner occupies the project. Builder's risk insurance is available in two forms: completed value or reporting.

The *completed value form* is written for the anticipated completed value of the project. Most projects use the completed value form (required by AIA and EJCDC documents), especially if the owner is inexperienced in dealing with construction projects or if only one project is in progress at a time.

The *reporting form* is written based on the project's actual value when the policy is written. Therefore, the reporting form coverage must be revised regularly (usually to coincide with each payment application), with the policy premium and insured value increasing at each update. The advantage of this type of insurance is that the payment of premiums is based on insured values at a given time. This condition is most advantageous if the values increase sharply during the final phases of construction. The requirement for filing regular reports of values may be cumbersome to some owners; however, failure to satisfy reporting requirements can leave the owner underinsured.

The reporting form works well for large projects with lengthy construction periods. An owner dealing with many projects at one time may also find the reporting form to be advantageous.

The owner should arrange for coverage of owner-furnished materials or equipment not included in the construction contract price. The owner should also determine whose insurance covers the value of the material or equipment in transit or stored by the contractor off-site during the project.

- AIA Document A201®: "Payment for materials and equipment stored on or off the site shall be conditioned upon compliance by the Contractor with procedures satisfactory to the Owner . . . and shall include the costs of applicable insurance, storage, and transportation . . . ."

- EJCDC® C-700: ". . . materials and equipment not incorporated in the Work but delivered and suitably stored at the Site or at another location agreed to in writing, the Application for Payment must also be accompanied by . . . evidence that the materials and equipment are covered by appropriate property insurance . . . ."

- ConsensusDocs® 200: ". . . applications for payment may include materials and equipment not yet incorporated into the Work but delivered to and suitably stored onsite or offsite including applicable insurance . . . ."

Property of the contractor stored on the owner's premises but off the construction site should be addressed in either the owner's property insurance or the contractor's property insurance. It is sufficient for the supplementary conditions to require the party holding title to secure insurance for property loss. In any event, property insurance is necessary to cover loss of material, whether stored on-site or off-site.

If the owner intends to furnish material or equipment to be incorporated into the project, care must be taken to secure coverage from the time the owner assumes title. The owner's property insurance may require adjustment for the storage of these materials, while the owner has the risk of loss.

AIA documents require the owner to obtain the builder's risk insurance because they have an insurable interest in the project. On the other hand, the EJCDC and ConsensusDocs Coalition place the requirement on the contractor. AIA Document A101® Exhibit A provides for transferring the obligation to the contractor. EJCDC® 200 allows the transfer of the obligation to the owner via the supplementary conditions. Owners with limited construction experience may find the administration of an insurance program burdensome, and they may be unable to obtain a ready source of coverage at favorable rates. Therefore, it may be advantageous for the owner to require the contractor to obtain the builder's risk insurance. However, owners dealing with many construction projects and having the necessary administrative support in place may prefer dealing with brokers and insurance carriers of their choice regarding business policy and cost control. Thus, they may obtain better rates than those available to a contractor.

The type of project may also influence the choice of who should provide builder's risk insurance. For example, an addition to an existing structure might be more economically covered by an extension of the owner's present coverage. In this type of project, the contract amount may be only a fraction of the property's value that could be lost in the event of a major fire. In this instance, any project-related insurance must be coordinated with the owner's existing property insurance to ensure that the completed facility's full value is protected. Further, there may be value in the contractor obtaining special insurance coverage to protect the contractor if the contractor is found liable for a fire that destroyed non-project areas in an existing building.

However, a completely new structure may be covered more economically by the contractor's builder's risk insurance. If the construction site involves special hazards (such as chemical processing), the owner's carrier may offer better terms because of familiarity with the risks involved. If the contractor provides builder's risk insurance, the potential exists for conflicts between the owner's insurance carrier and the contractor's insurance carrier.

Owner-provided builder's risk insurance may afford cost-saving opportunities for large and complex projects. Multiple-prime contracts in which each prime contractor is required to obtain insurance may duplicate policy costs that can otherwise be saved by combining coverage into a single owner-purchased policy. For example, experience on large road construction projects involving multiple-prime contracts has demonstrated overall insurance premium savings when the owner purchases the insurance. In the case of a project with multiple-prime contracts where the owner does not provide the builder's risk insurance, the supplementary conditions should identify which of the prime contractors is to provide the insurance. The selected prime contractor must include in the coverage the value of the other prime contracts. The contractor providing the insurance should furnish a copy of the policy (or proof of coverage) to the other prime

contractors. In cases dealing with multiple-prime contracts, the all-risk type of coverage may not be available. Regardless of who obtains the builder's risk policy, a single policy should be issued to cover the owner's, contractor's, and all subcontractors' insurable interests to avoid duplication of premiums.

Insurance coverage may be priced by the contractor and by the owner. Shopping for insurance may be feasible if the project is for a private owner or if the contract price is negotiated. The savings, if any, may compensate for the administrative demands. In the case of competitively bid public work, this approach is not feasible since the owner accepts the insurance obtained by the contractor. The economies of a competitive bid, if any, may not compensate for the administrative demands. The project's loss performance may likely affect the future rates of the party that procures the policy. The owner, in consultation with an insurance advisor, should determine preferences.

The inclusion of many parties under a single policy requires a plan for the administration of loss sums due to several of the insureds. The current practice requires the owner to adjust all losses, receive all loss payments, and distribute settlements to either the general contractor for division among the subcontractors or to each prime contractor in a multiple-prime contract project, as their interests may appear.

Subcontractors involved in the project can purchase an installation floater, which usually covers property only during the period of installation. The purpose of an installation floater is to insure the subcontractor's materials and work before the project is completed and accepted by the owner. Installation floaters are generally required when expensive equipment or materials are involved, such as generators, chillers, or similar items. Installation floaters are usually not required if the builder's risk policy names the subcontractor and has broad-based coverage that includes equipment installed in the project. Partial occupancy of a project before completion of the construction changes the insurer's risk. Therefore, partial occupancy should not begin without first obtaining the insurance carrier's permission. Regardless of who provides the property insurance, AIA Document A101® Exhibit A requires the insurance carrier providing the property insurance to be contacted before occupancy and written notice

DOMAIN 1
Planning,
Development,
& Organization

DOMAIN 2
Coordination

DOMAIN 3
Procurement,
Contracting,
& General
Requirements

DOMAIN 4
Research

DOMAIN 5
Analysis
& Evaluation

DOMAIN 6
Production

to be received from the carrier stating that necessary changes in coverage have been made. The EJCDC position is that proper endorsement should be obtained to ensure protection.

7.3.3.2 Equipment Breakdown Insurance

Insurance companies have traditionally separated certain risks from others. One example of such separation is *equipment breakdown insurance*, formerly referred to as *boiler and machinery insurance*. The equipment breakdown coverage insures against loss resulting from accidents to boilers and pressure vessels, machinery (e.g., elevators, pumps, manufacturing equipment), electrical equipment (e.g., transformers, generators), HVAC equipment, and computers and communications equipment identified in the policy. The policy may also include damage to others' property. In the past, this type of policy was issued separately from the builder's risk policy. However, builder's risk insurance policies usually include coverage for equipment, negating the need for separate coverage. AIA and EJCDC documents previously required this type of coverage; however, the most current documents no longer specifically list it as a required type of insurance.

7.3.3.3 Contractor's General Property and Equipment Insurance

The builder's risk policy covers the construction's value, but it does not cover the value of the tools and equipment used to build the project. Loss of tools and equipment can affect the progress and, perhaps, the quality of the work. Therefore, the owner should require the contractor to obtain insurance covering construction equipment and tools used on the project or show the financial ability to replace them. This type of insurance covers the cost of tools and equipment damaged by vandalism or a work accident; however, it does not cover losses due to theft or normal wear and tear. Mobile equipment, such as bulldozers, cranes, backhoes, and forklifts, are not covered by the contractor's automobile insurance; therefore, the contractor's general property and equipment insurance is provided to cover these expensive assets.

7.3.3.4 Loss-of-Use, Business Interruption, and Delayed Completion Insurance

All three of these protect the owner from financial losses due to a covered cause. In essence, the cause prevents the owner or renter from conducting regular business or carrying out their daily lives, which results in lost income or increased expenses, respectively. *Loss-of-use* and *business interruption* coverage are essentially the same things but are applied differently.

Loss-of-use coverage is typically associated with residential buildings, such as private homes or leased apartments. It covers living expenses, such as temporary housing, food, and moving costs should a homeowner's or renter's place of residence becomes uninhabitable due to fire, natural disaster, or another covered event.

Business interruption (also called *business income insurance*) coverage applies to businesses that suffer a loss of income due to the business's inability to conduct normal operations. Like loss-of-use coverage, business interruption coverage provides compensation for lost revenue and business expenses, such as mortgage or lease payments, employee payroll, and relocation costs.

Delayed completion provides the same protection as the other two but is limited to construction delays arising from the same perils as those insured against under a builder's risk coverage; thus, it is typically included in the builder's risk coverage as an endorsement or extension. The owner may elect to have this coverage throughout the construction period, and because of the untested performance of a new facility, extend the coverage for a period following construction. AIA Document A101® Exhibit A states that the owner may purchase and maintain such insurance at the owner's option.

7.3.3.6 Subrogation

The objective of comprehensive insurance planning is to create a network of policies to protect the collective and separate interests of parties engaged in the construction project. Subrogation in favor of insurance companies is a right that can significantly disrupt the relationships of the parties involved.

Subrogation allows the insurer to assume the insured party's rights against others in exchange for payment of the loss or damage. For example, suppose an owner suffers losses resulting from a fire when a new electrical transformer malfunctioned. The owner is insured against fire by insurance company "A" and files a claim for the fire damage. "A" investigates and

pays the full loss. However, in the investigation, "A" determines that the transformer was not installed as required by the manufacturer's instructions or that the electrical engineer improperly designed it. With the loss having been paid, the subrogation clause takes effect, and insurance company "A" obtains the rights to all the claims the insured (owner) could bring against the other parties for the damages. The insurance company then becomes a subrogee that can now file suit against either the contractor or the engineer as appropriate to satisfy the claim.

Through subrogation, one party's settlement can become another party's lawsuit. Because of the threat of litigation, this situation may adversely affect the owner's relationship with the contractor and the A/E for the project's balance. To prevent this situation, current contract practice suggests that all parties involved in the project waive all claims against one another to the extent covered by insurance. Because of this waiver, the right of subrogation does not arise. All parties involved in the construction contract should check whether such a waiver violates any term or condition of their individual insurance policies.

7.3.4 Controlled Insurance Programs

The multiple types of insurance required for a construction contract can be complicated and confusing for some participants. A way to simplify the construction insurance bureaucracy is through a *controlled insurance program* (CIP) and sometimes referred to as *wrap-ups*. CIPs consolidate most if not all of the required insurance for a construction project into a single policy. This single policy provides the necessary coverages for all or most parties involved in a construction project. There are two types of CIPs available: OCIP (purchased by the owner) and CCIP (purchased by the contractor).

The most significant advantage of using a CIP is the cost savings it can generate for large commercial construction projects. However, smaller projects benefit from CIPs due to their simplicity and having a streamlined claims process. A rolling wrap-up CIP can be established for owners with multiple construction projects that allow projects to be rolled into and out of the CIP as they are started and completed.

DOMAIN 1
Planning,
Development,
& Organization

DOMAIN 2
Coordination

DOMAIN 3
Procurement,
Contracting,
& General
Requirements

DOMAIN 4
Research

DOMAIN 5
Analysis
& Evaluation

DOMAIN 6
Production

None of the standard contract document forms from the AIA, the EJCDC, or the ConsensusDocs Coalition include CIPs. Therefore, if this type of program is proposed for a project, the standard contract document forms need to be significantly modified. These modifications should be done under the advice of an insurance advisor and legal counsel.

7.3.5 The Additional Insured

A liability policy protects persons named on the policy agreement. These persons are called named insureds. When so named, a person is entitled to legal defense for covered claims and policy payment of damages on the insureds' behalf for the legal liability arising from a covered occurrence.

When injury or damage results from the contractor's construction operations, other parties, together with the contractor, can be exposed to lawsuits. This "shotgun lawsuit" phenomenon can draw numerous parties, including the owner and the A/E, into litigation. The intention may be to sort out the responsible parties and thereby serve the interests of justice. However, the sorting process is expensive for the named parties involved in the project but not responsible for the damage.

The contract documents should require the owner and the A/E to be named additional insureds under the contractor's liability coverage. It must be understood that the insurance company does not expand the coverage of the policy by that extension. An additional insured is merely afforded the policy's benefits for the contractor's operations (the named insured). The acts, errors, or omissions of the owner and the A/E are not covered under the contractor's policy. Errors and omissions coverage must be provided by the individual firm's professional liability policy.

This additional insured endorsement to the contractor's policy is not a substitute for the owner's protective liability insurance. An owner's policy coverage is likely to be greater than that obtained by being named an additional insured in the contractor's policy.

7.3.6 Obtaining and Incorporating Insurance Information

The general conditions published by the AIA, the EJCDC, and the ConsensusDocs Coalition do not contain dollar amounts of insurance values to be used on the project. If not provided for in the general conditions, the proper place to include insurance values is in the supplementary conditions because the requirements vary from one project to the next. However, in the case of AIA documents, the amounts are added to the exhibit to the owner-contractor agreement. The actual coverage amounts must be obtained from the owner and inserted in the appropriate locations. This information should be requested early enough to allow the owner time to consult its insurance advisor and reply to the A/E with sufficient time for the information to be incorporated into the supplementary conditions when the A/E prepares them. When performing work for a repeat client or with an owner constructing multiple projects, the A/E should request each project's insurance information.

The insurance instruction request forms published by EJCDC are recommended for documenting the transfer of insurance information from the owner to the A/E. The EJCDC form is EJCDC® C-052, *Owner's Instructions Concerning Bonds and Insurance for Construction.* The EJCDC also publishes a prototype letter, EJCDC® C-051, *Letter to Owner on Bonds and Insurance for Construction,* that can be used to request the information.

Since the AIA has moved detailed insurance requirements to the owner-contractor agreement using AIA Document A101® Exhibit A, the A/E may have no involvement in preparing documents establishing minimum insurance requirements. Similarly, the ConsensusDocs general conditions are a part of the owner-contractor agreement; thus, the A/E would likely have no involvement with the preparation of that form either.

If used for establishing minimum insurance requirements, the supplementary conditions can be treated the same as a master guide specification section with spaces left blank for insurance information and other modifications as recommended by either the AIA or EJCDC and used in the A/E's practice. The A/E should use the language recommended in either the AIA or EJCDC guides when preparing supplementary conditions. The portion of the supplementary conditions dealing with insurance information should be identical to the request form used. It should include blank spaces where information is transferred from the request form to the supplementary conditions.

Upon receipt of the completed EJCDC® C-052 or other form provided by the owner, the A/E should insert the insurance information into the appropriate place in the supplementary conditions. If the form has missing information or appears incorrectly completed, the A/E should send it back to the owner, requesting clarification or completion. The A/E should not try to guess the intent of the owner. The A/E is not the owner's insurance advisor, nor does the A/E's liability insurance provide coverage for specifying insurance information; however, the addition of insurance values is a usual modification to the general conditions if the standard form allows for it.

7.3.7 Glossary of Insurance Terms

The following definitions related to construction insurance are from the Glossary of Insurance and Risk Management Terms (except where indicated) published by the International Risk Management Institute (IRMI) (https://www.irmi.com/glossary).

All-Risk Coverage. Property insurance covering loss arising from any fortuitous cause except those that are specifically excluded. This is in contrast to named perils coverage, which applies only to loss arising out of causes that are listed as covered.

All Risks, Difference-in-Conditions. A policy maintained by a general contractor (or subcontractor) to fill coverage gaps created by a project owner's (or general contractor's) maintenance of its own builder's risk program.

Bodily Injury (BI). Liability insurance term that includes bodily harm, sickness, or disease, including resulting death.

Builder's Risk Policy. A property insurance policy that is designed to cover property in the course of construction.

Business Interruption Insurance (Business Income Insurance). Commercial property insurance covering loss of income suffered by a business when damage to its premises by a covered cause of loss causes a slowdown or suspension of its operations.

Claim. Used in reference to insurance, a claim may be a demand by an individual or corporation to recover, under a policy of insurance, for loss that may come within that policy.

Claims-Made Policy. A policy providing coverage that is triggered when a claim is made against the insured during the policy period, regardless of when the wrongful act that gave rise to the claim took place.

Commercial Comprehensive General Liability (CGL) Policy. A standard insurance policy issued to business organizations to protect them against liability claims for bodily injury (BI) and property damage (PD) arising out of premises, operations, products, and completed operations; and advertising and personal injury (PI) liability.

Completed Operations. Under a general liability policy, work of the insured that has been completed as called for in a contract, or work completed at a single job site under a contract involving multiple job sites, or work that has been put to its intended use.

Contractual Liability. Liability imposed on an entity by the terms of a contract. As used in insurance, the term refers not to all contractually imposed liability but to the assumption of the other contracting party's liability under specified conditions.

Controlled Insurance Program (CIP). A centralized insurance program under which one party procures insurance on behalf of all (or most) parties performing work on a construction project or on a specific site.

Coverage. Used synonymously with "insurance" or "protection."

Employer's Liability Coverage. This coverage provided by part 2 of the workers' compensation policy provides coverage to the insured (employer) for liability to employees for work-related bodily injury or disease, other than liability imposed on the insured by a workers' compensation law.

Endorsement. An insurance policy form that either changes or adds to the provisions included in one or more other forms used to construct the policy, such as the declarations page or the coverage form.

Equipment Breakdown Insurance. Coverage for loss due to mechanical or electrical breakdown of nearly any type of equipment, including photocopiers and computers.

Exclusion. A provision of an insurance policy or bond referring to hazards, perils, circumstances, or property not covered by the policy.

General Aggregate Limit. The maximum limit of insurance payable during any given annual policy period for all losses other than those arising from specified exposures.

Hold-Harmless Agreement. A provision in a contract that requires one contracting party to respond to certain legal liabilities of the other party. The most commonly used types of clauses are:

- *Limited form* — Where Party A holds Party B harmless for suits arising out of Party A's sole negligence. Party B is thus protected when it is held vicariously responsible for the actions of Party A.

- *Intermediate form* — Where Party A holds Party B harmless for suits alleging sole negligence of Party A or negligence of both parties.

- *Broad form* — Where Party A holds Party B harmless for suit against Party B based on the sole negligence of A, joint negligence of A and B, or the sole negligence of B. Broad form hold harmless agreements are unenforceable in a number of states.

Indemnify. To make compensation to an entity, person, or insured for incurred injury, loss, or damage.

Indemnity. Compensation to a party for a loss or damage that has already occurred, or to guarantee through a contractual clause to repay another party for loss or damage that might occur in the future.

Indemnitee. The person or organization that is held harmless in a contract (by the indemnitor).

Construction
Specifications
Practice Guide

DOMAIN 1
Planning,
Development,
& Organization

DOMAIN 2
Coordination

DOMAIN 3
Procurement,
Contracting,
& General
Requirements

DOMAIN 4
Research

DOMAIN 5
Analysis
& Evaluation

DOMAIN 6
Production

Indemnitor. The person or organization that holds another (the indemnitee) harmless in a contract.

Installation Floater. Inland marine coverage on property (usually equipment) being installed by a contractor.

Insurable Interest. An interest by the insured person in the value of the subject of insurance, including any legal or financial relationship.

Insurance. A contractual relationship that exists when one party (the insurer), for a consideration (the premium), agrees to reimburse another party (the insured) for loss to a specified subject (the risk) caused by designated contingencies (hazards or perils).

Insured. The person(s) protected under an insurance contract.

Liability Insurance. Insurance paying or rendering service on behalf of an insured for loss arising out of legal liability to others.

Limit of Liability (Limit of Insurance). The most that will be paid by the insurer in the event of a covered loss under an insurance policy.

Longshoremen and Harbor Workers Act (LHWCA) of 1927. A federal law that provides no-fault workers' compensation benefits to employees other than masters or crew members of a vessel injured in maritime employment — generally in loading, unloading, repairing, or building a vessel.

Loss. (1) The basis of a claim for damages under the terms of a policy. (2) Loss of assets resulting from a pure risk. Broadly categorized, the types of losses of concern to risk managers include personnel loss, property loss, time element loss, and legal liability loss.

Monopolistic Fund States. Jurisdictions where an employer must obtain workers' compensation insurance from a compulsory state fund or qualify as a self-insurer (as is allowed in two of the jurisdictions). The monopolistic fund states are North Dakota, Ohio, Washington, and Wyoming.

Named Insured. Any person, company, or corporation or any of its members specifically designated by name as insured(s) in the policy as distinguished from others who, although unnamed, are protected by the policy definition. A named insured under the policy has rights and responsibilities not attributed to additional insureds, such as premium payment, premium return, notice of cancellation, and dividend participation.

Named Perils Coverage. A property insurance term referring to policies that provide coverage only for loss caused by the perils specifically listed as covered. It contrasts with "all risks coverage," which applies to loss from all causes not specifically listed as excluded.

Occurrence. In a commercial general liability (CGL) coverage form, an accident, including continuous or repeated exposure to substantially the same general harmful conditions.

Other States Coverage. Workers' compensation and employers' liability insurance coverage for an insured's employees traveling through or temporarily working in states other than the insured's home state, as specifically listed in item 3.C of the information page of the policy.

Owner's and Contractor's Protective (OCP) Liability Coverage. A stand-alone policy that covers the named insured's liability for bodily injury (BI) and property damage (PD) caused, in whole or in part, by an independent contractor's work for the insured.

Peril. Cause of a loss.

Policy. A written contract of insurance between the insurer and the policyholder. It is typically composed of a declarations page, policy form, and endorsements or riders that amend the policy form.

Property Damage (PD). As defined in the general liability policy, physical injury to tangible property, including resulting loss of use, and loss of use of tangible property that has not been physically injured.

Property Insurance. First-party insurance that indemnifies the owner or user of property for its loss, or the loss of its income-producing ability, when the loss or damage is caused by a covered peril, such as fire or explosion.

Replacement Cost Coverage. A property insurance term that refers to one of the two primary valuation methods for establishing the value of insured property for purposes of determining the amount the insurer will pay in the event of loss.

Reporting Form Coverage. Property insurance that allows an insured with fluctuating inventory values to establish a limit of insurance adequate to cover the highest possible exposed value but to pay a premium based on the actual values exposed.

Subrogation. The assignment to an insurer by terms of the policy or by law, after payment of a loss, of the rights of the insured to recover the amount of the loss from one legally liable for it.

Waiver of Subrogation. An agreement between two parties in which one party agrees to waive subrogation rights against another in the event of a loss. The intent of the waiver is to prevent one party's insurer from pursuing subrogation against the other party.

Workers' Compensation. The system by which no-fault statutory benefits prescribed in state law are provided by an employer to an employee (or the employee's family) due to a job-related injury (including death) resulting from an accident or occupational disease.

XCU Exclusion. (Not defined by IRMI.) A common exclusion from liability coverage for damages to others caused by blasting and explosion, collapse of structures, and underground excavation damage to property.

DOMAIN 4:
RESEARCH

Chapter 8

PRODUCT
RESEARCH &
SELECTION

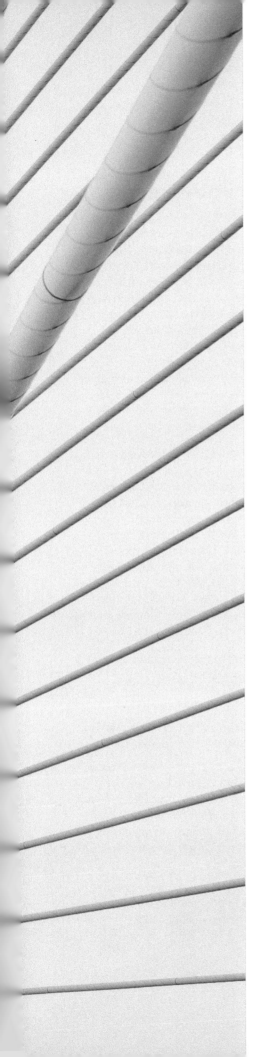

8.1 Introduction to Product Research and Selection

After the owner conceives the project parameters, the architect/engineer (A/E) must research the products, materials, and systems needed to complete the project and select products/suppliers suitable to meet the project's goals. The result of this research and selection step is to select products from suppliers, determine product-related requirements, and develop a design to incorporate the selected products.

There are many strategies and methods to evaluate products and select suppliers, and different organizations and A/Es use a variety of approaches. Regardless of the evaluation method used, the overall objective of the product research and selection process is to identify suitable products to meet the project's goals and maximize value to the owner.

8.2 Elements of Research

Regardless of who writes the specification sections in the project manual or how master guide specifications are developed, products must be researched, selected, evaluated, coordinated with other products, specified clearly and consistently, and coordinated with code requirements.

Deciding what products to specify requires organized and progressive compiling of researched information beginning with the preliminary design phases. Specifying products for construction is much like specifying goods for any other purpose. Selection is based on evaluating products against specific criteria derived from the project's requirements, applicable codes, and industry standards. There are several factors to consider in evaluating a product:

- Product performance criteria
- Product quality
- Manufacturer
- Installation and code requirements

Construction
Specifications
Practice Guide

DOMAIN 1
Planning,
Development,
& Organization

DOMAIN 2
Coordination

DOMAIN 3
Procurement,
Contracting,
& General
Requirements

DOMAIN 4
Research

DOMAIN 5
Analysis
& Evaluation

DOMAIN 6
Production

- Product availability and project schedule

- Cost

- Project conditions

During the design phase, the design team works with other stakeholders and participants to do the following:

- Research the owner's project requirements and relevant information produced during the project conception phase.

- Research the applicable requirements of the authorities having jurisdiction (AHJ) and local codes.

- Propose products to satisfy the owner's project requirements and the applicable building code requirements.

- Collect various forms of product information, including manufacturer data sheets, product drawings, manufacturer specification information, quotes, product standards, and reference standards to evaluate the products that best satisfy the project requirements and enhance stakeholder and participant understanding of the specified products.

- Identify and incorporate product information into the design.

- Develop written documents to detail the product information's technical aspects, including preliminary project descriptions, design narratives, or specifications.

- Summarize product quotes to aid with estimating project construction cost.

- Evaluate product sustainability.

8.3 Identifying Products

The A/E must make informed decisions regarding products, materials, and components to include in the design. Researching product information is not difficult, but it can be time-consuming and involve multiple sources, steps, and resources. Today, most product information is readily available online from manufacturers, authorities having jurisdiction (AHJ), and product standards websites. However, some of

the more traditional methods of obtaining product information, such as printed catalogs and trade shows, are still used.

It is important to note that the information from printed catalogs and other printed materials could contain inaccurate product information if the printed copies are not the most recent versions from the manufacturer. Personal interaction and direct communication with the local product representative remains a common method of gathering and evaluating product information. Product representatives have product knowledge that is not easily communicated on a manufacturer's website or product datasheet. (See Section 3.9 for additional information on working with product representatives.)

A generic product type that satisfies design criteria and meets project conditions must first be identified before specific products can be researched and evaluated. An example of a generic product is "ductile iron pipe for a sewer force main." A specific product example is "ductile iron pipe (8-inch diameter, pressure class 150, exterior asphaltic coating, interior cement lining, restrained push-on joints, ANSI/AWWA C150/A21.50 and ANSI/AWWA C151/A21.51)." Once a generic product selection is made, the research of additional product details can begin.

The steps involved in product research and evaluation include the following:

- Identify the type of product required.

- Establish product requirements by identifying the desired performance and design criteria.

- Research products by comparing significant aspects of the product, including product characteristics, quality, performance, aesthetics, availability, installation requirements, initial installed costs, operational costs, maintenance costs, code requirements, and applicable reference standards.

- Identify appropriate products by compiling a preliminary list of products and manufacturers that satisfy the design requirements and local codes.

8.3.1 Conduct Research for Product Selection

The A/E typically makes the final selection of products either alone or as the result of group discussions with the design team, owner, contractor, or all three. The A/E usually influences aesthetic products and manufacturer choices based on successful previous projects and product research. The owner or contractor may have experience with multiple manufacturers or suppliers and explicit preferences for suppliers they like to work with based on those previous experiences. The mechanical, plumbing, and electrical designers usually influence product selections for their systems based on applicable code requirements and previous experiences. In most cases, the A/E is heavily involved in the product specifying process and is expected to exercise professional judgment when selecting products. Product selection is one of the most important responsibilities of A/Es and specifiers. Here are the primary factors to consider in researching products:

- Economic implications of each choice
- Industry conditions and availability of products
- Sourcing
- Federal, state, and local code requirements
- Product suitability for project conditions
- Product representative
- Applicable product standards

8.3.2 Final Product Selection

If the documents are performance-based or list multiple acceptable products, the contractor may perform final product selection after the contract is awarded. In these cases, the A/E and the owner may not know which products were selected by the contractor until product information is submitted during construction. If the construction contract requires the contractor to list the products/manufacturers that their bid is based on, when bidders submit their bids for a project they must also include a list of the products/manufacturers they plan to use. Often this list is only for key products and is not all-inclusive. The A/E may also ask the bidder/proposer in a post-bid/proposal interview upon which products their bid/proposal was based.

Following are major aspects to be considered in the final selection of a product:

- Owner project requirements and project conditions
- Product characteristics and product quality
- Supply chain risk and equipment lead time
- Compatibility with other selected products
- Manufacturer
- Installation requirements and construction trades needed for installation
- Installed cost
- Operating cost and automatic or manual operation
- Maintenance requirements and maintenance cost
- Warranty requirements and manufacturer responsive to respond to warranty issues

Even if the selected construction products appear similar and may comply with the design intent, the products have different characteristics and most likely are not identical. The A/E is responsible for determining what degree of variance in product characteristics can be allowed and still be acceptable to meet the design intent. The A/E must identify products that meet the project design criteria, code requirements, and reference standards. Products not meeting code requirements or criteria for the intended installation should not be included in the project.

Overall, the A/E should know the product's elemental composition and quality and be aware of its advantages and limitations.

8.4 Economic Implications of Each Choice

A cost-effective facility is an important goal for the owner, and each product choice's economic

DOMAIN 1
Planning,
Development,
& Organization

DOMAIN 2
Coordination

DOMAIN 3
Procurement,
Contracting,
& General
Requirements

DOMAIN 4
Research

DOMAIN 5
Analysis
& Evaluation

DOMAIN 6
Production

implications must be evaluated. However, defining product cost-effectiveness can be a difficult challenge.

To a large degree, it is left to the A/E to select the many items specified for the project, affecting the project's cost. The A/E should be aware of the economic impact of the requirements stated in the specifications. Some A/Es fail to distinguish between the characteristics of a given material when used for different purposes. For example, the grade of redwood specified for an entrance door pull and the grade of the redwood strip specified for the edge of the parking lot paving should not be the same. Avoid elaborate and expensive requirements for items that are not critical to the success of the project. The specifier should consider selecting requisite grades of materials for the specific part of the project and not specify extravagant items where they are not appropriate.

Researching the economic implications of product choice should reveal the following information:

- Whether a product is domestic or imported

- Where the product is produced, warehoused, or both

- Product lead times and if delivery delays may be expected

- If trained installers are available in the project location

- Whether replacement parts are readily available or are excessively expensive

- How selected product options affect the project cost

Domestic products often have shorter and more reliable delivery schedules compared to imported products. Imported products may or may not be more cost-effective than domestic products due to different product quality. The availability of critical materials and components can impact the delivery schedule, and the A/E should research which specified products have longer lead times than more common products. The need for prompt delivery is paramount in owners' minds because they bear a financial cost for each day the project is not complete.

But suppose a product with a longer lead time is needed to achieve the design goal. In that case, the owner may decide to bear the additional financial cost even if a faster way is available to perform the desired function. For example, a local product may come in a color that would satisfy most of the project requirements. However, the owner requires a specific color only available from another manufacturer with

a longer lead time. If the owner requires the specific color with the longer lead time, they need to consider if they can wait for the extra time to get the product, despite the extra cost.

Products must be operated and maintained; thus the type of product specified influences the cost and ease of operation or maintenance. A product's expected maintenance cost should be researched and discussed with the owner before the product is specified. A product may have a low initial cost but require expensive, labor-intensive maintenance. Products often include parts that are designed to be replaced or consumed as part of routine service. Additionally, a low-initial-cost product could have routine maintenance that requires a high-cost component to be regularly replaced to maintain reliable operation.

The different product options and associated costs should be researched and evaluated with the owner's projection of the project's life to determine suitable products. It is often possible to use a product in different ways and to include different product options, and some product options are more expensive than others. If low capital cost is the owner's primary goal, then basic product options are often specified. On the other hand, a high initial cost of a product with enhanced product options may have low installation and maintenance costs.

The initial capital cost may not always be the dominant factor in selecting products. For many projects, the life cycle cost may be a more appropriate measure of value. The projected regularity of product repair or replacement caused by normal product deterioration is a factor in determining how product options affect the project cost. The availability of authorized or experienced installers and maintenance technicians in the project area should be a factor in estimating product life cycle costs.

8.5 Industry Conditions and Availability of Products

The A/E should consider the availability of the products being specified. A product available today may not be available some months later when

the project is under construction. Similarly, some products require longer delivery times and may not be appropriate for projects with short construction periods or when early completion of the project is crucial. If the A/E is aware of items that may be susceptible to significant availability or price fluctuations, these factors should be considered when making product selections.

Another consideration is the availability of skilled workers within specific geographic areas. It may not be appropriate to specify a specialized construction technique for a project located in an area where workers skilled in the specialized technique are not available to do the work. The A/E should consider whether standard available products and colors meet the owner's aesthetic standards or whether custom products and colors are needed. Custom design and custom colors often take more time to produce and have longer lead times than a manufacturer's standard product design. The availability and cost of maintenance supplies should be considered during product evaluation. The cost and availability of maintenance services offered by the manufacturer should also be considered.

8.6 Use of Schedules During Product Selection

Schedules can be used to help document the results of product research and product evaluation. After product evaluation, an approved product data schedule is included in the specifications section or on the drawings. Schedules help simplify communication by presenting data in a tabular form or a matrix. The location and content of schedules may vary widely among A/E firms. When placed in a specification section, schedules are included at the end of PART 3 — EXECUTION. Although not technically part of the execution, the schedules are placed there for convenience in specification preparation, although they may be included in the specifications or drawings.

Examples of schedules are pipe schedules, equipment schedules, hardware schedules, and sealant schedules. Schedules that include materials from

DOMAIN 1
Planning,
Development,
& Organization

DOMAIN 2
Coordination

DOMAIN 3
Procurement,
Contracting,
& General
Requirements

DOMAIN 4
Research

DOMAIN 5
Analysis
& Evaluation

DOMAIN 6
Production

multiple specification sections should be included in the drawings or included in a separate specification.

An example schedule is shown in Figure 8.1.

8.7 Research Sourcing for Selected Products

There are multiple instances in the contract documents where it is preferred to list the selected manufacturers in the product specification. For certain products, it may be required to identify the manufacturers' qualifications and product sourcing in addition to naming the manufacturers. Evaluate the following when researching the sourcing for selected products:

- Country of origin (domestic vs. imported), which can affect delivery time, testing, availability of parts, and warranty service

- Manufacturer's longevity

- Manufacturer's financial stability and track record

- Distribution network and local product representatives

- Availability of and statement of product performance criteria

- Extent of product testing and certifications

- Extent of technical services and availability of local repair services

- Warranty and service

- Sustainability benefits and certifications

8.8 Research Applicable Code Requirements

The A/E needs to understand federal, state, and local codes applicable to the design. There might be instances where some codes create conflicts that require interpretation by the AHJ. AHJs are the organizations, agencies, or departments that have control over an aspect of construction within an area in which they are given responsibility.

The A/E should reference applicable codes and identify requirements that must be met for the project to comply with the code. Some A/Es may meet with AHJs before applying for permits to obtain a local interpretation of a proposed design to satisfy

Figure 8.1
A specification example of an exposed piping schedule for chlorine gas disinfection

SERVICE	DIAMETER (INCH)	MATERIAL	INTERIOR LINING	EXTERIOR COATING	PRESSURE CLASS/ THICKNESS
Chlorine (liquid)	1	Carbon Steel	N/A	Painted	SCH 80
Chlorine (gas)	1, 1 ½, 2, 2 ½	PVC	N/A	N/A	SCH 80
Chlorine (gas)	1	Carbon Steel	N/A	Painted	SCH 80
Sulfur Dioxide (liquid)	1	Carbon Steel	N/A	Painted	SCH 80

code requirements or when modifications from codes are being requested. Meetings with AHJs may also be necessary when an interpretation is sought that is different from specified code requirements. A meeting with an AHJ may require design drawings, references, product literature, ratings of materials, and product certifications to describe the project details for the modification or interpretation being requested. If the A/E anticipates a need for an interpretation, the information should be forwarded to the AHJ for review before the meeting. The process of obtaining a code modification may require coordination with product representatives or reviews of other projects that have received a similar code modification. The product representative can provide technical assistance to the A/E and provide an equivalent product to help meet code requirements.

Codes vary from state to state and differ between local jurisdictions. For instance, a city may adopt codes different from those of the county in the same area. The A/E should be aware of applicable codes and inform the owner of their potential effects on the project.

The *International Building Code* (IBC), published by the International Code Council (ICC), establishes minimum regulations for building systems using prescriptive and performance-related conditions.

The IBC provides a model code with a development process that offers an international forum for design and construction participants to discuss performance and prescriptive code requirements. Local governments can then adopt and modify the model IBC as needed. By working with design and construction professionals, product manufacturers, building officials, AHJs, concerned citizens, and other interested groups, these organizations endeavor to be on the leading edge of available research, design concepts, and building products providing safety. (Refer to Section 4.4 of the *Project Delivery Practice Guide* for more information on codes, regulations, and standards.)

The A/E must have a thorough knowledge of the codes governing the project and consider their impact on the design from the earliest stages through the completion of the construction documents. Specifiers must also be cognizant of when the next version of the code becomes effective, according to the AHJ.

8.9 Evaluate Product Suitability for Project Conditions

All product selection decisions based on product suitability should be recorded, and the A/E must direct or be made aware of product selection decisions. This process requires systematic and progressive compiling of information, beginning with the early design phases. Selecting suitable products for a construction project is like selecting products at a store. Product suitability is based on evaluating the products against specific criteria derived from the owner's requirements and the design intent. Suitable products must be coordinated among design team (or project team) members to ensure the product is suitable for all design disciplines.

Once generic products are determined to be suitable, each type must be investigated to determine how to incorporate it into the design. If the product type is available from more than one manufacturer, investigate several manufacturers to determine acceptability. Cost savings to the owner may be achieved by allowing competition among acceptable

JOINT	TEST	REMARKS
Threaded	Hydrostatic Test (150 psi), Chlorine Pipe Test	Grade B, Type S ASTM A-106. Provide ammonia type unions with lead gaskets
Threaded	Chlorine Pipe Test	Chlorine Vacuum
Threaded	Hydrostatic Test (150 psi), Chlorine Pipe Test	Grade B, Type S ASTM A-106. Provide ammonia type unions with lead gaskets
Threaded	Hydrostatic Test (150 psi), Chlorine Pipe Test	Grade B, Type S ASTM A-106. Provide ammonia type unions with lead gaskets

DOMAIN 1
Planning,
Development,
& Organization

DOMAIN 2
Coordination

DOMAIN 3
Procurement,
Contracting,
& General
Requirements

DOMAIN 4
Research

DOMAIN 5
Analysis
& Evaluation

DOMAIN 6
Production

products and documenting the selection criteria in the specifications. Some project types, especially public projects, have owners that require competition unless special *sole source* permission is granted.

Products are affected to a varying extent by the conditions they are exposed to during the construction and facility management phases of a facility's life cycle. The specifier should ascertain the other consultants' determinations of characteristics of the project site. These may include the following:

- Environmental severity classification

- Energy code climate zone

- Wind load calculations according to American Society of Civil Engineers/Structural Engineering Institute (ASCE/SEI) Standard 7, *Minimum Design Loads for Buildings and Other Structures*

- Project site proximity to saltwater or likelihood of exposure to de-icing chemicals

The specifier should research the manufacturer's product information, test reports, and other available information for characteristics related to environmental exposure. Before making a selection, these characteristics should be compared to the prevailing project site conditions to determine the product's expected performance. Products are designed and manufactured to withstand a limited set of project conditions, including the following:

- Installed location on site

- Temperature

- Humidity

- Wind and solar exposure

- Seismic risks

- Atmospheric pressure

- Exposure to corrosive gases, hazardous chemicals, or possible contamination

- Interior applications

- Exterior applications

- Space constraints

- Frequency of use

- Security, vandalism, or theft concerns

- Owner's or manufacturer's maintenance program

Few products can reasonably withstand every project's conditions, but many products can perform satisfactorily within a reasonable set of limits. When conditions are unusual, a custom product designed to perform accordingly may be required. The A/E, owner, and product representative may collaborate to determine a product's suitability for the prevailing project conditions.

8.10 Review Key Product Selections with Product Representatives

Manufacturers that supply materials, products, and equipment to construct facilities are a varied group with different team members to support their products. In addition to making and selling their products, manufacturers are motivated to promote their innovations and products. Because products are continually improving, manufacturers make a significant contribution to the design and construction industry by advancing knowledge and techniques. Manufacturers have a vested interest in purchasers and users of their products. They want them to understand the qualities, characteristics, and potentials of their products, as well as their installation.

Manufacturer product representatives perform a crucial role in communicating technical information to the A/E, and they provide a valuable service to future product end-users. When the A/E begins research, the product representative is often consulted to determine product details and product viability. Quick, accurate, and dependable answers to questions are necessary for efficient progress through this process, and these answers can usually be obtained from the product representative. The A/E should view the product representative as an information resource with comprehensive knowledge of the product types they represent. Product representatives are a valuable part of the product selection process.

Product representatives should be able to reference applicable codes and identify requirements that must be met for the project to comply with local codes. In addition to online publications and physical samples, manufacturers typically make their research and development departments available for inquiries and strive to provide high-quality customer service for owners, the A/E, and contractors. Some manufacturers demonstrate a commitment to their products' quality by training and certifying, licensing, or approving those individuals and companies that install their products.

The A/E should determine if the manufacturer recommends the product for the use intended for the project. The product's documented properties and limitations should be compared against the design criteria established for the project. For instance, a particular submersible sewage pump should not be specified if the pump cannot operate within the specified operating flow range and total dynamic head conditions required by the design criteria and expected operations.

Most manufacturers and product representatives are aware that current and accurate technical information is required to design and construct projects; they are therefore conscientious about providing customer service to the A/E and owners

that make product selection decisions. Many manufacturers offer suggested proprietary or guide specifications to relieve the A/E from researching and writing a particular specification section. These specifications from manufacturers must be reviewed carefully to determine whether they have biases for a particular product and whether they accurately state the necessary information. (See Table 1.1 in Chapter 1 for a comparison of manufacturer guide specifications to other available master guide specifications.) Typically guide specifications are gathered from multiple manufacturers of similar products, and the guide specifications are compared to determine any manufacturer biases. The A/E uses the guide specifications from the manufacturers to write a detailed specification suitable for the project.

In much the same way that the continuing evolution of the internet has caused major pattern shifts in how the construction business handles information, the product information world has been permanently changed by the availability of information to the design professions and the building industries. Although product manufacturers still provide printed product information, much of their product information is available on the manufacturers' websites. Printed catalog libraries in A/E offices are being phased out in favor of online electronic libraries.

Manufacturer websites generally provide the following types of information about their products:

- Catalogs

- Product datasheets

- Installation instructions

- Safety Data Sheets (SDSs)

- Environmental Product Declarations (EPDs)

- Health Product Declarations® (HPDs)

- Test reports

- Evaluation service reports

- Drawing details and building information model (BIM) objects

- Manufacturer guide specifications

- Contact information for product representatives

- Continuing education presentations, seminars, and whitepapers

Some online sources have made the search for construction product manufacturers easier by creating online catalogs. These online catalogs list manufacturers and are typically organized according to MasterFormat®, with hyperlinks to the manufacturers' websites.

8.11 Research Applicable Product Standards

After preliminary product selections, the A/E continues to refine the product selections through the design development phase and construction documents phase. Product standards influence product selection by introducing quality control of the product. Product standards are a series of related standards that have become an accepted framework for developing a basis of product quality.

Product representatives should be familiar with available products from various manufacturers other than those they represent. Because relatively few projects name only one manufacturer, product representatives should be prepared to name

other qualified competitive sources. Product representatives usually prefer to compete against qualified products rather than risk competing against potentially low-cost but inferior products.

In contrast to mandatory codes and regulations, reference standards are voluntary. However, some codes and regulations adopt reference standards. The model code-writing bodies use reference standards because there has been considerable research and testing put toward their development. The model code-writing bodies cannot perform the same research and testing degree as the reference standards developers. The specifier should consult the appendices of the respective building codes for a helpful list of referenced standards.

Reference standards are not generally developed by governmental agencies. Rather, they are typically created and maintained by an organization, whether it is an association, society, institute, manufacturers group, or installer group that is directly involved in some way with the manufacture or installation of the materials, products, and equipment subject to the reference standard. Reference standards are the common language for the industry to establish minimum standards. If a reference standard is specified, then it can predict the result of a construction activity. For instance, if the specifications for a concrete structure require compliance with American Concrete Institute (ACI) 350, then the concrete structure is suitable to convey, store, or treat environmental liquids such as water, wastewater, and non-hazardous solid wastes.

8.11.1 Reference Standards

A reference standard is usually incorporated into the project's specifications by referring to its developing association name, number, title, or other commonly used designation (see Section 14.1.3 for reference standard specifying). This method is preferable to the inclusion of the standard's full text, which is usually copyrighted. For example, "ASTM E3038–20, *Standard Practice for Assessing and Qualifying Candidates as Inspectors of Firestop Systems and Fire-Resistive Joint Systems*" may be reproduced without the written approval of the authoring organization.

There are many advantages for the use of reference standards, including the following:

DOMAIN 1
Planning,
Development,
& Organization

DOMAIN 2
Coordination

DOMAIN 3
Procurement,
Contracting,
& General
Requirements

DOMAIN 4
Research

DOMAIN 5
Analysis
& Evaluation

DOMAIN 6
Production

Quality assurance. Organizations that develop standards are experts in their respective fields of interest, and their standards are the product of extensive research, experience, and lessons learned.

Uniformity. Standards represent the consensus of a national network of manufacturers within a field of interest.

Reduced conflict and duplication. To reduce duplication and conflict between standards, ANSI coordinates standards development and adopts and promotes the standards developed by its accredited members.

Reduced work. Incorporating standards into the specifications by reference saves the time required for writing a detailed and lengthy specification. A reference standard should be reviewed, and its content and purpose understood, before including it in the specifications.

Users of reference standards should be familiar with the following issues:

Applicability. Selection of reference standards that are most appropriate for the product and application. Avoid referencing non-applicable reference standards.

Quality. Reference standards often define quality in terms of minimum requirements.

Design Criteria. The minimum requirements may be so restrictive that they exclude most commercially available materials, or they may be so liberal that nearly anything produced can meet the requirements.

Availability. Users should maintain a current library of reference standards specified and understand the specified standards and how they apply to the product.

Duplication and Conflict. Requirements of one standard may conflict with another when two or more standards are used for a given product, increasing the possibility of using an inferior product.

Optional Provisions. Reference standards contain optional provisions, including categories, classes, or groups from which applicable properties must be selected.

Multiple Standards. Reference standards usually name other related standards. Users must understand the additional references' effect; otherwise, conflicts of information and optional provisions may undesirably affect the project.

8.11.2 Sustainability Standards

The sustainability of a product over the product's entire anticipated lifespan should be evaluated during product selection. The A/E also should understand the sustainability and environmental impact of the products being evaluated.

There are different publicly available sustainability standards used to evaluate the sustainability of building materials and products. The A/E also should research the sustainability metrics of products and determine if a more sustainable product can be cost-effective to achieve the project's goals. Most sustainability standards use a life cycle assessment to summarize the environmental impact of the product. The sustainability standards evaluate the product's environmental performance against a comparable framework used for similar products.

In addition to sustainability standards, ecolabels are used to identify sustainability performance quickly. Ecolabels are marks placed on product packaging to help consumers quickly and easily identify those products that meet specific environmental performance criteria. Private companies, trade associations, and environmental organizations typically manage ecolabels. Examples of ecolabels include Carpet and Rug Institute's CRI Green Label Plus™, Underwriters Laboratories' GREENGUARD, Forest Stewardship Council®'s FSC Chain of Custody Certification, and Green Seal™.

8.12 Product Research and Selection Process

Product research is necessary to identify and incorporate product information into the design. Multiple facets of a product are evaluated to determine its suitability to meet the project's goals. The A/E researches the owner's project requirements and relevant information produced during the project conception phase to establish a baseline for product evaluation. Design teams research the AHJ and local codes' applicable requirements to determine which products are suitable for the project. Product representatives work with the A/E to propose products to satisfy the owner's project requirements and the applicable building code requirements. Throughout the research phase, the A/E collects various types of product information to help evaluate the products that best satisfy the project requirements and enhance stakeholder and participant understanding of the specified products. This information may include manufacturer datasheets, product drawings, manufacturer specification information, quotes, product standards, and reference standards. Product information and product budgetary quotes are used to aid with estimating project construction costs.

After a product is selected, the A/E uses the research gathered during product evaluation to develop written documents (i.e., preliminary project descriptions, design narratives, or specifications) to detail the product information's technical aspects. Regardless of the research methods used, the product research and selection process's overall objective is to select suitable products to meet the project's goals and maximize value to the owner.

DOMAIN 5:
ANALYSIS & EVALUATION

Chapter 9

PRODUCT
EVALUATION

9.1 Product Evaluation Overview

Specifications are the principal device (alongside the drawings) to define the project and therefore deserve special attention for their role in evaluating systems that meet project requirements. The specification details allow the specifier to evaluate and select products according to the project's design intent. The specifier analyzes the products, especially for complex equipment and new technologies, to ensure they are appropriate for the project. In short, the specifier uses the owner's needs and requirements to evaluate systems, assemblies, and materials that meet project requirements. Besides the design intent, the proposed systems are evaluated against code requirements, climate conditions, constructability, reference standards, quality, and cost. The following sections discuss the recommended process to evaluate and analyze systems, assemblies, and materials being proposed for the project.

9.2 Evaluating Systems, Assemblies, and Materials

Some products affect the performance of other products and also subsequent product selections. To make the product selection process efficient, the architect/engineer (A/E) should evaluate major systems and subsystems first, and then evaluate smaller components based on their product quality and performance abilities and compatibility with prior product selections. Product evaluations can be used to evaluate complete systems and assemblies as well as components and construction products. Increased competition for products included in systems and efficient construction materials may also provide cost savings. The primary goal of evaluating systems, assemblies, and materials is to determine the applicability of available products and the compatibility of different products and systems to meet the project requirements. Systems, assemblies, and materials are evaluated with the following project components:

DOMAIN 1
Planning,
Development,
& Organization

DOMAIN 2
Coordination

DOMAIN 3
Procurement,
Contracting,
& General
Requirements

DOMAIN 4
Research

DOMAIN 5
Analysis
& Evaluation

DOMAIN 6
Production

- Compliance with project requirements and design intent

- Consistency with project drawings

- Compliance with code requirements

- Compatibility with desired constructability and construction sequence

9.2.1 Evaluating Products for Compliance with Project Requirements and Design Intent

Many factors influence the selection and incorporation of products into a project. Throughout this product evaluation process, participants of varying responsibility and authority make or influence product selections. The design process is a critical evaluation influencing the outcome of product selection, and one of the main goals is to ensure the selected products satisfy the project requirements. The owner sets the requirements for the details and design of the project that further create requirements that influence product selection decisions. Then the A/E evaluates products for compliance with the owner's project requirements.

Typically, the A/E performs multi-phased evaluations throughout the design phase that create a progressive evaluation leading to a final product selection. The product evaluation begins during the schematic design phase and when the A/E or owner makes conceptual product decisions for the primary products to define the functional project requirements. Then, detailed product information is collected and reviewed during the subsequent design phase to evaluate a product's compliance with project requirements. The A/E develops the specifications and drawings for the selected products after determining the products comply with the project requirements.

9.2.2 Review of Project Drawings

The drawings should be reviewed as they are being prepared to ensure all systems, assemblies, and materials are addressed in the specifications. The drawings also show how certain products are incorporated into the project, giving the specifier information on installation methods and suitable accessory materials. This review is also a good time to coordinate terminology used on the drawings and the types of written notes provided.

A particular material or component may appear many times throughout the drawings but is specified in only one location. Only generic notes should be used on the drawings to identify, but not describe, a material or component, which helps simplify and coordinate the documentation process. Overly detailed notes may obscure the drawings and increase the possibility of inconsistencies and duplications.

Detailed written information should be reserved for the specifications so that minor changes during the development of the documents can be accommodated by revising only the specifications. For example, if the drawings have been noted to include concrete pavers, a design decision changing to brick pavers would necessitate finding and changing several drawing notes in addition to the specifications. However, if the drawings had indicated only unit pavers, those notes would be unaffected by the change, and only the specifications would have to be modified.

Minimizing the number of required changes to written information on the drawings diminishes the opportunities for discrepancies among the various drawings and between the drawings and specifications. Whenever a change of materials is made, the corresponding symbols must be changed throughout the drawings, so symbols referring to a generic class of material, such as concrete or wood, are preferable over symbols referring to specific materials, such as walnut or oak. Thus, a change in wood species, for example, would not affect the drawings. Also, when more than one type of a generic class of materials is used, such differentiation can be shown in the drawings with short notations such as "Wood-A" and "Wood-B." Items of equipment, such as pumps or valves, should be identified on the drawings by a short generic name or coded symbol. For example, power roof ventilators (PRVs) might be indicated by "PRV-1" and "PRV-2." The graphic representation on the drawings should be only a representative outline rather than a detailed drawing.

Proprietary product information should not appear on drawings unless a closed proprietary specification limits the options to a single product. Even when specifications refer to products by their proprietary names, the notes on drawings should remain generic. If proprietary names are used on drawings,

acceptance of a substitution could require revision of each proprietary reference by addendum or contract modification.

Material systems should also be identified on the drawings with only generic notes. For example, either a four-ply built-up roof with gravel surfacing or a loose-laid and ballasted ethylene, propylene, diene monomer (EPDM) roof could be noted on the drawings simply as a "roof membrane." Suppose more than one type of roof membrane is used in a project. In that case, the drawings should identify them as roofing "Type A," "Type B," "Type C," and so on, where the letter symbolizes a specific system described in the specifications. Where different design strengths are specified for structural steel, reinforcement, concrete, or other structural elements, the drawings may indicate the boundaries between the materials of different capacities, which also may be designated as "Type A," "Type B," etc.

Ensure that drawings do not cross-reference the specifications with notes such as "refer to specifications" or "manhole cover — see specifications." Drawings and specifications are complementary parts of the same set of contract documents, and including references from one to the other is not recommended. However, it is acceptable to refer to specific specification sections. For example, a note on a floor plan could state "provide firestopping at wall penetration — see specification Section 07 84 00." This concept is consistent with similar techniques on drawings, where one drawing references another specific drawing or detail in the drawing set.

The drawings should not attempt to define the work of specific subcontractors or trades. However, the drawings may be used to indicate the extent of alternates, areas of construction phasing, limits of work, and specific items of work by the owner or by separate contract. Ensure these are appropriately incorporated in the correct Division 01 section.

On multiple-prime contract projects, the drawings can be used to designate work of separate contracts. Although these items may be graphically delineated on the drawings, the written descriptions and scope of work requirements should be defined in Division 01 — General Requirements and PART 1 — GENERAL of the specification section.

DOMAIN 1
Planning,
Development,
& Organization

DOMAIN 2
Coordination

DOMAIN 3
Procurement,
Contracting,
& General
Requirements

DOMAIN 4
Research

DOMAIN 5
Analysis
& Evaluation

DOMAIN 6
Production

9.2.3 Evaluating Products for Compliance with Code Requirements

The A/E continues to refine the product evaluation during the design development stage and reviews the project's regulatory requirements. Regulatory requirements influence product selection by introducing codes and standards that have a direct influence on product selection. If a product complies with the project's code requirements, there is less likelihood that it is unsuitable for the desired design intent and likely does not create a substantial risk to the owner. Product compliance with code requirements is necessary to eliminate products that create unreasonably hazardous or dangerous conditions. A product that fails to comply with an applicable code or safety rule or any other specified standard should not be included in the project.

Some product features are crucial for safe project operation, and many of these features cannot be quickly evaluated simply by visually examining the product during the design phase. Such features need to be evaluated and tested, with assurance provided to the owner or A/E that the product complies with code requirements and that compliance is consistent from product to product. For example, suppose the owner determines that a return activated sludge forcemain system must withstand average pressures of at least 250 psi. In that case, the owner needs assurance that none of the system components, like a valve seal or pipe seal, will fail to withstand such pressure. The owner and A/E cannot easily determine whether a part meets this requirement by merely looking at it; they rely on compliance with code requirements to ensure a product is suitable for the project.

Given a large number of national and international codes, many codes have redundant and overlapping requirements. In a few areas, particularly building construction, there are sometimes more than two standards that, while not identical, define functional requirements for the same type of product. This redundancy makes it especially important to know which aspects of the product are covered in the code compliance evaluation and which standard is referenced in the specifications. Requirements in two different codes covering the same product

may be very different. To understand the code compliance evaluation, the A/E needs to be aware of which standards are used to meet the project requirements.

9.2.4 Evaluating Products for Constructability and Sequencing

The A/E must understand that neither the section titles nor their arrangement is organized by scopes of work and do not control how the project's work is assigned to various construction trades and subcontractors. For example, the cold-formed metal framing for an exterior wall may involve welders and ironworkers. At the same time, carpenters or lathers may erect non-load-bearing metal wall framing for gypsum board partitions. Although MasterFormat® division and section titles may correlate with the activities of traditional contractor groups, it is not the intent of MasterFormat® to assign work to specific construction trades or design disciplines. Conversely, the subcontractor and the installing trade should not influence the arrangement of the specification sections. Published standard conditions of the contract further emphasize this philosophy within their requirements.

Evaluating products for constructability and sequence aims to provide a coordinated effort between design, product evaluation, and construction that produces a construction sequence that meets the project's requirements. Utilizing the overall project schedule and a list of major equipment, the constructability evaluation must develop a set of dates and milestones for input to the sequence evaluation. Product procurement dates and supplier delivery requirements must be evaluated to confirm that the proposed construction sequence requirements are met.

Installation techniques to reduce labor or increase efficiency through new, modified, or enhanced products, or unique application of products, are evaluated to determine if there is a benefit to the project. For instance, the exterior piping work (i.e., exterior piping installation, insulation of exterior piping, and heat-tracing of exterior piping) could be consolidated into a single subcontractor work package to create efficient sequencing and coordination instead of using a separate subcontractor for each discipline of the exterior piping work.

Projects with multiple pieces of the same type of equipment should take advantage of the efficiencies of repetitive activities through sequencing similar work activities together. When evaluating the design and construction sequencing of products, the A/E should also evaluate system commissioning and start-up requirements. By evaluating the product's start-up requirements, the A/E establishes that the overall project schedule will integrate commissioning and start-up sequencing with design and construction sequencing.

9.2.5 Value Analysis

Value analysis identifies areas of potential cost savings and benefits for the consideration and evaluation by the project team. The quality, performance, budget, and schedule of the products are among the project information to consider when evaluating products in the value analysis process. Budget requirements and maintenance costs directly influence decisions by establishing price parameters for products. The A/E sets priorities on budget decisions for each product based on many factors that vary with each project. The project schedule also has a direct influence on the product decisions and value analysis process. If the time allotted for product evaluation or value analysis is limited, the options that the A/E evaluates may also be limited. This limitation, in turn, can increase the occurrences of substitution requests and often increases construction prices. Another schedule factor to include in the value analysis is product delivery and availability. If a product has limited availability or has a long lead time for delivery, then the product schedule needs to be evaluated to determine how it fits into the project schedule.

Additional details for value analysis and life cycle costs can be found in the *Project Delivery Practice Guide*, Section 4.2.3.2.

9.3 Impact of Project Conditions on Materials and Methods

Materials and methods management is an important element in product evaluation. Materials represent a high cost to the owner, so minimizing procurement or purchase impacts presents important opportunities to benefit the owner. Material and method impacts are not just a concern during the construction phase; decisions about materials and methods are also determined during the initial planning and design phases. For example, long lead materials can be procured early in the project schedule to reduce the impact on the overall schedule and project conditions. Project conditions, such as the time of year or project location, may impact the availability of materials and consequently may influence the project schedule, especially in projects with a tight construction timeframe. Sufficient time for procuring the specified materials must be allowed in the project schedule. For projects with short schedules, more expensive manufacturers may be employed to save time in the product's schedule and reduce the impact on the overall project schedule.

The project conditions determine if there are cost or schedule benefits to assembling items off-site and then delivering them to the site. For instance, fabricated support members, such as steel beams and columns for buildings, are typically pre-manufactured in an off-site facility before delivery to the site, simplifying the field erection procedures. Welded or bolted connections are partially connected to the fabricated support members and are then cut to the necessary dimensions before delivery to the site. Similarly, steel tanks, pre-fabricated buildings, pump skids, control panels, and pressure vessels are often partially or fully fabricated in an off-site shop. If the selected product includes work that can be done in a shop where working conditions can be better controlled before delivering the product to the site, it is often beneficial to the owner to use that product, assuming that the product can be shipped to the site after fabrication.

9.3.1 Impact of Interior Conditions

There are several components to evaluate when selecting products for interior conditions, such as the quality of the building air, heating, ventilation, lighting, and noise. Products located inside buildings can be vulnerable to the interior conditions inside the building and experience negative effects if the products are not suitable for the interior climate. If a product selected is not suitable for the interior climate, then the product could deteriorate and reduce the useful life of the building. The A/E should evaluate products that improve a building's energy efficiency and interior conditions, mainly by efficiently reducing the energy needed for heating, lighting, and equipment operation. To prevent materials and products from needing to be replaced too often and becoming costly maintenance items, A/Es should evaluate material durability within the project's interior conditions, especially for the materials that experience a lot of wear, such as flooring.

9.3.2 Impact of Exterior Conditions

The products selected for the project must be designed to suit the exterior conditions at the site. The impacts of the environmental conditions on the products are evaluated to determine product suitability for the site. For instance, frequent wet weather events or intense storms make it more important to direct stormwater away from the site and control stormwater release on the site or select products suitable for wetter climates. A milder climate with high humidity fluctuations will reduce the durability of building materials if the materials are not suitable for mild climates. High groundwater levels, proximity to water bodies, and risk of storm surges all need to be considered when evaluating products for the project.

Exterior conditions are some of the factors to consider in material and method selection during product evaluations. Often buildings and products that have not taken local environmental conditions into consideration result in a project that performs poorly and requires high levels of maintenance to maintain reliable operation. Materials and methods also must be compatible with specific regional and local cultural and aesthetic conditions. For example, a stucco wall and flat roof type residential construction, typically seen in the southwestern United States, is not typical in the Midwest. In the Midwest, the climate is colder, and homes typically use wood framing, vinyl siding, and pitched roofs.

9.4 Application of Reference Standards

A standard is a document established by consensus that provides rules, guidelines, or characteristics for activities or their results as defined in the International Organization for Standardization/ International Electrotechnical Commission (ISO/ IEC) Guide 2. Standards are incorporated by reference into the specifications and thus become commonly known as *reference standards.* They are published by trade associations, professional societies, standards-writing organizations, governments, and institutional organizations. Typical authors are architects, engineers, scientists, technologists, manufacturers, and product users who are extremely knowledgeable about the particular reference standard subject. Where applicable, use standards listed in the model or local codes to ensure acceptability with the authority having jurisdiction (AHJ). Depending on how it is listed in the codes, a reference standard may be considered either a code requirement or a guideline to gain acceptance by the AHJ.

Reference standards include the following types:

- **Basic material standards** such as ASTM International (ASTM) B211/B211M, *Standard Specifications for Aluminum and Aluminum-Alloy Rolled or Cold Finished Bar, Rod, and Wire*

- **Product standards** such as Engineered Wood Association (APA) PS-1, *Structural Plywood*

- **Design standards** such as American Concrete Institute International (ACI) ACI 318, *Building Code Requirements for Structural Concrete*

- **Workmanship standards** such as ASTM E2112, *Standard Practice for Installation of Exterior Windows, Doors and Skylights*

DOMAIN 1
Planning,
Development,
& Organization

DOMAIN 2
Coordination

DOMAIN 3
Procurement,
Contracting,
& General
Requirements

DOMAIN 4
Research

DOMAIN 5
Analysis
& Evaluation

DOMAIN 6
Production

- **Test method standards** such as ASTM E119, *Standard Test Methods for Fire Tests of Building Construction and Materials*

- **Codes** such as American National Standards Institute/American Society of Mechanical Engineers (ANSI/ASME) A17.1, *Safety Code for Elevators and Escalators*

- **Installation standards** such as National Fire Protection Association (NFPA) 13, *Standard for the Installation of Sprinkler Systems*

- **Performance standards** such as ASTM F1487, *Standard Consumer Safety Performance Specification for Playground Equipment for Public Use*

- **Life safety standards** produced by organizations such as International Code Council, Inc. (ICC), NFPA, and UL

Reference standards are incorporated into the specifications by referring to a number, title, or other designation. The provisions of standards so referenced become a part of the specifications just as though included in their entirety. Their incorporation into the specifications by reference saves the A/E the work of writing elaborate and lengthy text. Accompanying these benefits are some liabilities:

- Inadequate reference standards coexist with stringent ones.

- Reference standards can create duplication and contradiction within the contract documents.

- Standards can contain embedded options.

- Standards generally refer to minimum requirements.

- Reference standards might contain undesired requirements.

- Various AHJs may enforce different editions of the same standard, which might have conflicting requirements.

9.4.1 Know the Standard

A reference standard should be reviewed and its content and purpose thoroughly understood before it is incorporated into the specifications. Other project requirements must be compatible with the reference standard, and the standard should be free of duplications and contradictions. If the reference standard does not meet these criteria, the A/E must choose between using the standard as a reference and defining exceptions to it or writing original requirements into the specifications.

The A/E should have access to the reference standards proposed to be cited in the specifications. Maintaining a current library of all reference standards may be expensive and a difficult task, but it is advisable to, at a minimum, obtain commonly referenced standards.

9.4.2 Duplications and Conflicts

Duplications and conflicts may occur when two or more reference standards are used for a given product. The requirements of one standard may conflict with another, thus creating an opportunity to use a product conforming to lesser requirements than those that were intended. Some reference standards contain provisions that, at first glance, appear to be an irrevocable part of the standard. However, a footnote or subsequent paragraph may void these provisions unless they are stated explicitly in the specifications.

Reference standards, especially those dealing with workmanship, may contain statements similar to those in the conditions of the contract or Division 01. When standards are referenced, the duplicated statements become part of the project specifications. Statements that differ in wording or intent from the requirements of the conditions of the contract or Division 01 can create ambiguities leading to conflicts. For example, the American Institute of Steel Construction, Inc. (AISC) *Code of Standard Practice* covers numerous contractor-owner and contractor-subcontractor relationships. The AISC Code also uses the words "owner" and "contract documents" in a different context than those used in the general conditions of a construction contract. These situations could easily contribute to misunderstandings.

In addition, other provisions often appear in reference standards, such as the following examples:

- "Spaces above suspended ceilings shall be ventilated."

- "During the installation of drywall tape, the building temperature shall be maintained at not less than 50 degrees F (10 degrees C)."

Statements such as these might conflict with other specification requirements and create confusion, misinterpretation, or contradictions. Wherever the wording or intent of such provisions differs, there exists a potential for disputes. Such provisions should be identified and excluded when the standard is used. Similarly, the A/E could state that when there is a conflict or discrepancy between a reference standard and the specifications or another referenced standard, the more stringent requirements shall apply. Such statements cannot be relied upon to handle all possible conflicts, however. The A/E needs to identify the duplications and ensure the specifications modify the references to eliminate contradictions.

9.4.3 Embedded Options

Many standards include several categories, classes, or groups from which applicable properties must be selected. These embedded options constitute choices that must be identified and modified to prevent discrepancies. For example, ASTM C150/ C150M, *Standard Specification for Portland Cement*, covers 10 cement types. The A/E should evaluate each choice. If the A/E does not specify the type, the selection is forfeited to the contractor, who can reasonably be expected to select the least expensive option.

9.4.4 Multiple Standards

Many standards contain references to other standards. They create conflicts of information and produce multiple choices in the same manner as single reference standards. The AISC Document *Specifications for the Design, Fabrication, and Erection of Structural Steel for Buildings* provides another example. This document refers to several ASTM standards and these refer, in turn, to still other ASTM standards. The essential point is that standards listed within other standards must not contain qualifications that contradict any other referenced standard or the project specifications.

There is no easy solution to this problem other than knowing and understanding the content of the additional referenced material.

9.4.5 Trades and Subcontracts

Reference standards may refer to a particular trade or a particular subcontractor. Construction contracts are usually written for one contractor, and a subcontractor's reference in a project specification should be avoided. Again, knowing the reference standard contents eliminates statements that contradict the requirements of the project specifications.

9.4.6 Level of Requirements

Reference standards often define minimum requirements. The minimum requirements may be so restrictive that they exclude most commercially available materials or are so liberal that nearly anything produced can meet them. Exceptions may be made to the reference standards to avoid these extreme situations.

9.5 Verify Warranty Requirements

There are two basic types of warranties used in construction projects:

- Construction warranties or guaranties, which cover products and workmanship. Construction warranties are usually extended warranties specified in various specification sections.

- Warranties that cover products only.

Warranties on goods are generally affected by a sales transaction. They are governed by the *Uniform Commercial Code* (UCC), other applicable state laws, and the specific terms of the warranties offered. The UCC is a general term used to describe the law governing the sale of goods and other commercial matters. Each state has adopted the UCC as the law in that state. Although the separate state enactments are similar, thereby providing uniform national law, some variations exist from state to state. (See Section 5.4 for more information on the UCC.)

Construction
Specifications
Practice Guide

DOMAIN 1
Planning,
Development,
& Organization

DOMAIN 2
Coordination

DOMAIN 3
Procurement,
Contracting,
& General
Requirements

DOMAIN 4
Research

DOMAIN 5
Analysis
& Evaluation

DOMAIN 6
Production

Definitions to terms used in this section can be found in the *Project Delivery Practice Guide*.

9.5.1 Guaranties and Warranties

The terms guaranty and warranty are commonly used interchangeably to describe the manufacturer's responsibility after delivery of a product and the contractor's responsibility after completion of construction. These same terms are also used for similar meanings in other contexts. According to *Black's Law Dictionary*, "guaranty" and "warranty" are derived from the same root and are, in fact, etymologically the same word, the "g" of Norman French being interchangeable with the English "w."

Though the two terms are frequently misapplied in business, the law has assigned slightly different meanings. Legally, a guaranty is a separate contract by a third party (analogous to a surety bond) who assumes responsibility if the principal fails to perform. Conversely, a warranty is an assurance by the principal that it will assume stipulated responsibilities for completed portions of the project. Thus, a manufacturer warrants its material, whereas the construction contractor provides a third-party guaranty for those same materials and a warranty

for the construction contractor's workmanship in installing them.

9.5.2 Construction Warranties

The subject of warranties is as technical and confusing as that of insurance. Although most A/Es have learned to avoid specifying insurance requirements, it is still common practice for A/Es to specify warranties. Those who do so on behalf of the owner must be as knowledgeable about warranties as they are about the product's physical properties and materials they specify.

Warranties specified for materials and equipment shall be in addition to, and run concurrently with, the contractor's general warranty and guaranty and requirements for the contract's correction period.

9.5.3 Terms and Conditions

Requirements that apply to maintaining valid warranties are referred to as *terms and conditions*. Standard general conditions published by the American Institute of Architects (AIA), Engineers Joint Contract Documents Committee (EJCDC), ConsensusDocs, and other organizations (including derivative documents) indicate that the contractor warrants that material and equipment furnished is new or good quality, free from defects, and conforms to the requirements of the contract documents. These warranty provisions indicate exclusions of defects and damage caused by insufficient or improper operation and maintenance, abuse, modifications, and normal wear and tear. It should be noted that none of these warranties includes a time limitation. The time limit varies depending on the location of the project and the laws governing the contract.

Although an exclusion limits the applicability of a warranty, a condition must be satisfied to make the warranty effective. If the condition is not met, the warranty is null and void. In the case of a roofing warranty, some requirements, such as proper use and adequate maintenance, may be stated as conditions rather than exclusions. In such cases, the manufacturer may disclaim liability even if the product failure has nothing to do with the failure to comply with the condition.

The one-year correction period provided in standard general conditions is simply a specific contractual obligation for the contractor and a remedy for the owner under the general contract. It is not intended to limit the effect of warranties provided in or required by the contract. The distinction between the contractor's obligations under the general warranty and its one-year specific correction obligations is not always made. Some contracts — most notably federal construction contracts that use warranty language provided in Federal Acquisition Regulations (FAR) — actually limit the contractor's warranty obligations to one year.

Extended warranties are sometimes required in the specifications covering items such as roofing. Unfortunately, many of the documents that purport to be guaranties or warranties are in fact little more than disclaimers of responsibility. It is virtually impossible to obtain a manufacturer's warranty that is as broad as a construction contractor's responsibilities during the correction period. Figure 9.1 illustrates a two-party agreement with contractual assurance by the contractor to the owner of a warranty obligation for a specified time period. With the use of AIA, EJCDC, and other standard general conditions, it is unnecessary to specify one-year warranties. Extended warranties are not provided for in AIA, EJCDC, ConsensusDocs, and other standard general conditions and must be appropriately

specified in PART 1 — GENERAL of the product specification section.

Figure 9.2 illustrates the relationship of the owner and the contractor and the requirements of a guaranty document similar to an insurance policy or a performance bond and involvement of a third party (guarantor or surety) to that contract.

9.5.4 Purpose

Construction warranties are usually required for several reasons:

- To protect the owner against faults, defects, or failures despite technical compliance with the terms of the contract

- To provide a remedy to the owner for non-conformance with the contract after completion and acceptance of construction

- To give the owner recourse against additional parties (manufacturers, subcontractors, and suppliers) who are not in a direct contractual relationship with the owner

- To extend the manufacturer's responsibility beyond the end of the correction period

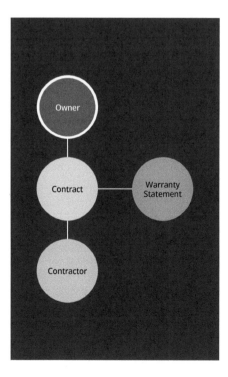

Figure 9.1
Example of
a Two-Party
Warranty
Relationship

DOMAIN 1
Planning,
Development,
& Organization

DOMAIN 2
Coordination

DOMAIN 3
Procurement,
Contracting,
& General
Requirements

DOMAIN 4
Research

DOMAIN 5
Analysis
& Evaluation

DOMAIN 6
Production

Figure 9.2
Example of a
Three-Party
Guarantor
Relationship

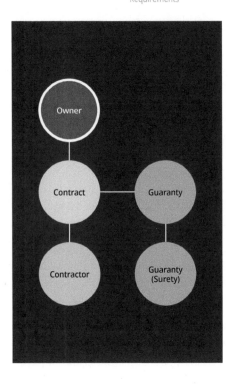

- To allow a remedy beyond the normal statute of limitations

The unpredictability of performance and replacement cost of some products, such as roofing, waterproofing, insulating glass units, compressors, and other equipment, causes many owners to insist on extended warranties. The A/E should carefully evaluate the decision to specify warranties based on the cost-benefit to the owner.

Many warranties are offered because of market conditions or as marketing techniques. Several years ago, the built-up roofing industry offered a third-party roof bond, which was considered little value. However, when the single-ply roofing systems became available with extended warranties, the built-up roofing industry began offering similar warranties to remain competitive. In some cases, when the performance and other requirements of two products are similar, the decision to purchase a particular product may be based on the available warranty.

To introduce a new product, some manufacturers offer an *extended warranty* as an incentive to have their product specified or accepted. Extended warranties also may be offered on products that do not quite measure up to the project specifications.

9.5.5 Benefits of Extended Warranties

For anyone to benefit from extended warranties, the manufacturer must be financially secure enough to cover its liabilities. Immediate benefits can be gained from an equitable extended warranty that could make it worth the owner's cost. These benefits include the qualification of the installer by the manufacturer, the manufacturer's involvement in the construction process, and insurance against failure.

One way to ensure these benefits is to specify and purchase the manufacturer's best system, which often means a 20-year system for built-up roofing. When A/Es specify systems with shorter warranty durations, they may find that, in some cases, roofing contractors can become approved installers by merely placing a phone call to the manufacturer. However, when a 20-year system with a full workmanship and materials warranty is specified, most manufacturers pre-qualify the installer and get involved in the construction process. The 20-year warranty means that the manufacturer has a vested interest in supplying a long-life roofing system that should provide trouble-free service when properly maintained by the facility owner.

9.5.6 Limitations and Exclusions

Product warranties are frequently perceived as providing increased legal and financial protection for owners against product defects, which is usually inaccurate. Most product warranties provide a limited warranty, which actually reduces the rights an owner may have by statute under a full warranty. Now that strict product liability has become a significant concern for manufacturers, the terms of warranties have become a principal mechanism for limiting manufacturers' liability for defective products or products that fail to perform as expected.

When an owner decides to insure a facility, the insurer can evaluate its risk in terms of geography, facility type, facility contents, quality of construction, and other criteria. The insurer can do this because a structure exists to evaluate. However, when a manufacturer sells a product, little is known of the exact circumstances under which its product is required to perform. Therefore, a manufacturer can limit its potential liability or choose not to accept the risks associated with its decision. Generally, manufacturers choose to limit their exposure and price their products accordingly.

Unless otherwise stipulated, materials are sold under a *full warranty*. According to the UCC, a full warranty includes a refund or replacement for the defective product and the labor to repair or replace the product, as well as any "consequential and incidental damages" that occur as a result of the failure of the warranted product. These damages could include damages to furnishings and adjacent construction and even profits lost by the owner because of damaged merchandise or the inability to conduct business under normal conditions. The cost of replacement and consequential and incidental damages can easily exceed the defective product's original cost. For example, a waterproofing material that fails to perform as warranted may cost less than a dollar per square foot. However, it could cost thousands of dollars to replace and repair damage in areas located below the waterproofing.

Most manufacturers find that the risks of a full warranty are more than can be accepted without increasing their product cost to uncompetitive levels. The UCC allows a buyer and seller to agree to a limited warranty with reduced remedies. There is seldom a real negotiation on the terms of a product manufacturer's warranty. Instead, a manufacturer typically disclaims its obligations to provide remedies under a full warranty and incorporates a limited warranty into its terms of sale. If the disclaimers are conspicuous in the product literature and on the product labeling, then specifying or purchasing a product normally implies the buyer's consent to the warranty limitations. Limited warranties also seek to avoid litigation by establishing in advance the terms and remedies available under warranty.

Common limitations in a warranty can exclude labor and consequential and incidental damages. Other conditions may establish criteria that the buyer must meet before the warranty is honored. For example, a manufacturer may require an extra fee to register the warranty, restrict the conditions of use for the product, or require installation by specially qualified contractors. Other provisions may limit rights under warranty to the original purchaser, which can be interpreted to refer to the contractor or a subcontractor, thus leaving an owner without recourse directly to the manufacturer. If the product warranty begins when the contractor purchases or installs the product, the owner receives less protection than if the warranty began at substantial completion. The A/E should study the disclaimers

Construction
Specifications
Practice Guide

DOMAIN 1
Planning,
Development,
& Organization

DOMAIN 2
Coordination

DOMAIN 3
Procurement,
Contracting,
& General
Requirements

DOMAIN 4
Research

DOMAIN 5
Analysis
& Evaluation

DOMAIN 6
Production

and limitations to determine what protection is provided under warranty and which of the owner's rights and remedies are taken away.

The A/E should also verify that warranty provisions comply with code requirements. As an example, one major roofing manufacturer's standard warranty excludes responsibility for damage caused by "winds of peak gust speeds of 55 miles per hour or higher measured at 35 feet above the ground." However, model building codes might list 70 mph as the minimum design sustained wind load and 85-mph three-second gusts.

Though a full warranty (materials and labor) is specified, there may be limitations that affect the warranty. For instance, in the case of waterproofing, the cost of removal and replacement of other materials that cover the waterproofing is generally not included in the manufacturer's warranty, or a sealant manufacturer may offer a 20-year warranty that is valid only if the sales receipt and original container are returned. Some warranties may cover replacing the initially installed product but not cover the replacement product itself, which leaves some parts of a project without the full extended warranty. Some products cannot be field modified without voiding their warranty, and others have strict limitations on how they may be modified. The financial capability of the manufacturer or supplier offering an extended warranty should always be considered. Warranty forms should be requested along with other submittals to verify all limitations, terms, and conditions.

As extended warranties are usually written from the manufacturer's perspective, even those issued in good faith invariably contain language that limits their coverage scope. Warranties usually exclude consequential damage to any facility component other than the warranted product itself. In many cases, coverage of a product or system is prorated. For each year of service the product or system has already provided, many warranties pay a smaller percentage of the repair or replacement costs.

When manufacturers delete exclusions from their warranties, they usually add other costs or terms and conditions to protect their interests. Prorated coverage, for example, is eliminated in no-dollar-limit roof warranties. In exchange

for paying full replacement costs for a defective system, the manufacturer requires the use of all or almost all of the manufacturer's products within a warranted system.

Given the number of ways that a manufacturer's obligations can be diminished or nullified, it would be a mistake to place marginal systems on a level with their more expensive competitors simply because both systems are warranted for the same number of years. In reality, the terms of one warranty may provide significantly more protection than the terms of another.

A/Es should carefully read warranties and determine what is covered and what is excluded. The exclusions are very important. Some roofing warranties exclude damage caused by ponded water and gale winds. Many manufacturers' warranties take away consumer protections customarily included in the UCC, including *implied warranty of merchantability or fitness for a particular purpose* (see Section 9.5.2). A manufacturer's warranty may restrict repairs of failures only up to the original installation cost, not replacement costs. An extended warranty is of little benefit if nothing is covered. For example, an implied warranty becomes worthless if the written warranty states that a roofing material may be unsuitable for roofing.

The only way to ensure that warranty dollars are being invested wisely is to compare the clauses and conditions of several warranties and identify those that could cause problems if the need to file a claim arises. For instance, clauses stating that the terms of the warranty are the owner's sole remedy nullify any added protection the owner would have had through implied warranties.

In addition to exclusions and limitations, the A/E should examine a manufacturer's ability and willingness to honor its warranties. An important factor is the financial backing of the warranty under consideration. Some manufacturers do not have or have not committed sufficient assets to satisfy all claims against their warranties. In either case, an owner may be left with a faulty product and no immediate remedy.

It is also essential to determine which companies have been in business long enough to have long-term experience with their products. A 20-year warranty issued by a company that has been in business for five years is questionable, just as a 20-year warranty on a new product is also questionable. In some cases, it may be useful to talk to facility owners with warranted systems from a specific manufacturer to determine its product history. Reports of continual repairs and slow or negative responses to warranty calls may indicate a problem with a product or system, or it may indicate that a company is in financial trouble. Sometimes the warranty provider is a broker, not the manufacturer. The A/E should determine whether the warrantor is from the same company that has provided the product or a broker. Also, the A/E should determine whether the product manufacturer financially backs the warranty.

The A/E should be aware of the limitations warranties place on repairs or alterations of warranted items. Usually, a repair or alteration to an item by a party other than the manufacturer or original installer may invalidate the warranty period's remainder.

The following exclusions and limitations should be of particular concern:

- **Language making the warranty the exclusive remedy.** These clauses reduce the possible remedies that the owner could seek if there is a problem.

- **Clauses limiting the scope of coverage.** A/Es should ask if the warranty covers materials only or workmanship as well.

- **Clauses limiting the assignability of the warranty.** Generally, the law assumes that a warranty is transferable if the facility is sold before the warranty expires. If the warranty specifically prohibits assignment and the facility is sold, the new owner is not covered by the warranty.

- **A requirement stating that the owner must sign the warranty document.** If the warranty is not effective until it is signed, there is a good chance it contains language that limits the owner's rights.

- **Warranties containing a deductible.** If included, determine when the deductible begins.

- **Clauses limiting the time the owner has to take legal action.** This type of clause applies to a manufacturer's breach of a warranty.

- **A requirement allowing the warrantor to recover legal costs.** This requirement applies in a proceeding involving the owner or contractor, whether the warrantor prevails or not.

- **Unfair dispute resolution procedures.** Used when a difference in opinion occurs regarding the manufacturer's warranty.

- **Clauses that exclude installation of the replacement product.** The installation of a replacement product may be cost-prohibitive for the owner.

Warranties are only as good as the manufacturer's reputation and become useless if the manufacturer goes out of business. Bonds may be considered for major items if extended warranty periods are required. Also, an insurance policy with coverage similar to the required warranty may be an acceptable alternative. The owner's insurance advisor should be consulted if this alternative is considered. Some warranties provide that the warrantor reserve the exclusive right to determine whether the warranty is applicable; in such a case, the A/E should try to determine whether a mechanism is available to appeal the rejection of a claim.

A comparison of manufacturers and their warranties could lead to selecting a product or system that has a good performance record but a very limited warranty. Unfortunately, many manufacturers are reluctant to negotiate the terms of their warranties. Therefore, the owner's options may be limited to accepting unfavorable conditions, using another product or system with an acceptable warranty, or choosing not to accept any manufacturer's warranty and relying solely on the provisions of the UCC.

Ultimately, an owner may accept an extended warranty on the manufacturer's terms. However, in the process of examining and comparing warranties, the owner may have learned what level of service can realistically be expected. More importantly, the owner has avoided the trap of assuming that a product's expected service life is equal to the length of its warranty.

Construction
Specifications
Practice Guide

DOMAIN 1
Planning,
Development,
& Organization

DOMAIN 2
Coordination

DOMAIN 3
Procurement,
Contracting,
& General
Requirements

DOMAIN 4
Research

DOMAIN 5
Analysis
& Evaluation

DOMAIN 6
Production

The A/E should address the problem of unwanted exclusions by listing acceptable exclusions in the specifications but requiring the A/E's approval of additional exclusions as a condition of acceptance of the product or its warranty. Specifications that generally require the contractor to "install according to the manufacturer's instructions" help preserve the owner's rights under warranty, but only if the contractor complies. Despite their limitations, warranties do instill buyer confidence in a product.

9.5.7 Remedies

The UCC permits the manufacturer to disclaim implied warranties of merchantability and fitness in writing and permits vendors to limit the duration of their responsibility and the remedies available to the buyer. The nature of those remedies and their limitations are the most essential features of warranties.

The A/E that requires the contractor only to submit the manufacturer's standard warranty could allow the manufacturer to limit its responsibility to an unreasonable level from the owner's standpoint. The owner may be better off having no warranty at all.

The time it takes to settle a claim can also cause problems. Most manufacturers have a procedure that contractors must follow to collect for repairs made under warranty. Suppose the contractor proceeds immediately to make repairs without waiting for the manufacturer's approval. In that case, the repairs may not be compensated by the manufacturer, placing the contractor in a difficult situation. Contractors may jeopardize long-standing business relationships if they do not respond quickly to an owner's request to repair a defective product. When the owner is a large company with many facilities that require some sort of repair work, contractors should not jeopardize future work by being unresponsive in emergency situations.

In a multicomponent system, the A/E should require the manufacturer issuing the warranty to accept system responsibility. The A/E should specify a warranted system, not a system with individually warranted components. When problems occur, the owner should not have to rely on the legal system to determine who is responsible for a product or workmanship failure. Because of the association

with remedial provisions, warranties are often thought of as a prescribed set of remedies promised by the warrantor rather than a representation of the warranted item's condition or performance. Some warranties may be prorated over the stipulated time period and may diminish in value over the duration.

9.5.8 Duration

The most commonly specified factor for warranties and the most common basis for comparing warranties is their duration. However, the duration may be one of the least important terms of the warranty, and the failure to address some of the other terms may leave the owner without the desired protection. By specifying only the duration for a warranty with no further requirements, the A/E has no basis for rejecting a warranty that has the specified duration but is unacceptable in other respects.

Expressed time limits are generally stipulated in product warranties. The time limits often bear no direct correlation with the expected service life of the product. In some cases, it is unrealistic to expect a product to serve satisfactorily for its warranty duration. Rather than rely on a warranty, the A/E should verify a particular product's performance history before specifying it for an application where the performance duration is critical. Another area worth analysis involves the extent of testing or other studies conducted by the manufacturer to verify that the system can reasonably be expected to function for the stated period.

9.5.9 Purchasing Warranties

Warranties effected by a sales transaction and governed by the UCC and other applicable state laws are referred to as purchasing warranties. Although purchasing warranties are seldom directly applicable to a construction contract, the UCC governs most transactions involving the sale of goods. The UCC attaches certain express and implied warranties to sales transactions and governs warranties provided by the seller. Any written warranty is called an *express warranty*. An *implied warranty* is derived from the nature of a transaction, applicable state law, and the position of the parties.

Construction
Specifications
Practice Guide

DOMAIN 1
Planning,
Development,
& Organization

DOMAIN 2
Coordination

DOMAIN 3
Procurement,
Contracting,
& General
Requirements

DOMAIN 4
Research

DOMAIN 5
Analysis
& Evaluation

DOMAIN 6
Production

Express warranties may consist of the following:

- An affirmation of fact or promise related to goods, such as a claim of performance

- A description of the goods, such as photos, drawings, or specifications

- A sample or model that becomes a basis of the agreement

Under the UCC, there are two implied warranties. The first is the *implied warranty of merchantability* or "implied warranty that goods are merchantable," which means that the consumer goods conform to the following:

- Pass without objection in the trade under the contract description

- Are fit for the ordinary purposes for which such goods are used

- Are adequately contained, packaged, and labeled

- Conform to the promises or affirmations of fact made on the container or label

The second is the *implied warranty of fitness for a particular purpose.* A warranty of fitness means that when the retailer, distributor, or manufacturer has reason to know any particular purpose for which the goods are required and, further, that the buyer is relying on the skill and judgment of the seller to select and furnish suitable goods, then there is an implied warranty that the goods shall be fit for the intended purpose.

These implied warranties are a part of every transaction unless the sale documents clearly state that they do not apply. The implied warranty of merchantability requires the goods are reasonably fit for the general purpose for which they are sold. The term merchantable means fair, average, medium quality (Richard A. Mann and Barry S. Roberts. *Smith and Roberson's Business Law*, 17th ed., Cengage, 2018; 479).

Regarding the implied warranty of fitness for a particular purpose, *Smith and Roberson's Business Law* states:

> The implied warranty of fitness for a particular purpose arises if at the time of sale the seller had reason to know the buyer's particular purpose and

> the buyer was relying upon the seller's skill and judgment to select suitable goods (480).

To illustrate the difference between the two types of implied warranties, compare a specification calling for a pump with another calling for a submersible pump. The pump seller impliedly warrants that it is fit (merchantable) for the ordinary purposes for which pumps are used. The submersible pump seller might also warrant that it functions under water (fitness for a particular purpose).

The UCC also governs how warranties may be disclaimed. Exclusion of the warranty of title must be by specific language, or the circumstances of the sale must be such that the buyer should not expect a warranty of title. Express warranties can be disclaimed in the same manner in which they are created, but warranty language takes precedence over disclaimer language in the event of a conflict. Implied warranties may generally be disclaimed by using a conspicuous written disclaimer or using the words "as is, with all faults" or similar language. Federal law requires that written warranties covering consumer products (often inapplicable to construction projects) fully and conspicuously disclose, in simple and easily understood language, the terms and conditions of such warranty, including whether the warranty is a full or limited warranty.

Sellers should be informed of the specific uses to be made of their goods. Their recommendations are being relied upon to obtain maximum advantage of the implied warranty of fitness. However, if the buyer requests or demands a particular brand, there is no implied warranty of fitness because the buyer is relying on the buyer's skill or judgment (Mann and Roberts 480).

When specifying warranties, the A/E should avoid the following:

- Relying on a warranty as a substitute for a thorough investigation of a product and its manufacturer

- Requiring warranty coverage that is not available for a particular product

- Requiring or permitting a warranty that weakens, rather than strengthens, the owner's rights

The A/E should be as familiar with standard warranties offered with products as with the physical qualities and performance characteristics of the products. The size, stability, and reputation of the manufacturer and its ability to make good on a warranty claim may be more important than the terms of the warranty itself.

The A/E should determine before producing the specification whether warranties are offered or are available, the terms of such warranties, whether the terms can be specified, whether the terms of standard warranties are negotiable, whether the owner can do without the warranty altogether, or whether the manufacturer requires acceptance of its warranty terms as a condition of sale.

In general, the best assurance of long-term product performance is a combination of good materials, appropriate design, and skillful workmanship. No warranty can compensate for the lack of these important aspects.

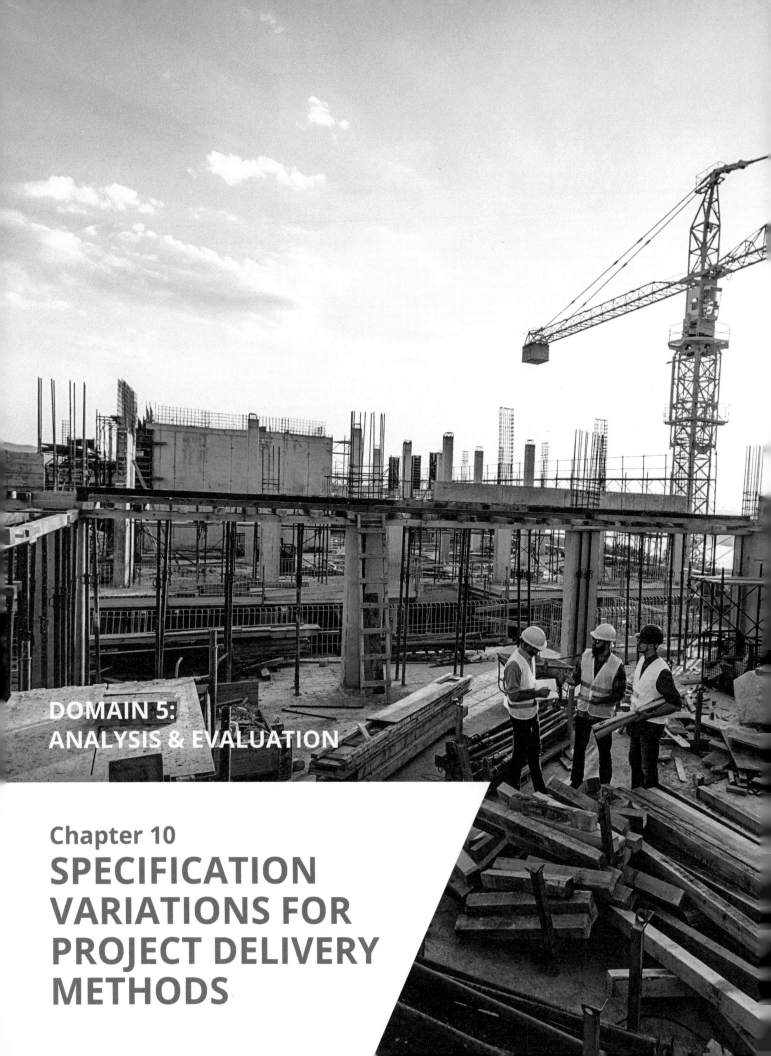

Chapter 10
SPECIFICATION VARIATIONS FOR PROJECT DELIVERY METHODS

10.1 Aligning the Specifications with Project Delivery Methods and Schedules

This practice guide is generally focused on the traditional design-bid-build project delivery method. However, other project delivery methods require some variation in the construction documents. Some project delivery variations may be simple, and others may require multiple project manuals and separate packages of drawings. Some variations result from the use of non-standard agreements or conditions of the contract. Although multiple-prime contracts might be utilized without construction management, they are discussed under the construction management advisor/agent option in Section 10.4. The procurement and contracting procedures may determine the type of documents required and the methods of specifying used. The owner typically provides information about contract procedures. American Institute of Architects (AIA) Document G612™, *Owner's Instructions to the Architect*, provides three forms for obtaining the appropriate information: Part A for the construction contract and Part B for bidding procedures.

For more information on the various project delivery methods, refer to Chapter 3 of the *Project Delivery Practice Guide*.

10.2 Document Variations for the Design-Bid-Build Project Delivery Method

The design-bid-build delivery method includes three options:

- Competitive Bid Option
- Competitive Proposal Option
- Negotiation Option

Construction
Specifications
Practice Guide

DOMAIN 1
Planning,
Development,
& Organization

DOMAIN 2
Coordination

DOMAIN 3
Procurement,
Contracting,
& General
Requirements

DOMAIN 4
Research

DOMAIN 5
Analysis
& Evaluation

DOMAIN 6
Production

Each of these options has slight variations, mostly in how the project is procured. Refer to the *Project Delivery Practice Guide* for detailed information on the design-bid-build delivery method and each of its options. Since this practice guide uses the competitive bid option as the baseline delivery method, this section focuses on the other two options: the competitive proposal option and the negotiated option.

The competitive proposal option is much like the competitive bid option, except that there are additional documents that proposers must submit along with their proposals. The owner uses these additional documents to evaluate the proposers to determine the best-qualified contractor for the project. Even after a contractor is selected, the owner and contractor may still negotiate the contract's final price.

The compilation and completion of a project manual are usually completed after negotiations have started during the early design phases for the negotiated option. The negotiations are frequently based on outline specifications and design development documents leading to a cost of the work with a guaranteed maximum price (GMP) agreement. The project manual and other construction documents are prepared to finalize the design, obtain required permits, and obtain actual prices for the work's cost. These construction documents might then form contract documents.

10.2.1 Project Manual Variations

There are some notable differences in project manual preparation between a project using the negotiated option and the other two options. The architect/engineer (A/E) will not necessarily be the sole decision-maker on all the items that would generally be the A/E's responsibility. Other project team members, especially the owner and contractor, often share decisions.

10.2.2 Division 00— Procurement and Contracting Requirements

This division experiences the most changes if either the competitive proposal or negotiated option is used. With the competitive proposal method, the documents are similar to those for the competitive bid option. Instead of bidding forms and documents, equivalent proposal forms and documents are provided. For the negotiated option, many of the forms and documents within the procurement requirements are unnecessary.

10.2.2.1 Procurement Requirements

MasterFormat® contains optional titles applicable to the competitive proposal option process. These titles include Request for Proposal and Request for Qualifications, as well as Instructions to Proposers. The inclusion of these documents can improve the proposal process by establishing procedures for clarifications, addenda, and a structured proposal form. These procurement requirements could be similar to the requirements for a traditional bid process, such as affirming that the proposer has visited the site and accounted for local conditions.

10.2.2.2 Contracting Forms

The owner-contractor agreement included in a project manual might be a standard form that eventually includes the negotiated amount determined after a request for proposals (competitive proposal option) or determined by informal negotiations (negotiated option). The A/E might not always participate in this process. The A/E, however, should request a copy of the owner-contractor agreement form to ensure that there are no conflicts between the agreement, the conditions of the contract, and Division 01. If the contract is negotiated between the owner and contractor, the A/E may not prepare contracting forms, bonds, and certificates. The negotiating contractor might prepare these forms. The A/E should review these forms to ensure that they do not contain responsibilities not included in the A/E agreement. The A/E should also inform the owner if the proposed agreement does not mention required responses to the A/E's responsibilities.

10.2.2.3 Conditions of the Contract

Even though negotiations are the primary aspect of the negotiation option (it could also be part of the competitive proposal option), the conditions of the contract affect the various participants involved. The conditions of the contract are the basis of the requirements provided in Division 01 and should be included in the project manual to establish that basis. Should the provisions of the conditions of the contract change through negotiation, then the A/E needs to review these changes to determine if any changes need to be made to Division 01.

The general conditions might be standard documents published by the AIA, the Engineers Joint Contract Documents Committee (EJCDC), or the ConsensusDocs Coalition. Some owners, especially large developers, prefer to use their own general conditions, which may be based on existing standard general conditions. In some instances, the negotiating contractor offers its own version of the conditions of the contract. If so, these conditions should be reviewed by the owner's legal counsel.

If the conditions of the contract are other than standard AIA, EJCDC, or ConsensusDocs Coalition general conditions, the A/E must carefully review the documents to understand their variations from the standard documents. Variations in the conditions of the contract might involve A/E and contractor roles that differ from those generally associated with standard agreements. These requirements or responsibilities must be reconciled. Requirements for insurance, bonds, and payments, including the process for payment applications and retainage, may be covered in the owner-contractor agreement and should not be repeated in the conditions of the contract. The owner-contractor agreement should be reviewed to ensure that conflicting requirements are not included in the conditions of the contract. If the owner-contractor agreement is not available to the A/E, the owner and contractor should prepare appropriate conditions of the contract for publication in the project manual.

10.2.3 Division 01 — General Requirements

Possible conflicts among the agreement, the conditions of the contract, and Division 01 requirements may occur, depending on the negotiations' outcomes. Division 01 requirements should be prepared in conjunction with the conditions of the contract. Special coordination might be necessary for some procedures that are negotiated, such as payment procedures, construction progress schedules, submittals, substitutions, warranties, and contract closeout.

10.2.4 Divisions 02 through 49 — Specifications

Writing specifications for the negotiated option would not be significantly different from those of the other two options. The decisions to utilize specific products might result from prior negotiations or value analysis; however, the specifications would be similar. If pricing and negotiations have determined specific products, then the specification might be written as proprietary, eliminating some level of detail.

10.3 Document Variations for the Construction Manager at Risk (CMAR) Project Delivery Method

CMAR provides professional management expertise during the project's design. With the CMAR project delivery method, the A/E does not prepare procurement documents. Instead, the construction manager prepares the procurement documents for each subcontract they plan to issue. Suppose the construction manager uses the fast-track scheduling technique. In that case, the construction manager may provide procurement documents for each work package issued, similar to the work packages used by the integrated project delivery (IPD) method (see Section 10.5).

DOMAIN 1
Planning,
Development,
& Organization

DOMAIN 2
Coordination

DOMAIN 3
Procurement,
Contracting,
& General
Requirements

DOMAIN 4
Research

DOMAIN 5
Analysis
& Evaluation

DOMAIN 6
Production

10.3.1 Project Manual Variations

Some differences in project manual preparation occur using the CMAR project delivery method. The A/E will not necessarily be the sole decision-maker on all the items that would generally be the A/E's responsibility. Decisions are often shared with other project team members, including the owner and construction manager.

10.3.2 Division 00— Procurement and Contracting Requirements

This division is likely to see little preparation effort on the part of the A/E. Owner-provided documents, such as geotechnical data and existing hazardous material information, may be included. Some procurement forms (e.g., wage rates) and contract forms (e.g., substitution request form, RFI form) may also be included. The construction manager may supplement this division with their forms and documents applicable to subcontractors. If these forms and documents are included, then the table of contents should list them.

10.3.2.1 Procurement Requirements

The construction manager may prepare the procurement requirements for packages. Regardless of who prepares the procurement requirements, the A/E should work with the construction manager on the necessary drawings and specifications to be included, whether issued as a single set of construction documents or in a series of multiple work packages. Working with the construction manager ensures that the work packages contain the required information.

10.3.2.2 Contracting Forms

Agreement forms are usually prepared by the construction manager and are usually the construction manager's standard subcontract forms.

10.3.2.3 Conditions of the Contract

The general conditions for the CMAR project delivery method are already established by the time the project manual is prepared. Since subcontractors are bound to the same contract provisions as the construction manager, a copy of the conditions of the contract should be included.

10.3.3 Division 01— General Requirements

Whether contract documents for a CMAR project are issued as a single set or as multiple work packages, specifications are subject to the same Division 01 requirements. Division 01 may be issued for multiple work package projects as a stand-alone package that all subsequent work packages reference, eliminating the need to publish Division 01 for each package. If a subsequent work package requires a revision to Division 01, that change can be issued with the work package. (See Section 1.2.4.3 for version control in working with multiple work packages.)

10.3.4 Divisions 02 through 49—Specifications

The A/E should prepare specifications to secure accurate pricing, whether as a single set or in multiple work packages. The level of detail of the specifications may be influenced by the construction manager or by the owner's project requirements. Some work packages may use the same sections as previously issued work packages. (See Section 1.2.4.3 for version control in working with multiple work packages.)

10.3.5 Conformed Documents

After all work packages are issued, the owner or the construction manager might require combining all work packages into one project manual for convenience. The A/E should be aware of this possibility from the beginning so that similar specification sections can be appropriately organized using the appropriate level of numbers and titles, and the drawings can be numbered with a logical system.

10.4 Document Variations for the Construction Management as Advisor/Agent Management Option

When the construction manager (CM) acts as an advisor to or agent for the owner but does not perform in the contractor role like in the CMAR project delivery method, that is referred to as a "construction manager as advisor" ("CMa" per AIA contract documents) or "construction manager as agent." The former applies to a construction manager hired by the owner to advise the owner throughout a project's duration. The latter places the construction manager in the role of the owner's agent, thus allowing the construction manager to make decisions on behalf of the owner.

In either case, the nature of construction management provides management services for the owner and can be implemented for any project delivery method. However, the CM as advisor/agent is well-suited for projects involving multiple prime contractors. Construction documents involving multiple-prime contracts may be released at different times and may require separate sets of documents, including a project manual and specific drawings. During the construction documents stage, the A/E may not prepare procurement documents. The construction manager may prepare these procurement documents for each bid/proposal package, including the bid/proposal solicitation, instructions to bidders/proposers, bid/proposal forms, and supplements, as well as a summary of work for each bid/proposal package or contract.

If the A/E agreement was based on construction management services, the A/E usually produces construction document packages identified by the construction manager to implement the multiple-prime contracts. If the fast-track scheduling technique is used, either with multiple-prime contracts or a single-prime contract, the A/E's document preparation time is likely to increase, even though the overall project schedule is reduced.

The construction documentation process is usually staggered for the fast-track scheduling technique to produce separate bid/proposal packages based on the required scheduling.

10.4.1 Project Manual Variations

Some differences in project manual preparation occur using a CM as advisor/agent management option to implement a multiple-prime project. The project manual may see little to no variation from a typical bid or proposal project for single-prime projects. Like other project delivery methods, the A/E will not necessarily be the sole decision-maker on all the items that would typically be the A/E's responsibility. Decisions are often shared with other project team members, such as the owner and construction manager.

10.4.2 Division 00 — Procurement and Contracting Requirements

The procurement and contracting requirements require modification to conform to the CM as advisor/agent management option. Standard documents from the AIA, the EJCDC, the ConsensusDocs Coalition, and the Construction Management Association of America (CMAA) provide specialized contract documents for this type of management option. For multiple-prime contracts, each bid/proposal package usually consists of procurement requirements (including a bid/proposal form appropriate to the package's scope) and contracting requirements (including the conditions of the contract).

10.4.2.1 Procurement Requirements

The construction manager may prepare the procurement requirements for the bid or proposal packages. Regardless of who prepares the procurement requirements, the A/E should work with the construction manager on the necessary drawings and specifications to be included in the packages and assist the construction manager in ensuring that the bid/proposal packages contain

DOMAIN 1
Planning,
Development,
& Organization

DOMAIN 2
Coordination

DOMAIN 3
Procurement,
Contracting,
& General
Requirements

DOMAIN 4
Research

DOMAIN 5
Analysis
& Evaluation

DOMAIN 6
Production

the required information. The process of obtaining separate bids or proposals for a multiple-prime project is not significantly different from that of the design-bid-build project delivery method using either the competitive bid or competitive proposal option, respectively.

Preparing procurement requirements for the CM as advisor/agent management option can be an extensive process when multiple packages are involved. The A/E is affected by how the construction manager chooses to issue bid/proposal packages. Some believe that full sets of procurement documents should be issued. The bid/proposal form or Section 01 12 00 — Multiple Contract Summary should indicate the scope of work for each contract. The advantage to issuing full sets is that each bidder/proposer may examine all requirements that might affect their bid/proposal. The disadvantages, however, are that the design has to be complete. A construction manager might issue only partial documents that describe the package being procured. The advantages are that bid/proposal packages may be issued while design work is still underway, and reproduction costs are usually lower. The disadvantage is that bidders/proposers may not be able to examine all related documents.

10.4.2.2 Contracting Forms

The construction manager usually prepares agreement forms for each bid/proposal package. The agreement form should be compatible with the owner-CM as advisor/agent agreement form.

10.4.2.3 Conditions of the Contract

The general conditions for CM as advisor/agent in a multiple-prime project require special provisions ensuring cooperation between and mutual responsibility among the multiple-prime contractors. Special provisions may require the construction manager to provide services such as consolidating multiple payment applications into a single application for the A/E to review. Some standard general conditions of the contract for the CM as advisor/agent management option are available from the AIA (CM as "adviser" per AIA spelling) and the CMAA (CM as agent).

Supplementary conditions may include the same modifications customarily required in a design-bid-build project delivery method. These modifications include requirements for insurance and bonds and the process for payment applications and retainage. Because the conditions of the contract are published with the first bid/proposal package, early preparation is required. With multiple-prime contracts, identical conditions of the contract should be issued with every package.

10.4.3 Division 01 — General Requirements

The A/E and construction manager must be alert to possible conflicts between the agreement, the conditions of the contract, and the Division 01 requirements. Division 01 requirements for multiple-prime contracts should be prepared with specific regard for each contract's scope. Special coordination is necessary for specific procedures such as payments, progress schedules, product submittals, quality control, substitutions, warranties, and contract closeout.

When separate bid/proposal packages are issued, not all Division 01 sections may be necessary for each bid/proposal package. Only the sections about the particular bid/proposal package should be issued with the respective package. For example, Section 01 45 36 — Testing Laboratory Services would not be issued in bid/proposal packages with no testing requirements. Particular Division 01 sections, such as allowances, alternates, testing laboratory services, temporary facilities and controls, field engineering, and operation and maintenance data, should be issued only with the appropriate bid/proposal packages. The Division 01 sections common to all bid/proposal packages, such as submittal procedures, product substitution procedures, and cleaning, should be included with each bid/proposal package.

The construction manager should be heavily involved in preparing Division 01. The Division 01 sections, for construction management project delivery, inform the owner and the various prime contractors about administrative procedures required for the project. Division 01 may also be used to assign temporary construction requirements to various contractors. The following sections are generally included in project manuals for multiple-prime projects:

Section 01 12 00 — Multiple Contract Summary. This section should identify the participants' responsibilities and long-lead items, construction documents packages, and site use.

Section 01 21 00 — Allowances. This section may be used to postpone design decisions. Allowances help the construction manager achieve accurate cost control, even if some products are not known. These unknowns should be minimized because the construction manager usually provides preliminary pricing. On multiple-prime projects, it is essential to include the allowances in the appropriate contract.

Section 01 32 00 — Construction Progress Documentation. This section includes requirements for critical path method network analysis with requirements for updating. Long lead items and milestone dates might be identified in the documents to ensure compliance with an overall project schedule.

Section 01 33 00 — Submittal Procedures. This section should be included for consistency in the information required for submittals. The construction manager's field representative usually maintains a complete set of submittals at the project site. The construction manager generally monitors submittals more closely to confirm the scope of work and delivery dates. Shop drawings, product data, and samples are received and checked for completeness by the construction manager and forwarded to the A/E or returned to the contractor for resubmittal.

Section 01 50 00 — Temporary Facilities and Controls. This section should coordinate site facilities and controls such as temporary utilities, parking areas, swing staging, field offices and sheds, sanitary facilities, hoists, telephones, fire protection, soil erosion, and other controls. Fences, barricades, walkways, project signs, and other minor temporary construction items should also be specified here, along with the responsibilities of each contractor. Assignment of temporary construction to an appropriate trade contractor may be specified in this section. It is usually necessary to include specification requirements for temporary facilities and controls that allow the construction manager to divide these responsibilities among the contractors.

Section 01 70 00 — Execution and Closeout Requirements. This section should be included

DOMAIN 1
Planning,
Development,
& Organization

DOMAIN 2
Coordination

DOMAIN 3
Procurement,
Contracting,
& General
Requirements

DOMAIN 4
Research

DOMAIN 5
Analysis
& Evaluation

DOMAIN 6
Production

for completing the construction manager and contractor's duties, such as submission of warranties and maintenance data and provisions for final cleaning and project record documents. The construction manager and the A/E may inspect the project for substantial completion. The results of this inspection are presented to the respective contractors for corrective action, if applicable, and to the owner for its information.

10.4.4 Divisions 02 through 49—Specifications

The A/E should prepare specifications to secure accurate contract bids/proposals. On multiple-prime contracts, the construction manager may request changes to define various contractors' responsibilities clearly. The level of detail of the specifications may be influenced by the construction manager or by the owner's project requirements. A specification section may be tailored differently for each bid/proposal package; therefore, a section with the same MasterFormat® number and title may vary slightly from one package to another.

For example, Section 05 50 00 — Metal Fabrications may contain only the miscellaneous metal related to each specific bid/proposal package. In this case, several metal fabrication sections are likely to be required for the entire project. Because each section may be different, each can be given a different Level 4 section number and title (e.g., Section 05 50 00.10 — Metal Fabrications for Building Envelope and Section 05 50 00.20 — Metal Fabrications for Interior Construction). However, some construction managers may prefer to use the same section for all bid/proposal packages and use Section 01 12 00 — Multiple Contract Summary to describe the scope of what is included in a particular bid/proposal package.

10.4.5 Combined Documents

The owner or the construction manager might require combining all construction documents packages into one project manual and set of drawings for convenience. The A/E should be aware of this possibility from the beginning so that similar specification sections can be organized using the appropriate level of numbers and titles, and the drawings can be numbered with a logical system.

10.5 Document Variations for the Integrated Project Delivery (IPD) Method

The IPD method integrates project stakeholders, technology, and business models that work collaboratively towards a common goal (a successful project) and share risks. The method uses one of the following contractual arrangements:

- Standard tripartite arrangement with separate agreements for owner-A/E and owner-contractor

- Multi-party agreement including the owner, A/E, and contractor

- Single-purpose entity (SPE) agreement where the owner, A/E, and contractor are members of a limited liability company

In practice, regardless of the contractual arrangement, the IPD method works similarly to the CMAR project delivery method using the fast-track scheduling technique and multiple work packages. The construction documentation process is usually staggered to produce separate work packages based on the project's required scheduling. Though the overall project schedule may be reduced, the A/E's document preparation time is usually longer.

10.5.1 Project Manual Variations

Some differences in project manual preparation occur using the IPD method. As a collaborative process, the A/E may not be the sole decision-maker on all the items that would generally be the A/E's responsibility. Decisions are often shared with other stakeholders.

10.5.2 Division 00 — Procurement and Contracting Requirements

This division is likely to see little preparation effort on the part of the A/E. Owner-provided documents, such as geotechnical data and existing hazardous material information, may be included. Some procurement forms (e.g., wage rates) and contract forms (e.g., substitution request form, RFI form) may also be included. The contractor may supplement this division with their forms and documents applicable to subcontractors. If these forms and documents are included, then the table of contents should list them.

10.5.2.1 Procurement Requirements

The contractor may prepare the procurement requirements for individual work packages. Regardless of who prepares the procurement requirements, the A/E should work with the contractor on the necessary drawings and specifications for each work package. Working with the contractor ensures that the work packages contain the required information.

10.5.2.2 Contracting Forms

Agreement forms are usually prepared by the contractor and are usually the contractor's standard subcontract forms.

10.5.2.3 Conditions of the Contract

The conditions of the contract for the IPD method are already established by the time the project manual is prepared. Since subcontractors are bound to the same contract provisions as the contractor, a copy of the conditions of the contract should be included.

10.5.3 Division 01 — General Requirements

Specifications for an IPD project are subject to the same Division 01 requirements as most other project delivery methods. Division 01 may be issued for multiple work package projects as a stand-alone package that all subsequent work packages reference, eliminating the need to publish Division 01 for each package. If a subsequent work package requires a revision to Division 01, that change can be issued with the work package. (See Section 1.2.4.3 for version control in working with multiple work packages.)

10.5.4 Divisions 02 through 49 — Specifications

The A/E should prepare specifications to secure accurate pricing. The detail level of the specifications may be influenced by the contractor or by the owner's project requirements. Some work packages may use the same sections as previously issued work packages. (See Section 1.2.4.3 for version control in working with multiple work packages.)

10.6 Document Variations for Design-Build Delivery Method

In the traditional design-bid-build delivery method, the contract documents are a part of the contract between the owner and the contractor. However, in the design-build delivery method, the owner's project requirements or project description are prepared by the owner. The owner might issue an RFP, conditions of the contract between the owner and design-builder, technical or performance specifications, and design requirements (including any schematic drawings). The design-builder responds to the RFP, negotiates an agreement, and eventually prepares the construction documents consisting of the specifications, drawings, and subsequent modifications. The construction documents may or may not be part of the contract documents between the owner and the design-builder, depending on the contract arrangements. However, they are usually submitted to the owner for approval. The A/E for the design-builder prepares the construction documents for a design-build project. Though performed in the design-builder's interest, the basic services provided by the A/E may be similar to those of a traditional

DOMAIN 1
Planning,
Development,
& Organization

DOMAIN 2
Coordination

DOMAIN 3
Procurement,
Contracting,
& General
Requirements

DOMAIN 4
Research

DOMAIN 5
Analysis
& Evaluation

DOMAIN 6
Production

contract. In all cases, the construction documents should be prepared following the principles in this chapter.

10.6.1 Division 00 — Procurement and Contracting Requirements

To obtain a design-build contract, the owner prepares the procurement and contracting requirements. However, the design-builder is responsible for preparing the procurement and contracting requirements for obtaining bids or proposals from subcontractors.

When the design-builder hires a contractor to perform the construction (e.g., developer-led design-build), the project may use any of the three design-bid-build delivery method options. However, most design-builders that contract out the construction are more likely to use the negotiation option since they tend to work with contractors with whom they have a relationship.

10.6.1.1 Procurement Requirements

The design-build contract between the owner and design-builder may be a negotiated contract resulting from an RFP from an owner. This process of selecting a design-builder may have occurred during the project delivery stage of the project. During the construction documents stage, the design-builder prepares any necessary procurement documents for subcontracts, including the instructions to bidders. The subcontract procurement requirements and construction documents might not vary significantly from procurement documents prepared for the design-bid-build or other project delivery methods.

10.6.1.2 Contract Requirements — Agreements and Conditions of the Contract

Standard agreements and conditions of the contract between the owner and the design-builder for design-build projects are available from the AIA, the EJCDC, the Design-Build Institute of America (DBIA), and the ConsensusDocs Coalition. The design-builder

may also have its own general conditions tailored for a specific project type. Most standard agreements are written for two phases: the preliminary design phase and the documents/construction phase. Most agreements incorporate the conditions of the contract into the form itself and therefore do not appear as separate documents.

10.6.2 Division 01 — General Requirements

The design-builder or a specifier working as a consultant to the design-builder should prepare the construction documents' general requirements. The Division 01 sections for a design-build project might involve both contractors and subcontractors. Division 01 may also be used to assign temporary construction requirements to various subcontractors. Some of the Division 01 sections that may apply to design-build contracts are summarized in the following paragraphs.

> **Section 01 10 00 — Summary.** This section should identify responsibilities and owner-furnished items, partial occupancy, and use of the site.
>
> **Section 01 21 00 — Allowances.** This section may be used to delay design decisions. Allowances permit the design-builder to achieve accurate cost control even if some products are not known. These unknowns should be minimized because one of the factors in selecting the design-build delivery method is that the project requirements are reasonably predictable.
>
> **Section 01 25 00 — Substitution Procedures.** This section should be included in the design-build construction documents. There are always circumstances that require substitutions. The substitution procedures should be managed so that the owner is aware of the substitutions and products ultimately included in the project.
>
> **Section 01 33 00 — Submittal Procedures.** This section should be included for consistency in the information required for submittals. In a design-build contract, the design-builder is usually required to maintain a complete set of submittals at the project site. The submittal procedure

in the design-build process is the same as in the design-bid-build project delivery method. Shop drawings, samples, and product data are received and checked by the design-builder and distributed by the design-builder to the A/E or returned to the subcontractor for resubmittal if there are problems. The owner should also receive a set of approved shop drawings.

Section 01 50 00 — Temporary Facilities and Controls. This section includes requirements for the use of parking and staging areas, storage sheds, trailers, hoists, sanitary facilities, fire protection, and temporary utilities. Fences and other barriers, walkways, project signs, and minor temporary construction items are also specified in this section. Assignment of temporary construction to an appropriate subcontractor may be specified in this section. It is usually necessary to include specification requirements for temporary facilities and controls, even if the design-builder performs the work. The owner may want to see this information as part of the contract documents.

Section 01 70 00 — Execution and Closeout Requirements. This section should be included to close out the design-builder's and subcontractors' duties at the end of a project. This section could include provisions for such items as submission of warranties, maintenance data, maintenance materials, project record documents, and final cleaning provisions. The design-builder inspects the project for substantial completion. The results of this inspection are presented to the owner for evaluation.

10.6.3 Divisions 02 through 49 — Specifications

The design-builder or a specifier working as a consultant to the design-builder should prepare specifications to secure accurate subcontract bids/proposals and ensure a clear definition of various subcontractors' responsibilities. The level of detail of the specifications may be influenced by the design-builder or by the owner's project description. The design-builder may desire brief specifications that allow wide latitude in product requirements and selections. On the other hand, the owner may have

stringent project requirements that dictate the specification detail required.

10.7 Document Variations for Owner-Build Project Delivery Method

An owner-build project may range from simple maintenance or rehabilitation to an entirely new facility. The documents are structured similarly to those of other delivery methods. A simple project may be procured the same as a design-bid-build project or separated into multiple contracts. An owner might even consider a simple design-build delivery method for a pre-engineered structure. Owners capable of preparing their own designs and documentation might have an in-house department with an A/E or facility manager. Documentation may be performed in-house or under agreement with an independent A/E. With the owner providing their own construction services, the construction documents may focus primarily on the information needed to obtain permits.

10.7.1 Project Manual Variations

Project manual preparation for owner-build projects is similar to that for other project delivery methods. A project may require a single project manual or several project manuals for multiple-prime contracts.

10.7.2 Division 00 — Procurement and Contracting Requirements

The procurement and contracting requirements for an owner-build project vary considerably. The inclusion of these requirements depends on what the owner plans to perform in-house and what contractors perform.

DOMAIN 1
Planning,
Development,
& Organization

DOMAIN 2
Coordination

DOMAIN 3
Procurement,
Contracting,
& General
Requirements

DOMAIN 4
Research

DOMAIN 5
Analysis
& Evaluation

DOMAIN 6
Production

10.7.2.1 Procurement Requirements

The procurement requirements are developed similar to other delivery methods and depend on the project's nature and whether it is to be bid, negotiated, or purchased. The owner might prepare its own procurement requirements for subcontract packages with specialty contractors.

10.7.2.2 Contracting Forms

The owner-contractor agreement included in a project manual might be a standard form or determined by informal negotiations. The A/E might not always participate in this process. The A/E might include the owner's standard documents that have been prepared by the owner's attorney or in-house legal department. A copy of the owner-contractor agreement form should be available to ensure no conflicts between the agreement, the conditions of the contract, and Division 01. If the A/E is in independent practice, the A/E should review these forms to ensure they do not contain responsibilities not included in the owner-A/E agreement. The A/E should also inform the owner if the proposed agreement does not require responses to the A/E's responsibilities.

10.7.2.3 Conditions of the Contract

The conditions of the contract may also be standard documents that have been prepared by the owner's attorney or in-house legal department. The conditions of the contract should appropriately reflect the aspects of similar project delivery methods. This situation means that provisions might be required to ensure coordination between multiple contracts or specific issues for purchases or services. The conditions of the contract affect the various participants involved. The conditions of the contract are the basis of the requirements established in Division 01. Conditions of the contract should be included in the project manual to provide continuity of these requirements.

If the conditions of the contract are not industry standard, such as those from the AIA, the EJCDC, or the ConsensusDocs Coalition, the A/E must carefully review the documents to understand their variations from the standard documents. Variations in the conditions of the contract might include A/E and contractor roles different from those generally associated with standard agreements. These requirements or responsibilities must be reconciled.

Requirements for payments and changes may be covered in the owner-contractor agreement and should not be repeated in Division 01. If the owner-contractor agreement is not available to the A/E, the A/E should determine appropriate circumstances to prepare the project manual.

10.7.3 Division 01— General Requirements

Possible conflicts among the agreement, the conditions of the contract, and the Division 01 requirements can occur, depending on their source and particular project requirements. Division 01 requirements should be prepared in conjunction with the conditions of the contract. Specific issues should address operations at existing facilities, including site use, security, personnel identification, and access to the work. Other issues may involve specific procedures such as payment procedures, construction progress schedules, submittals, substitutions, warranties, and contract closeout.

10.7.4 Divisions 02 through 49—Specifications

Writing specifications for this delivery method are not usually different; however, some owners have specific requirements for products that have become standard in their identity or operations. The decisions to utilize specific products might require the owner's specific approval. If the owner requires specific products, then the specification might be written as proprietary, eliminating a detail level.

**DOMAIN 6:
PRODUCTION**

Chapter 11

PROJECT MANUAL
PRODUCTION

11.1 Project Manual Concept

The term *specifications* is often used to describe the collection of construction documents and project requirements. However, some of the documents are not specifications at all.

The documents commonly referred to as the specifications contain much more than that name implies. The procurement requirements, contracting forms, and conditions of the contract are usually included, but they are not specifications. In most cases, these are prepared by, or in coordination with, the owner and the owner's legal counsel and insurance advisor. This information, along with the specifications, is a collection of certain written construction documents and project requirements whose contents and functions are best implied by the title *Project Manual*. The project manual concept provides an organizational format and standard location for all the various documents involved. For effective coordination, document and section titles and their use sequence should be the same for each project. With different project delivery methods, some documents become unnecessary. For example, in the owner-build delivery method and with negotiated contracts, bidding requirements are not applicable. Figure 11.1 shows an example of the recommended order of information and documents in a typical project manual.

11.2 Specifications Production

Specifications may be produced in a variety of ways, depending on individual office practice, the type of work generally performed, the number of projects produced, and the size of the architect/engineer's (A/E's) firm:

- In small firms, a principal assumes responsibility for specifications preparation.

- Medium-sized firms of 20 to 70 people might employ a full-time specifier.

- Large firms may maintain a complete specifications department of several people.

DOMAIN 1 — Planning, Development, & Organization
DOMAIN 2 — Coordination
DOMAIN 3 — Procurement, Contracting, & General Requirements
DOMAIN 4 — Research
DOMAIN 5 — Analysis & Evaluation
DOMAIN 6 — Production

Figure 11.1
Typical Project
Manual
Arrangement per
MasterFormat®

PROCUREMENT AND CONTRACTING REQUIREMENTS

DIVISION 00

INTRODUCTORY INFORMATION

- 00 01 01 Project Title Page
- 00 01 05 Certifications Page
- 00 01 07 Seals Page
- 00 01 10 Table of Contents
- 00 01 15 List of Drawing Sheets
- 00 01 20 List of Schedules

PROCUREMENT REQUIREMENTS

- **00 10 00 SOLICITATION**
- 00 11 13 Advertisement for Bids
- 00 11 16 Invitation to Bid
- **00 20 00 INSTRUCTIONS FOR PROCUREMENT**
- 00 22 13 Supplementary Instructions to Bidders
- **00 30 00 AVAILABLE INFORMATION**
- 00 31 13 Preliminary Schedules
- 00 31 19 Existing Condition Information
- 00 31 32 Geotechnical Data
- **00 40 00 PROCUREMENT FORMS AND SUPPLEMENTS**
- **00 41 00 Bid Forms**
- **00 43 00 Procurement Form Supplements**
- 00 43 13 Bid Security Form
- **00 45 00 Representations and Certifications**

CONTRACTING REQUIREMENTS

- **00 50 00 CONTRACTING FORMS AND SUPPLEMENTS**
- **00 52 00 Agreement Forms**
- **00 60 00 PROJECT FORMS**
- **00 61 00 Bond Forms**
- **00 62 00 Certificates and Other Forms**
- **00 70 00 CONDITIONS OF THE CONTRACT**
- **00 72 00 General Conditions**
- **00 73 00 Supplementary Conditions**

SPECIFICATIONS

- **DIVISION 01**   **GENERAL REQUIREMENTS SUBGROUP**
- **DIVISION 02-19**   **FACILITY CONSTRUCTION SUBGROUP**
- **DIVISION 20-29**   **FACILITY SERVICES SUBGROUP**
- **DIVISION 30-39**   **SITE AND INFRASTRUCTURE SUBGROUP**
- **DIVISION 40-49**   **PROCESS EQUIPMENT SUBGROUP**

Note: This example does not show a complete list of possible documents for inclusion in a project manual. See *MasterFormat* ® for further information.

- A project-team approach may be used, with one person coordinating the writing efforts of several people working on the same project.

- An internet-based consulting service may be retained on an as-needed basis.

- Any firm, regardless of its size and capacity, may elect to retain an independent specification consultant (such as a member of the Specifications Consultants in Independent Practice [SCIP] organization) on a project-by-project basis or for all projects designed by the firm.

- Most building product manufacturers (e.g., architectural door hardware, elevators, curtainwall assemblies) provide technical services that include generic and project-specific specifications for their product lines. Manufacturers' product specifications generally require thorough review and editing to remove proprietary information embedded in the specification. Proprietary information applicable to only one manufacturer may not be permitted per governmental procurement regulations for public projects or by the owner for private projects.

- Many online building product services also offer free outline and short-form specifications generated from the designer or specifier's checklist selections.

In all instances, someone by choice or assignment assumes the specifier's role and becomes responsible for assembling the project specifications. Like architectural designers, some of these specifiers may find that they have a predilection for writing specifications proficiently.

11.2.1 Developing Specifications

The techniques used in the preparation of specifications usually involve developing sections from product reference materials or editing sections from master guide specifications. (See Section 1.3 for developing and organizing office master guide specifications.) Regardless of who writes the specification sections or how they are developed, products must be researched, selected, evaluated, coordinated with other products, specified consistently and clearly, and coordinated with the drawings.

DOMAIN 1
Planning,
Development,
& Organization

DOMAIN 2
Coordination

DOMAIN 3
Procurement,
Contracting,
& General
Requirements

DOMAIN 4
Research

DOMAIN 5
Analysis
& Evaluation

DOMAIN 6
Production

11.2.2 Gathering Information

Before beginning to write a section of specifications, the specifier must have the necessary information about that product, equipment, system, or assembly. Two kinds of information are needed. The first is information regarding the specific project requirements that may be obtained from the following:

- Owner's specific requirements such as mandatory products, standard forms, and standard details, and designation of a green building rating system and target goal

- Owner's intent to use FM Global to insure the structure (this drives mandatory use of FM Global standards)

- The A/E design team's drawings

- A specifications notebook or checklist with recorded product selections by the designer

- A preliminary project description (PPD) or outline specification prepared earlier

- Detailed cost estimate

- If a public project, the original government request for proposal, with amendments and attachments

- Applicable laws and building codes

The second kind of information the specifier needs is reference materials about the products and construction methods applicable to the particular specification section being edited. Sources include the following:

- Manufacturer's information, which includes product data and guide specifications on company websites; hard-copy product data binders; and product manuals, catalogs, and other literature

- Handbooks, pamphlets, and other educational and reference material published by trade associations whose members are manufacturers, fabricators, and installers

- Reference standards available from trade associations, government agencies, and national standards associations

- Information available from technical and professional societies such as the American Institute of Architects (AIA); the American Society of Civil Engineers (ASCE); the American Society of Mechanical Engineers (ASME); the American Society of Heating, Refrigeration, and Air-Conditioning Engineers (ASHRAE); Construction Specifications Institute (CSI); and the National Society of Professional Engineers (NSPE)

- Commercial master guide specifications (see Section 1.3)

- Product representatives who supply technical information and expertise

- Information available from contractors, subcontractors, and special consultants

- Personal experience of the members of the project team

- Specifications for similar construction projects where similar products and methods were used (*Caution:* Similar project specifications should be used only for reference as products and methods of installation may have changed, manufacturers or products may no longer exist, reference standards may be discontinued, and applicable codes may have changed.)

Many manufacturers offer suggested proprietary or guide specifications to relieve the A/E from some effort in researching and writing a particular specification section. These specifications must be reviewed carefully to determine whether they have biases and accurately state the necessary information. Manufacturer's suggested specifications that provide product-specific performance and installation data are often made available to A/Es on their websites and through online construction material directories. Although many design and contractor team members are involved in selecting and purchasing products and systems, the person producing the project specifications is most likely to request comprehensive technical assistance. Product representatives should be able to perform the following tasks:

- Provide generic descriptions of products and systems.

- Understand the work of other trades that affects the proper installation and performance of the product.

- Identify the reference standards that relate to the product.

- Describe related work associated with the product.

- Assist in determining system, assembly, or product options and accessories.

- Identify modifications necessary to integrate a system or product in a project.

- Answer questions concerning delivery, storage, and handling of products.

- Explain installation procedures.

- Explain product and system installations.

- Identify the required certifications.

- Discuss requirements for field quality control.

- Answer questions regarding composition and manufacturing processes to produce products.

- Provide a guide specification in a format compatible with the A/E's computer system.

- Provide information regarding codes and regulations related to the use of a product or process.

- Assist in obtaining authorities having jurisdiction (AHJ) approval for installation of a product or process.

- Provide product samples.

- Provide CAD drawings.

- Provide BIM Objects.

11.2.3 Reviewing the Procurement and Contracting Requirements

Ensure copies of the procurement requirements and contracting requirements are available if applicable to the project delivery method. Documents that are most relevant during the preparation of the specifications include, but are not limited to, the following:

- **00 31 13 — Preliminary Schedules.** This document may identify any phasing for the project for work packages to determine a planned sequence of preparing sections.

- **00 31 32 — Geotechnical Data.** This document provides information necessary to specify several sections, such as waterproofing, earthwork, and pavements.

- **00 70 00 — Conditions of the Contract.** This document has the most influence on preparing Division 01 sections but may also influence provisions within PART 1 — GENERAL and PART 3 — EXECUTION of some sections.

Refer to Chapter 2 for additional information on project manual coordination.

11.3 Documenting Specification Information

Most specifiers develop their own methods of assembling and recording specification information. Following are some common methods:

Notes or Email Memoranda by the Project A/E to the Specifier. Some project A/Es pass product information to the specifier by memoranda, similar to Figure 11.2. Product information memoranda or emails should be filed under the appropriate section within the MasterFormat® titles of the specifications. The minutes of various meetings may also provide information affecting the specifications.

Product Notebook. The product notebook may be the traditional binder or a directory of folders within a computer filing system. In preparing specifications, the A/E should refer to the product notebook for information and catalog cuts collected during the design stage. This notebook serves as a compilation of products selected for the project, so there is less need to query the project A/E about decisions already made.

Specification Checklists. Some firms use a specification checklist, as shown in Figure 11.3.

DOMAIN 1
Planning,
Development,
& Organization

DOMAIN 2
Coordination

DOMAIN 3
Procurement,
Contracting,
& General
Requirements

DOMAIN 4
Research

DOMAIN 5
Analysis
& Evaluation

DOMAIN 6
Production

Figure 11.2
Sample
Specification
Memorandum

SPECIFICATION MEMORANDUM

CSI

PROJECT: ROBERTSON SQUARE

PROJECT NUMBER: 0312

DIVISION: 06 - WOOD, PLASTICS, AND COMPOSITES

SECTION: 06 42 00 - WOOD PANELING

PANELING IN THE EXECUTIVE OFFICES AND THE LIBRARY WILL BE BOOKMATCHED WALNUT VENEER.

JIM MITCHELL
PROJECT ARCHITECT

3/15/10
DATE

These forms list items by appropriate section and serve as reminders to the A/E. A comprehensive specification checklist must be compiled gradually, based on experience. A checklist of the proposed materials for a project may be circulated among the design team to prepare drawings and make notations. The A/E uses these lists to collect information, to start any necessary research, and as a basis for the product notebook. Checklists often prompt the project A/E to record the necessary information. This process results in thorough specification notes and less time spent collecting information.

Specification Worksheets. If a comprehensive specification checklist is not used, the A/E may prepare separate worksheets for each specification section. A list of specification items shown on the drawings should be recorded on these sheets. Each drawing should be reviewed separately, and information available from

previous notes, preliminary project descriptions, outline specifications, or a combination of these should be added to the worksheets. If errors, conflicts, or omissions are detected, comments should be made on the drawings, in the notebook, or on the worksheets for correction and coordination. A meeting among project participants is usually the appropriate method of resolving such problems, and decisions made should be promptly noted on the worksheets or specification notebook.

Preliminary Project Description (PPD). These descriptions based on systems and assemblies may have been created for a project during schematic design and could be used as a checklist in preparing the project specifications.

Outline Specifications. As done with PPDs, the outline specifications based on products and activities may also have been created for

Figure 11.3
Sample
Specification
Coordination
Checklist

SAMPLE COORDINATION CHECKLIST:

SECTION 08 31 13—Access Doors and Frames

- Location and size of each access door and floor door required.

- Locations of fire-rated access doors and their required fire-resistance ratings.

- Construction details such as those for masonry, gypsum board assemblies, plaster, tile, and acoustical surfaces in which access doors will be installed.

- Schedule of access doors.

- Hand of the access door and clearance around doors.

- Details of nonstandard units that require custom fabrication.

- Identification of custom units and standard units fabricated from other than the usual materials or finishes.

- Locations of floor fire doors painted yellow with the following warning painted in black letters on the surface: FIRE DOOR—DO NOT STORE MATERIALS ON SURFACE.

- Details of safety railings on the floor doors.

DOMAIN 1
Planning,
Development,
& Organization

DOMAIN 2
Coordination

DOMAIN 3
Procurement,
Contracting,
& General
Requirements

DOMAIN 4
Research

DOMAIN 5
Analysis
& Evaluation

DOMAIN 6
Production

a project during design development. These may be more up-to-date and may also be used as a checklist in preparing the project specifications. (See Chapter 12 for more information on outline specifications.)

11.4 Specifications Organization and Preparation

Several decisions are required at the outset of the development of a specification section. On small, limited-scope projects, remodeling work, and work under the control of an owner-builder, the decision may be made to use a shortform specification or to record only the basic product selections and requirements. Conversely, highly detailed language may be needed for some sections where requirements are critical or have been the subject of extensive investigation. The owner's specific project requirements should be reviewed again at this time, along with any requirements imposed by outside sources, such as regulatory agencies.

11.5 Basic Procedural Decisions

Before the specifier can begin editing master guide specification sections or writing original sections for a project, the specification's type and organization must be decided. The Engineers Joint Contract Documents Committee (EJCDC®) 1910-16, *Uniform Location of Subject Matter*, is a useful reference for coordinating portions of the construction documents. For each subject included in the construction documents, the recommended primary and secondary locations for information are provided. Suggested cross-references to other locations are also included. The information or requirements stated in secondary locations supplement rather than duplicate those stated in primary locations.

11.6 Format

Information collected should be developed in the three-part SectionFormat®. This three-part format provides consistency in the presentation of information and, at the same time, allows flexibility for adapting to a wide variety of construction projects. Only one specific requirement or action should be addressed in each article, paragraph, or subparagraph to permit easy reference. If changes are necessary, items can be modified or deleted with minimum disruption of other text or cross-references. (See Chapter 13 for more information on formats used with specifications.)

11.7 Method of Specifying

A decision must also be made regarding the appropriate method of specifying: descriptive, performance, reference standard, or proprietary. At times, more than one method may be necessary for the same project manual. The specifier should be careful about combining methods in a single product specification. Doing so can create redundancy and result in a conflict incapable of resolution. (See Chapter 14 for more information on specifying methods.)

The specifier should evaluate the complexity of the specification required for the project. A project manual may contain a combination of sections that vary in their complexity. On small projects, remodeling projects, or more substantial work under an owner's control, the decision may be made to use shortform specifications. (See Section 12.2 for more information on shortform specifications.) In some cases, sections containing an entire division's requirements—which document only basic decisions, selections, and requirements—may be used. Conversely, highly detailed sections may be needed where requirements are complex, unique, or extensive. Some master guide specifications include sections of varying content. The most appropriate text or version for each section should be selected based on the project requirements. The project requirements might also dictate the method or methods of specifying that can or should be

DOMAIN 1
Planning,
Development,
& Organization

DOMAIN 2
Coordination

DOMAIN 3
Procurement,
Contracting,
& General
Requirements

DOMAIN 4
Research

DOMAIN 5
Analysis
& Evaluation

DOMAIN 6
Production

used. If a project is for a government agency, non-restrictive methods are generally required, and it is essential to be aware of this requirement before beginning to prepare specifications.

11.8 Specification Language

Competent specification writing requires the correct use of vocabulary and grammar and the correct construction of sentences and paragraphs. As legally enforceable contract documents, construction specifications should be prepared with regard and respect for their legal status. Following are the four Cs for effective communication:

- **Clear.** Use proper grammar and simple sentence construction to avoid ambiguity.

- **Concise.** Eliminate unnecessary words, but not at the expense of clarity, correctness, or completeness.

- **Correct.** Present the information accurately and precisely. Select words that convey exact meanings.

- **Complete.** Do not leave out important information and adequately coordinate with other related sections.

Specifications should also be coordinated—sometimes referred to as the fifth "C"—with all stakeholders. (See Section 15.4 for more information on specification language.)

11.9 Preparing Specification Sections

Specification sections may be newly written, derived from a previous project specification, or edited from a master guide specification. With commercial master guide specifications, editing rather than writing is usually the primary means for producing project manuals or specifications. Copies of previous project specifications should be used only for reference and should not be edited for a new project. A previous specification section may not contain necessary options, materials, or standards and may

have changed since the specification was written, or the product may no longer be available. In addition, copied sections might not reflect changes made by addenda or contract modifications.

11.9.1 Division 01— General Requirements

Early distribution of a draft version of Division 01— General Requirements to consultants and other contributors to the specifications helps eliminate overlapping requirements and omissions. (See Chapter 3 for a more detailed discussion of general requirements.)

11.10 Preliminary Review

Members of the project team should review draft versions of the specifications to identify errors and oversights and update content to align with new or revised drawings. (See Chapter 2 for more specific examples on preliminary reviews and what to look for in coordinating draft versions of specifications.)

11.10.1 Proofreading

Proofreading should be performed by someone familiar with construction terminology and who is competent to identify incorrectly selected editing options or statements out of context. The proofreader should review the selected options, revisions, new paragraphs, sentences, statements, and sections added or deleted.

11.11 Final Preparation, Publication, and Distribution

When no further substantial changes in content or extent are expected, and project manual documents have been drafted, the project manual's final preparation can begin. Final preparation includes processing edited content into a final draft of the project manual for final review and subsequent revision and publishing.

Sending header, footer, and other formatting information in advance to other consultants writing specifications lessens the time needed for final production.

Although printing hard copies of the project manual and drawings is rarely required, it is still good practice to organize the project manual into separate volumes when the page count exceeds 700 pages. Page counts greater than 700 pages are impractical to bind together in a single volume when printed copies are required. The number of volumes and content of each volume should be identified on the cover page(s) and table of contents. Separate volumes may also be used for addenda, modifications, or multiple-prime contract construction projects.

11.11.1 Inclusion of Agreement and Conditions of the Contract into Project Manual

Even though standard agreement forms published by professional societies, other organizations, and agencies may be utilized, the A/E should avoid including the agreement by reference only. It is more appropriate to include the actual agreement forms in the project manual. Referencing an incorrect or outdated form is eliminated if the forms are bound into the project manual.

Include the conditions of the contract (general and supplementary conditions) along with the agreement. Although the conditions of the contract should have been coordinated early in the project's development, the A/E needs to verify that the conditions of the contract are the appropriate version for the project delivery method.

11.11.2 Table of Contents

The completed sections, schedules, reports, and other documents and forms are assembled for inclusion in the project manual. The project manual table of contents is prepared by carefully recording the section numbers and titles and, in some firms, the number of pages of each. Another common

approach is to generate the table of contents early in the design process and maintain it throughout production to help organize the project manual's production. Going through the project manual and cross-checking sections with the table of contents is a part of quality control before publication and distribution.

11.11.3 Reproduction and Distribution

The processed specification text should be transmitted to the owner for final review and comment. If changes are required, the text should be returned for revision. If changes are not required, the draft becomes the final copy for reproduction. When requested by the owner, reproduce the approved project manual and construction drawings in a number sufficient for procurement purposes and funding approvals by financial institutions. Copies should also be distributed to each project team member and regulatory agencies for the permit and other approvals.

11.11.4 Archive Electronic Files for Version Control

Revisions to specifications should be distributed and archived in a neutral format, such as the portable document format (PDF) or internet-based posting, for easy access and usability. The specifier should use a consistent file naming protocol for version control. Consider using the optional yyyy-mm-dd convention prescribed by ISO 8601, *Data Elements and Interchange Formats — Information Interchange — Representation of Dates and Times*. There should be appropriate security features to prevent the modification of the contract documents by means other than those expressly designated.

A revision log that captures the project name and owner's or A/E's project number, specification section number and title, and a brief description of the changes should be archived for use in updating office master guide specifications to capture lessons learned.

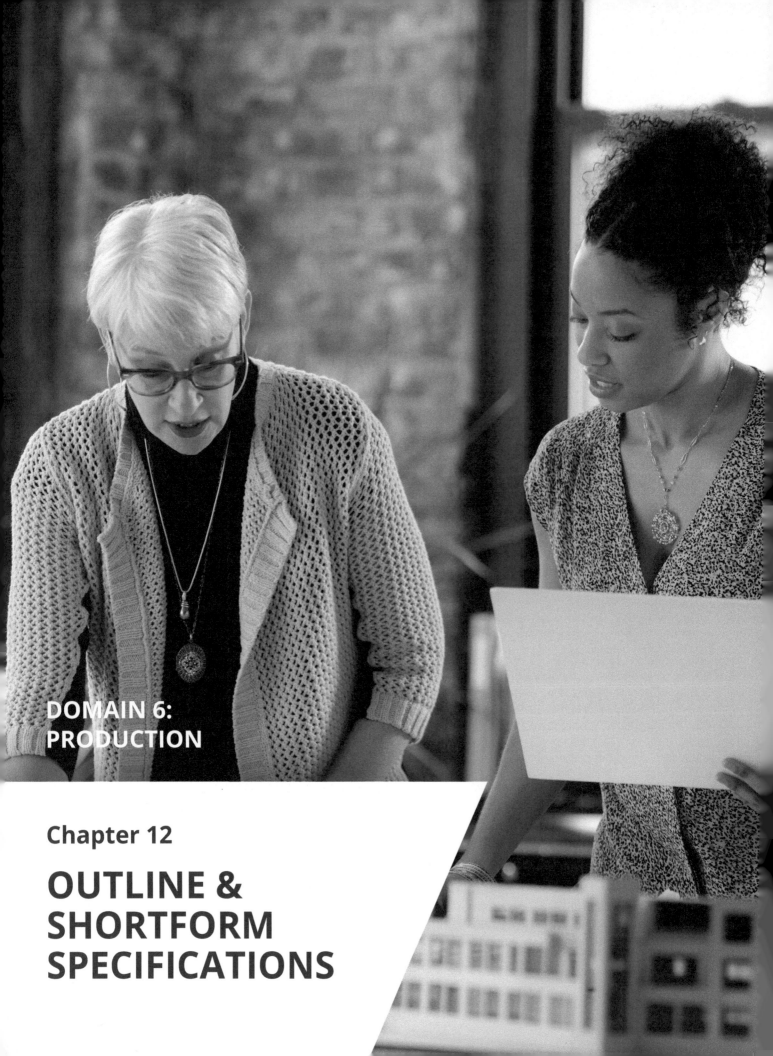

DOMAIN 6:
PRODUCTION

Chapter 12

OUTLINE & SHORTFORM SPECIFICATIONS

12.1 Outline Specifications

The architect/engineer's (A/E's) early design decisions on materials, manufacturers (when known), products, equipment, unique or special fabrications, and general level of quality are recorded in outline specifications, usually during the design development phase. With the design drawings, outline specifications are prepared in the early stages of the design process to assist in progressing the design and developing and updating estimates of probable construction cost, schedules, and value analysis. The structure and content are intentionally brief, including concise descriptions of manufacturers, products, manufactured units, materials, equipment, and assemblies. Outline specifications are not intended for use as contract documents. (More detailed information on outline specifications is provided in Section 4.6.2 of the *Project Delivery Practice Guide*.)

12.1.1 When to Use Outline Specifications

Outline specifications are best suited for the design development phase when selecting materials and products is very active. They may also be used earlier in schematic design if required by the owner, or when the A/E has much experience with the building type. Outline specifications set a base level of quality that may be used in establishing a guaranteed maximum price (GMP) for projects using the design-bid-build negotiation option or construction manager at risk (CMAR) project delivery methods.

12.1.2 Purpose of Outline Specifications

Outline specifications can benefit the design team, owner, and contractor in several ways:

- To further document design decisions made during design development

- To expand on preliminary project descriptions (PPDs) prepared during the schematic design phase

- As a checklist in preparing project specifications

DOMAIN 1
Planning,
Development,
& Organization

DOMAIN 2
Coordination

DOMAIN 3
Procurement,
Contracting,
& General
Requirements

DOMAIN 4
Research

DOMAIN 5
Analysis
& Evaluation

DOMAIN 6
Production

- As a guide for owners, cost estimators, construction managers, and authorities having jurisdiction in understanding design decisions on materials, manufacturers, products, equipment, and special fabricated items or assemblies

- To control clarity of the construction documents

- As a tool for coordinating the terminology used on the drawings and in the specifications

- To provide criteria for products, materials, and other provisions that have a special cost consideration or impact

- As a reference for the owner's specific requirements, if any, for manufacturer or performance

12.1.3 Characteristics of Outline Specifications

The brevity of outline specifications provides only the essential information necessary to establish a clear understanding of the project's materials, products, systems, equipment, and general requirements for use by A/Es, owners, lenders, cost estimators, and contractors. An outline specification section for a specific material, product, or system can be as brief as a few sentences but is usually a single page, with some reaching two to three pages per section. Outline specifications use MasterFormat® as the organizational structure and should be as close as possible to the final project manual's organization. SectionFormat® may or may not be used; however, the sequence of information within each section should follow SectionFormat® to assist with producing project specifications.

12.1.4 Outline Master Guide Specifications

When available, outline master guide specifications can save the A/E time preparing office master outline specifications and outline project specifications. Creating an office master for outline specifications using commercially available outline master guide specifications reduces production time, ensures a comprehensive list of sections, and increases quality consistency. Use of outline master guide specifications has benefits in format,

organization, and sequence of information similar to SectionFormat®. Outline master guide specifications establish a consistent level of detail in describing the quality of materials, products, equipment, and assemblies. As with editing other types of specifications, the challenge is to edit the outline master guide specifications to align with the A/E practice's needs. The A/E can modify the outline master guide specifications to fit their unique practice while maintaining an easily recognized organization and format for information and a consistent detail level.

12.1.5 Writing Outline Master Guide Specifications

One method of writing outline master guide specifications is to start with the A/E office's or owner's master guide specifications and delete the content with no or little bearing on the project cost. The remaining content can be further edited to reduce the information to simple sentences and take full advantage of the streamlining method. (See Section 12.1.7 for more information on converting full-length and shortform specifications into outline specifications, and Section 15.4.17 for more information on streamlining.)

Another method is to start with commercially available outline master guide specifications and edit them to align with the A/E firm's practice or owner's instructions for use. If the office has master guide specifications, ensure the outline specifications editing reflects the edits made to the master guide specifications.

12.1.6 Outline Project Specifications

Outline project specifications are project-specific. They become the record of early design decisions and establish a base level of quality for cost estimating purposes. When used in this way, outline project specifications can improve the entire project team's efficiency by reducing potential changes in the construction documents' subsequent development.

Not all information is known in the early design phases, but the outline project specifications should document what is known or anticipated. These outline specifications may be a required early design deliverable to the owner. However, they are also a tool to record early decisions made by the A/E, set early cost estimates for the project's unique requirements, and enable design team coordination.

12.1.7 Converting Full-Length or Shortform Master Guide Specifications to Outline Specifications

Use the following techniques for converting full-length or shortform master guide specifications into outline specifications when there are no available outline master guide specifications from commercial sources:

Discard most of PART 1 — GENERAL and PART 3 — EXECUTION requirements. Maintain only the unique requirements that increase costs, such as mock-ups and installation warranties in PART 1 and contractor-provided field quality control testing in PART 3 (e.g., low-voltage electrical conductance testing for membrane roofing).

Remove reference standards. However, retain those that are for unique standards of material quality or testing that would affect costs.

Condense text by using streamlining techniques. Eliminate text that is not driving cost or schedule.

Focus on PART 2 — PRODUCTS. Retain content directly applicable to materials, products, and manufacturers (when known).

- Retain only the information that is required to establish basic product and installation quality.

- Include special fabrication or workmanship required to achieve the intended level of quality.

- Include special or custom finishes.

- Include reference standards that are unique to the material or system.

DOMAIN 1
Planning,
Development,
& Organization

DOMAIN 2
Coordination

DOMAIN 3
Procurement,
Contracting,
& General
Requirements

DOMAIN 4
Research

DOMAIN 5
Analysis
& Evaluation

DOMAIN 6
Production

12.1.8 Commercially Available Outline Master Guide Specifications

Like full-length and shortform specifications (discussed in the next section), outline specifications are also offered from commercial sources. Since CSI provides no standard format for outline specifications, these commercial sources' products use their own format. Commercial outline specifications are usually based on the provider's library of full-length specifications. If a specifier uses commercial master guide specifications, it is best to use the companion library of outline specifications to ensure consistency across specification types.

12.2 Shortform Specifications

Projects of limited scope and extent may require less detailed descriptions than those provided by a typical full-length specification. Similarly, for projects with a negotiated contract or design-build delivery method, a specification with reduced detail may be appropriate. In these cases, an A/E may choose, or an owner may request, to use a shortform specification. Although the name might imply that documents are less than complete, the specification must provide sufficient detail to describe the project's requirements. It must provide, at minimum, a code-compliant level of information. Unlike the preliminary project descriptions or outline specifications that are part of the early design phases, a shortform specification is a legally enforceable contract document. Shortform specifications should be viewed as the process of logically and consistently editing full-length specifications into a compact form.

12.2.1 When to Use Shortform Specifications

Shortform specifications might be used for any project, though some types of projects lend themselves more readily than others:

Small Projects. Projects of limited extent and cost. The use of full-length specifications may

not be consistent with the scope of the project drawings. In such cases, shortform specifications would be justified as long as the desired level of detail is consistent throughout the specifications. Similarly, shortform specifications can be used effectively on projects that use standard materials and traditional construction details, as they generally require less descriptive detail in the specifications.

Design-Negotiate-Build Project Delivery. Where a contractor has had previous experience with the owner or A/E on a similar project type, there is usually better communication, so the chance of misunderstanding is lessened. The shortform specification can be practical because the contractor is familiar with the owner's detail level, and less descriptive detail may be acceptable in the specifications.

Construction Management Project Delivery. Multiple-prime contracts may present coordination complications, and unless the shortform specification is written to cover such situations, full-length specifications are usually more suitable.

Design-Build Project Delivery. The detail provided by the shortform specifications depends mainly on the completeness of the owner's project requirements. Shortform specifications can be used effectively in design-build projects because the single contract and single focus of accountability provide many negotiated contract features. Because the A/E and the contractor are associated, coordination and communication are improved, which reduces the chance of misunderstanding, and less administrative detail is usually required. The detail level is purposely reduced to decrease cost and increase flexibility in product selection, subcontract negotiation, and installation. Items such as shop drawings, samples, testing, inspection, and extended warranties may not be included in the specifications unless required by the owner or by code. The owner has limited influence, and much of the decision-making is done by the design-build entity.

Owner-Build Project Delivery. Because the administrative activities and installation details are reduced to the minimum, the A/E has less influence and the owner does more of the decision-making.

Interior Design and Tenant Improvement Projects. These projects may involve installing standard finishes, furnishings, and equipment. Unless the materials or systems used are unusual, there is usually no need for detailed product descriptions or execution requirements. The use of reference standards may specify an acceptable level of detail.

Single-Prime Contract. Simple projects can work better with shortform specifications because there are generally fewer complex administrative issues.

Projects Where a Shortform Specification Is Specifically Requested. The owner should be informed of the reduced detail of the specifications and their limitations.

12.2.2 Purpose of Shortform Specifications

The purpose of shortform specifications is to provide a concise set of construction specifications commensurate with the size and extent of a project and to reduce the level of detail where it is appropriate. Project specifications can be as brief as a collection of detailed notes on the drawings (as shown in Figure 12.1) or as long as a traditional full-length specification. Depending on the level of detail used, a shortform specification is located somewhere between these two extremes.

A full-length master guide specification can be condensed into a shortform specification by combining closely related sections and the careful removal of requirements unnecessary for limited scope projects. Correctly developed, the resulting shortform specification is concise without the omission of critical information. As with full-length specifications, the imprudent removal of language from a specification to shorten its length can reduce detail to the point of sacrificing quality control. Thus, preparing a shortform specification requires the competence, skill, and technical knowledge of an A/E who is experienced as a specifier and who knows construction standards.

12.2.3 Characteristics of Shortform Specifications

Shortform specifications are a part of the contract documents' written portion and share the same characteristics as full-length specifications. These shortform specifications should accomplish the following:

- Express the design intent and a consistent level of project detail despite their short length.

- Include information necessary to achieve the design intent and the required level of detail. However, not all requirements can be described briefly, and text should not be condensed solely for the sake of brevity. The level of project requirements expressed by the shortform specifications must be consistent with the detail necessary to meet the owner's project requirements.

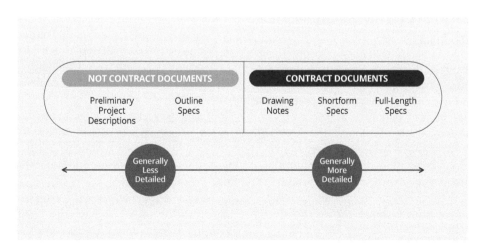

Figure 12.1
Level of Detail

DOMAIN 1
Planning,
Development,
& Organization

DOMAIN 2
Coordination

DOMAIN 3
Procurement,
Contracting,
& General
Requirements

DOMAIN 4
Research

DOMAIN 5
Analysis
& Evaluation

DOMAIN 6
Production

- Be capable of being priced. Like typical specifications, they should be clear, concise, correct, and complete.

- Be made specific to a project. The specifications should be coordinated with local codes, construction practices, and the owner's project requirements.

- Be complementary with the drawings.

- Be fully enforceable as a contract document.

- Be consistent with the level of drawing detail.

Shortform specifications are made cost-effective by communicating the project requirements in the shortest possible form. They are compact and easy to read, and the language is concise and direct. Because there is less written material to review, coordination and document review are simplified. Less time and cost are usually required to assemble and edit shortform master guide sections.

Shortform specifications might impose limitations. The level of construction detail may be more challenging to maintain because there is less descriptive content. The A/E should carefully determine the amount of detail necessary for each specification section. The A/E must be skilled, knowledgeable, and experienced as a specifier to ensure that essential items are not omitted and unnecessary detail is not retained. The risk of error might increase as the detail decreases, and the A/E, not the owner, assumes this risk. The A/E and the owner should agree on an acceptable level of requirements for the project and determine the degree of specification detail required accordingly.

12.2.4 Shortform Master Guide Specifications

As seen in Figure 12.2, creating project specifications from a shortform master guide specification usually takes less time than editing a full-length specification because of the ability to work from a previously created abbreviated master document. The shortform master guide specification has already been edited and prepared in a condensed format. Although a project may have a unique situation that requires adding items to the specification, the editing of the shortform master guide decreases the likelihood of omitted items, and the level of project detail

is maintained throughout the specification. The following steps should be taken to create a shortform master guide specification for a given project type.

12.2.4.1 Establish Project Types and Level of Detail

The A/E should determine the extent of the project type and establish the detail level of the various specification sections. This process helps determine which method of specifying is best suited to achieving the required detail. Where the project's extent requires a greater degree of detail, full-length specification sections should be used. The shortform master guide specification for each project type can have Level 2 and Level 3 MasterFormat® section titles. Combinations of master sections may be used within a project manual:

- A broad Level 2 MasterFormat® title for each section can be used when less content is required to describe the work. For example, a section for cast-in-place concrete may include concrete forms and accessories, reinforcement, and finishing; a plaster section may include both gypsum plaster and Portland cement plaster.

- Several focused Level 3 MasterFormat® sections may be used for those instances when a greater level of content is required that cannot be provided by a single Level 2 section. For example, instead of a Level 2 precast concrete section, use two Level 3 sections, such as plant-precast architectural concrete and site-precast architectural concrete.

- A single section may cover all the titles within a division, and a single section can become the division itself. This method can be used when the project is of limited scope. For example, Section 03 00 00 — Concrete includes all aspects of concrete work, including forms and accessories, reinforcement, and finishing.

12.2.4.2 Establish a Master Section List for the Project Type

Determine which sections apply to the project type. MasterFormat® should be used as the standard organizational system to establish numbers and titles for the sections. The master list should show preferred numbers and titles that have been

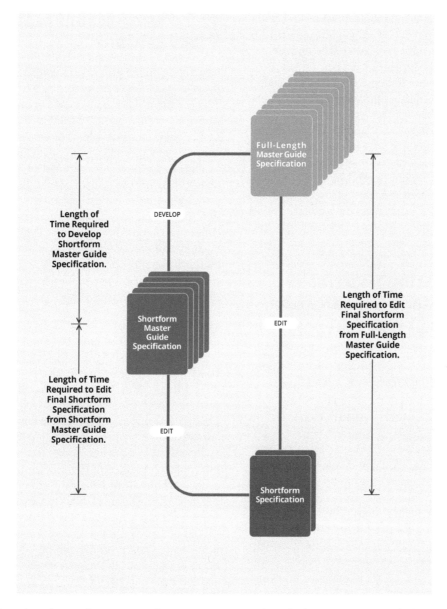

Figure 12.2
Comparison
of Time
Requirements

permanently assigned to each section, with gaps in the numbering to allow for other project-specific sections. The following list provides examples of information for each section. Each A/E or specifier develops its own system loosely based on this concept.

- Provide a description of each section.
- Identify the work included in related sections.
- Provide the current status of each section, including the date of initial preparation and the latest revision.

- Identify the party responsible for preparing and updating the section.
- Determine the order of priority for completion of each section.

12.2.4.3 Develop a Standard Shortform SectionFormat® and PageFormat®

A standard section and page format should be developed for a shortform master guide specification. A standard shortform format presents text clearly and at a density best suited for the brief descriptions

DOMAIN 1
Planning,
Development,
& Organization

DOMAIN 2
Coordination

DOMAIN 3
Procurement,
Contracting,
& General
Requirements

DOMAIN 4
Research

DOMAIN 5
Analysis
& Evaluation

DOMAIN 6
Production

to be read easily. As indicated by Figure 12.3, the three-part SectionFormat® should be used with no more than two levels of paragraphs under each article. A third level may be used occasionally for listing items, but their use should be avoided wherever possible. Using the three-part headings is recommended because they act as organizational markers to help locate and coordinate information quickly. They also serve as a reminder to maintain consistency throughout the project manual. Figure 12.3 illustrates article headings for shortform specifications. The A/E would decide the choice of articles and format based on the extent required for the particular project. Figure 12.4 illustrates a shortform specification using SectionFormat® and PageFormat®.

12.2.5 Writing Shortform Master Guide Specifications

The selected sections of the shortform master guide specification should be written using the streamlining method. (See Section 15.4.17 for more information on the streamlining method.)

12.2.5.1 Establish Division 01— General Requirements

Division 01 sections should be developed using only those articles that apply to the project type and adding others needed to cover situations usually encountered for the project type (e.g., cutting and patching for renovation work). Use Division 01 to specify coordination and quality assurance items. When the project requirements allow for less complexity, the Division 01 sections might be combined into one section, as shown in Figure 12.5.

12.2.5.2 Update the Shortform Master Guide Specification Regularly

The shortform master guide specification must be updated together with the traditional full-length master guide specifications. Doing so avoids coordination and consistency errors when sections from both full-length and shortform sections are combined in a project specification.

12.2.6 Shortform Project Specifications

Depending on the project's size and extent, the A/E must decide the scope of each section. MasterFormat® Level 3 and Level 4 numbers and titles for sections should be combined under a Level 2 title when possible. With any combination, the A/E should decide whether it is convenient or efficient to do so. The use of broad Level 2 numbers and titles reduces the length of specifications by combining similar paragraphs in the section. The A/E should maintain the intent and level of project detail consistently throughout the specification, regardless of the resulting length of the individual sections. The shortform section's length can vary from a partial page to several pages, depending on the project requirements.

The A/E should decide which of the articles shown in SectionFormat® can be omitted and which can be logically combined. Division 01 sections should be coordinated with the procurement requirements, contracting requirements, and the other specification sections. PART 1—GENERAL of each section in Divisions 02 through 49 should be limited to the administrative and procedural requirements that apply only to that portion of the work and not repeat information provided in Division 01. Include articles such as submittals and quality assurance only when necessary to elaborate further on the generalized requirements outlined in Division 01. The A/E should be careful not to reduce detail in Division 01 below the level of project requirements; however, because administrative requirements often constitute significant cost items, include only those necessary to the project.

12.2.7 Techniques for Converting Full-Length Master Guide Specifications to Shortform

Standard full-length master guide specifications may be edited into a shorter format by deleting detail deemed excessive to secure project requirements. The following techniques help condense the remaining text.

Figure 12.3
Example of
Shortform Section
Article Headings

PART 1 — GENERAL

1.01 Section Includes
1.02 Price and Payment Procedures
1.03 Administrative Requirements
1.04 Action Submittals
    A.   Shop Drawings
    B.   Product Data
    C.   Samples
1.05 Closeout Submittals
1.06 Quality Assurance
1.07 Field [or] Site Conditions
1.08 Warranty

PART 2 — PRODUCTS

2.01 Manufacturer
2.02 Description
2.03 Material
2.04 Fabrication
2.05 Finishes
2.06 Accessories

PART 3 — EXECUTION

3.01 Examination
3.02 Preparation
3.03 [Erection][Installation][Application]
3.04 Field or Site Quality Control
3.05 Attachments

End of Section

Schedules

Construction
Specifications
Practice Guide

DOMAIN 1 — Planning, Development, & Organization
DOMAIN 2 — Coordination
DOMAIN 3 — Procurement, Contracting, & General Requirements
DOMAIN 4 — Research
DOMAIN 5 — Analysis & Evaluation
DOMAIN 6 — Production

Figure 12.4
Example of
Shortform Section

SECTION 03 30 00
CAST-IN-PLACE CONCRETE

PART 1—GENERAL

1.01 SUMMARY

    A. Section includes cast-in-place concrete for interior slabs on grade.

1.02 SUBMITTALS

    A. Concrete mix design.
    B. Concrete delivery slips.
    C. Samples.

PART 2—PRODUCTS

2.01 CONCRETE MATERIALS

    A. Portland Cement: ASTM C150, Type I.
    B. Normal-Weight Aggregate: ASTM C33, uniformly graded.
    C. Water: Potable.
    D. Reinforcing Bars: ASTM A615, Grade 60, deformed.
    E. Welded Wire Fabric: ASTM A185, welded steel wire fabric, flat sheets.
    F. Supports for Reinforcement: Comply CRSI specifications.

2.02 CONCRETE MIX

    A. Comply with ACI 301, ASTM C94, and ASTM C116 for normal-weight ready mixed concrete as follows:
        1. Compressive Strength (28 Days): 4000 psi (27.6 MPa).
        2. Slump: 4 inches (100 mm).

2.03 CONCRETE ACCESSORIES

    A. Moisture Retaining Cover: 10 oz. burlap laminated to 4 mil polyethylene sheet.
    B. Vapor Retarder: 15-mil high density polyethylene, perm rating not to exceed 0.006 gr/ft^2/hr.

PART 3—EXECUTION

3.01 CONCRETE PLACEMENT AND FINISHING

    A. Comply with recommendations in ACI 304R for measuring, mixing, transporting, and placing concrete.

    B. Control Joints: Saw-cut joints 1/4 of slab depth not to exceed 10 feet in any direction.

3.02 CONCRETE FINISHING

    A. Slab Finish: Trowel finish.
    B. Flatness/Levelness Requirements:
        1. Specified overall Value: FF 30/FL 23.
        2. Minimum Local Value: FF 25/FL 20.
    C. Curing Method: Moisture-retaining cover.

END OF SECTION

Project name/Project no./date   03 30 00-1   Cast-In-Place Concrete
(optional information)

Figure 12.5
Example of
Division 01 —
General
Requirements
within a Single
Section

Division 01
General Requirements

Section 01 00 00
General Requirements

PART 1—GENERAL

01 10 00	**Summary**	1.01 Summary of Work
		1.02 Work Restrictions
01 20 00	**Price and Payment Procedures**	1.03 Allowances
		1.04 Alternates
		1.05 Contract Modification Procedures
		1.06 Payment Procedures
01 30 00	**Administrative Requirements**	1.07 Project Management and Coordination
		1.08 Construction Progress Documentation
		1.09 Submittal Procedures
		1.10 Sustainable Design Submittals
01 40 00	**Quality Requirements**	1.11 Quality Assurance
		1.12 Quality Control
		1.13 Sustainable Standards Certifications
01 50 00	**Temporary Facilities & Controls**	1.14 Temporary Utilities
		1.15 Construction Facilities
		1.16 Vehicular Access and Parking
		1.17 Temporary Barriers and Enclosures
01 60 00	**Product Requirements**	1.18 Basic Product Requirements
		1.19 Product Substitution Procedures
		1.20 Product Delivery Requirements
01 70 00	**Execution and Closeout**	1.21 Cleaning and Waste Management
		1.22 Starting and Adjusting
		1.23 Protecting Installed Construction
		1.24 Closeout Procedures
		1.25 Closeout Submittals

PART 2—PRODUCTS
Not USED

PART 3—EXECUTION
Not USED

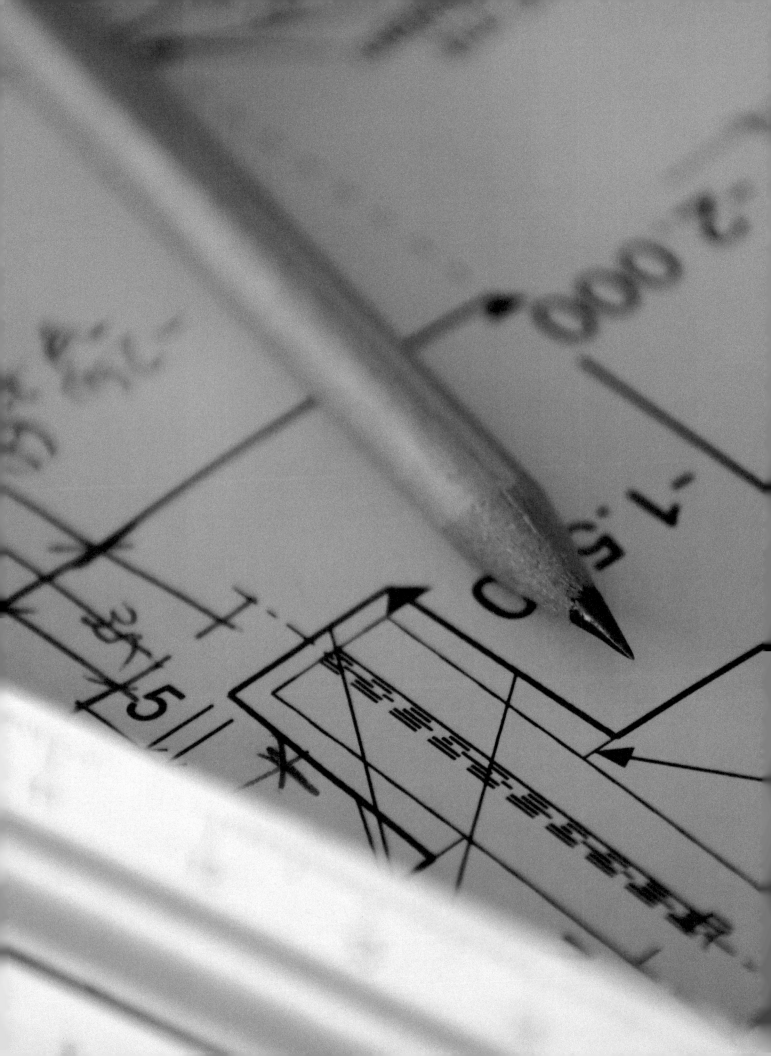

Eliminate administrative details in PART 1. Eliminate excessive cross-referencing of related sections. Delete titles of reference standards when the standard is included in other text by abbreviation and number. Delete specific submittal details.

Combine and edit related sections into a single section. For example, combine wood doors, plastic doors, and steel doors under one section if the subjects allow this reduction of detail without compromising understanding.

Combine and edit related articles or paragraphs and delete excessive details. For example, using the preceding door example, it may be possible to combine the hardware item descriptions.

Combine and edit sentences within an article or paragraph and delete redundant wording. For example, using the preceding door hardware example, the hardware finish descriptions might be combined into a single sentence without ambiguity.

Condense the text by using the streamlining method. Be clear and concise with language, using short imperative or declarative sentences; use lists for materials, manufacturers, and references; and use the colon in place of "shall be" when preparing lists.

Use reference standards to save text space and set a minimum level of project requirements and workmanship.

Place schedules on the drawings. Sometimes it is more practical to do this rather than reproduce them in the specification. However, in some cases it may be more costly to produce and print schedules on the drawings than in the specifications. The US National CAD Standard® (NCS) recommends the inclusion of schedules as part of the drawing set. NCS does, however, state that schedules developed as electronically generated databases or spreadsheets can be incorporated into the drawing set or specifications. Other schedules that are part text and part symbol or diagram that might be best placed on the drawings.

Follow SectionFormat® as closely as possible. Use the least number of paragraph levels.

Follow PageFormat® as closely as possible. Use the least number of indentations.

12.2.8 Commercially Available Shortform Master Guide Specifications

Shortform master guide specifications are available commercially. Before using these in a project, they should be scrutinized to determine what is not covered. Determine the level of detail they represent and the type of project for which they would be appropriate. The guide specifications should then be modified as necessary to tailor the sections to the firm's practice and maintain a consistent level of detail.

Chapter 13

ORGANIZING USING FORMATS

13.1 Introduction to Formats

It is not practical to include sufficient notes on construction drawings to describe product quality and installation methods in detail. Separate written descriptions, referred to as specifications, more effectively communicate this type of information. The drawings and specifications are complementary.

Specifications define the qualitative requirements for products, materials, workmanship, and administrative requirements upon which the project is based. A simple definition of the word *specify* is to describe or define in detail. A specification is a precise statement describing the characteristics of the work. Whether specifying brick walls, curtain wall assemblies, buildings, or bridges, the specifications must describe the desired results entirely so that the work can be constructed per the contract requirements. Specifications in this context are different from other types of technical data and product descriptions available from project manufacturers that may also be referred to as specifications. Specifications are not just descriptions of products, but detailed descriptions of products' results with effort applied to these products to produce a work result, for example, the product carpet versus the work result of carpeting.

The Construction Specifications Institute (CSI), Construction Specifications Canada (CSC), and other related organizations developed several standards to organize all of the information that needs to be addressed—from project conception throughout its life cycle. These standards, called formats, can be employed for various applications. The chief advantage they carry is a standardized means of organizing, storing, retrieving, and communicating this enormous body of data.

13.2 Hierarchy of Formats

The various formats establish an organizational hierarchy. Figure 13.1 illustrates these relationships.

OmniClass® is a multi-table system for organizing information used by the architectural, engineering,

DOMAIN 1
Planning,
Development,
& Organization

DOMAIN 2
Coordination

DOMAIN 3
Procurement,
Contracting,
& General
Requirements

DOMAIN 4
Research

DOMAIN 5
Analysis
& Evaluation

DOMAIN 6
Production

Figure 13.1
Hierarchy of
Formats

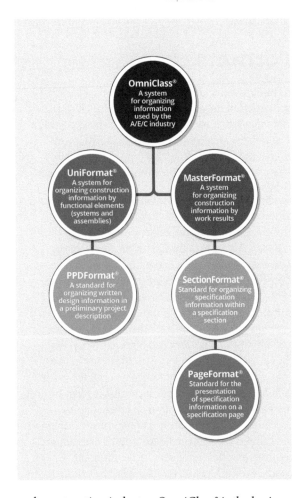

methods, and is utilized more often during the later design and construction stages of a project. However, information organized by MasterFormat® is also used throughout the facility life cycle. The primary purpose of MasterFormat® is to organize the project manual, reference keynotes, and detailed cost estimates.

Both MasterFormat® and UniFormat® are also designed to work within OmniClass®, a multifaceted pure classification system that provides the capability for wide-ranging information storage and retrieval applications.

MasterFormat® establishes the organizational structure for the documents and sections within a project manual. Each document and section has its unique number and title. A section is further divided into the three PARTs defined in **SectionFormat®**. **PageFormat®** provides a consistent format for each page within a specification section. This simple hierarchy helps the architect/engineer (A/E) place information within the project manual and helps the user of the project manual find the information. For example, if a contractor or supplier wants to know what types of windows are required for a project, it is a simple process to find the answer:

- What is the general category of information? Division 08 — Openings

- What is the specific category of information? Section 08 52 00 — Wood Windows

- What is the detailed information? PART 2 — PRODUCTS, Windows: horizontal sliding, plastic-clad, wood units with double glazing

13.3 OmniClass®

OmniClass® uses a multi-table framework for organizing all forms of information used or encountered in the construction industry. The 15 OmniClass® classification tables can be used together or individually to manage information about all aspects of the facilities that comprise the built environment over their entire life cycle. OmniClass® concepts are derived from internationally accepted standards developed by the International Organization for Standardization (ISO) and supported by the International Construction

and construction industry. OmniClass® is the basis for deriving relational applications. This system supports and empowers the transfer and use of information in the construction marketplace, ultimately serving all participants who work to sustain the built environment throughout a facility's entire life cycle.

UniFormat® organizes construction information based on the elements of a facility, otherwise known as systems and assemblies. These systems and assemblies are characterized by their function without identifying in detail the products that compose them. UniFormat® is chiefly employed in the early design phases of a project for preliminary project descriptions (formatted per PPDFormat®) and performance specifying; it is frequently used for cost estimating.

MasterFormat® breaks the same information down by work results, or construction practices that result from a combination of products and

Information Society and the International Alliance for Interoperability.

These concepts are described in detail in two ISO standards in particular:

- ISO 12006-2, Organization of Information about construction works — Part 2: Framework for classification of information, and ISO/PAS (Publicly Available Specification).

- ISO 12006-3, Organization of Information about construction works — Part 3: Framework for object-oriented information exchange, which, when taken together, define bases for organizing, managing, and transferring information about the built environment. These standards were also followed in the development of Uniclass: Unified Classification for the Construction Industry, a faceted classification system similar to OmniClass®, created in the United Kingdom in 1997. Additional ISO-compatible classification systems are being developed in other countries.

The scope of OmniClass® is designed to address objects of every scale through the entire built environment. MasterFormat® and UniFormat® address specific topics from specific viewpoints; the scope of OmniClass® is much broader. Where OmniClass® tables address similar topics, these legacy formats are incorporated within the scheme. MasterFormat® is incorporated as the basis of the OmniClass® table for work results, and UniFormat® is the basis of the table for elements.

13.3.1 Basis of Organization

The OmniClass® tables are organized by segregating information about the built environment into a set of discrete, coordinated tables. Each table's information is organized based on a specific facet, or view, of the information for the subject matter addressed by that table.

Following are the OmniClass® tables:

Table 11 — Construction Entities by Function

Table 12 — Spaces by Function

Table 13 — Construction Entities by Form

Table 14 — Spaces by Form

Table 21 — Elements

Table 22 — Work Results

Table 23 — Products

Table 31 — Phases

Table 32 — Services

Table 33 — Disciplines

Table 34 — Organizational Roles

Table 35 — Process Aids

Table 41 — Information

Table 42 — Materials

Table 49 — Properties

Entries in the OmniClass® tables are arranged hierarchically. Tables are organized from broader high-level concepts to more specific lower-level, or granular, concepts. The OmniClass® tables taken as a whole also comprise an implied hierarchy of subjects, a progression from the general to the specific, with tables that deal conceptually with whole construction entities coming before the tables that dissect those objects into their composite elements, viewed from a variety of conceptual facets. The numbering of the entries in the OmniClass® tables consists of pairs of numbers for each level of hierarchy represented. The hierarchical organization of the OmniClass® tables allows for the classification of topics at differing degrees of detail or extent. A system of signs, or delimiters, combines the numbers representing entries from different tables, allowing the classification of more complex objects with more specificity.

13.3.2 Applications

OmniClass® tables address topics and activities in construction information. At the most superficial level, a single OmniClass® table can be used to organize a small collection of similar material. For instance, a small collection of product literature could be organized according to Table 23 — Products. For a more extensive collection, designators from more than one table can be used to qualify and refine entries, enabling information to be recalled according to user needs with far greater precision. For classifying extensive, complex collections of information, designators from multiple tables can be combined using OmniClass® delimiters to define

UniFormat®

2010 EDITION
A Uniform Classification of
Construction Systems and Assemblies

conceptual relationships between table entries and classifying a wide variety of concepts contained within various data sources.

13.4 UniFormat®

UniFormat® is a uniform classification system for organizing preliminary construction information into a standard order or sequence based on systems and assemblies. By establishing a uniform list of identifiers and titles, UniFormat® promotes standardization and facilitates information retrieval. UniFormat® can be used to organize Preliminary Project Descriptions, preliminary cost estimates, and drawing detail filing in the early stages of a facility's life cycle.

UniFormat® organizes construction information based on physical parts of a facility called systems and assemblies. These systems and assemblies are characterized by their function without identifying the products that compose them. Systems and assemblies present a view of a proposed facility separate from the view presented by a breakdown of building materials, products, and activities.

13.4.1 Basic Organization

UniFormat® classifies information into nine Level 1 categories:

Project Description
A   Substructure
B   Shell
C   Interiors
D   Services
E   Equipment and Furnishings
F   Special Construction and Demolition
G   Building Sitework
Z   General

These nine categories can be used to arrange preliminary project descriptions and preliminary cost information. Category Z, General, is designated by the last letter of the alphabet, so the classification can expand beyond building construction. When the list is so expanded, this category remains last. When included in project manuals, elemental (system

and assemblies) performance specifications can be located in MasterFormat® under Section 01 80 00 — Performance Requirements, in an order taken from these basic UniFormat® categories.

The UniFormat® numbering system is as follows:

Level 1	A	SUBSTRUCTURE
Level 2	A10	Foundations
Level 3	A1010	Standard Foundations
Level 4	A1010.10	Wall Foundations
Level 5	A1010.10.CF, or A1010.10.03 30 00	Continuous Footing

Titles in Levels 1 through 3 can be applied to most preliminary project descriptions (PPDs) and preliminary cost estimates. Levels 4 and 5 are available for use on detailed, complex projects. Level 4 and 5 titles and detailed listings provide a checklist to ensure a comprehensive and complete application of UniFormat®.

At Level 1, the hierarchy comprises the major categories of construction information separated by their special function. These special functions include the nine Level 1 categories. The letters and titles of Level 1 categories are fixed and should not be changed when used in an application.

The first category, Project Description, does not have a letter designation, which allows it to appear first in the list of titles and distinguishes its contents from the other titles. The Project Description category is not a building system or assembly. Instead, it is a collection of basic information that allows users to introduce the project before reading details of systems and assemblies. Project Description contains bidding, proposal, and contract requirements and allows UniFormat® to be used as a stand-alone contracting structure for construction projects, especially design-build applications.

UniFormat® divides Level 1 categories into classes of information by separating them into the constituent parts that compose them. This method of classifying is known to information specialists as decomposition.

Level 2 classes carry the letter of their parent category, plus a two-digit number. Alphanumeric designations and titles of Level 2 classes are also fixed and should not be changed in application.

DOMAIN 1
Planning,
Development,
& Organization

DOMAIN 2
Coordination

DOMAIN 3
Procurement,
Contracting,
& General
Requirements

DOMAIN 4
Research

DOMAIN 5
Analysis
& Evaluation

DOMAIN 6
Production

Levels 3 and 4 are developed by further subdividing Level 2 classes. These subclasses carry the alphanumeric designation of their parent category and class, plus another two-digit number with the two-digit Level 4 numbers being set off by a decimal point. Alphanumeric designations and titles of Level 3 and 4 subclasses are also fixed and should not be changed in application. The user can create alphanumeric designations for Level 4 subclasses unassigned within a group of Level 3 subclasses.

Numbers and titles at Level 5 offer specialized design solutions of their parent Level 4 subclasses. Particular materials may be identified (e.g., concrete and steel) to differentiate one specialized solution from another. Titles at Level 5 are examples of information included in their Level 4 subclass.

No alphanumeric designation is assigned. Extensions may be assigned by the user. User-assigned Level 5 numbers should carry their parent Level 4 subclasses' alphanumeric designation, plus a two-digit number or the corresponding MasterFormat® number. Level 5 and, sometimes, Level 4 titles begin to correspond to the concepts contained in MasterFormat® numbers and titles. The numbering system can expand to allow for additional numbers and titles at any level. This flexibility allows UniFormat® to expand in the future and allows users to add titles and numbers for subjects not in the current edition. User-defined numbers and titles that fit within the established framework of UniFormat® can be added. Appendix D provides a list of Levels 1, 2, and 3 alphanumeric designations and titles from UniFormat®.

13.4.2 Applications

UniFormat® has many applications beyond those described next. UniFormat® is best suited for applications when the details of construction assemblies are not known. Other potential uses of UniFormat® include scheduling, value analysis, building performance, recording design data, structuring codes, as well as monitoring and managing design programs and costs.

13.4.2.1 Preliminary Project Descriptions (PPDs)

UniFormat® provides a system to describe a project by its basic systems and assemblies before

the particular materials and methods have been chosen. A/Es use this document to organize project descriptions and help estimators formulate early cost estimates. (See Section 4.5.2 of the *Project Delivery Practice Guide* for a detailed discussion on PPDs and CSI's PPDFormat®.)

Following are the basic underlying ideas behind the concept of the PPD:

- Written descriptions of the schematic design should be organized around systems and assemblies that correlate to general industry cost estimating methods for this phase.

- Written descriptions should allow design professionals to provide sufficient information for cost estimating without the necessity of making final design decisions.

- Written descriptions should document qualitative requirements for the project appropriate to the level of decision-making and detail in the design.

- Using an industry-standard organizational format provides a checklist to help design teams ensure all appropriate subjects are included.

In addition to providing more detail for preparing Preliminary Project Descriptions, PPDFormat® has additional material to respond to the following changes in the industry:

- Coordination with the latest edition of UniFormat®

- Building Information Modeling (BIM)

- Integrated Project Delivery (IPD)

13.4.2.2 Preliminary Cost Estimates

UniFormat® also serves as the basis for organizing preliminary cost estimates and aligns with the organization of PPDs. Familiarity with UniFormat® allows users to relate a PPD to cost data easily. There are commercially available cost data systems based on UniFormat®.

13.4.2.3 Drawing Detail Filing

UniFormat® also serves as a system for filing and retrieving drawing details. Because most details include multiple materials classified using MasterFormat®, it is challenging to file details under that system. UniFormat®, by contrast, is organized by elements, systems, and assemblies that relate to the element, system, or assembly depicted in a drawing detail. UniFormat® is used for the internal filing and retrieval of drawing details in an office that creates or uses drawing details—it is not proposed for use to identify details in a set of drawings.

13.5 MasterFormat®

MasterFormat®, jointly developed by the CSI and CSC, is an organizational structure providing numbers and titles for the variety of subject matter necessary for the construction, operation, and maintenance of a facility. MasterFormat® provides a system of six-digit and eight-digit numbers and titles for organizing construction information into a standard order or sequence. By establishing a master list of numbers and titles, MasterFormat® promotes standardization, facilitates the placement and retrieval of information, and improves construction communication. (See Appendix C for a list of MasterFormat® numbers and titles.)

13.5.1 Basic Organization

The numbers and titles in MasterFormat® are organized into two groups:

- Procurement and Contracting Requirements Group
- Specifications Group

The first group, Procurement and Contracting Requirements Group, is the location for introductory information and procurement information. It is also the location for information defining the relationships, responsibilities, and processes for construction. The second group, Specifications Group, provides the locations to describe administrative requirements and the physical aspects of construction.

13.5.2 Divisions

MasterFormat® arranges related construction practices, or work results, into a series of Level 1

titles called divisions. Several of these divisions are without contents or titles; they are reserved for potential future expansions in content. Central to the arrangement and use of MasterFormat® groups and the sections that make them up is that all of the different work results are addressed equally. The more basic or common divisions are generally placed near the beginning of MasterFormat®. These contain work results likely to be specified in all types of construction.

For example, all new building construction projects have contractual requirements and general requirements and are constructed using some types of materials. Later in MasterFormat® come the sub-groupings of divisions that contain work result sections that apply only to specific types of projects (building construction, heavy civil work, process plant construction, and the like). The only exception to this general rule is civil work; all projects reference sections in the Site and Infrastructure Subgroup, located in the "30-series" of divisions, for their civil work.

The basic organizational structure of MasterFormat® groups and subgroups, including division numbers and titles, is as follows:

Procurement and Contracting
Requirements Group
Division 00—Procurement and
Contracting Requirements
Specifications Group
General Requirements Subgroup:
Division 01—General Requirements
Facility Construction Subgroup:
Division 02—Existing Conditions
Division 03—Concrete
Division 04—Masonry
Division 05—Metals
Division 06—Wood, Plastics, and Composites
Division 07—Thermal and Moisture Protection
Division 08—Openings
Division 09—Finishes
Division 10—Specialties
Division 11—Equipment
Division 12—Furnishings

DOMAIN 1
Planning,
Development,
& Organization

DOMAIN 2
Coordination

DOMAIN 3
Procurement,
Contracting,
& General
Requirements

DOMAIN 4
Research

DOMAIN 5
Analysis
& Evaluation

DOMAIN 6
Production

Division 13 — Special Construction

Division 14 — Conveying Equipment

Division 15 — (Reserved)

Division 16 — (Reserved)

Division 17 — (Reserved)

Division 18 — (Reserved)

Division 19 — (Reserved)

Facility Services Subgroup:

Division 20 — (Reserved)

Division 21 — Fire Suppression

Division 22 — Plumbing

Division 23 — Heating, Ventilating, and
Air-Conditioning

Division 24 — (Reserved)

Division 25 — Integrated Automation

Division 26 — Electrical

Division 27 — Communications

Division 28 — Electronic Safety and Security

Division 29 — (Reserved)

Site and Infrastructure Subgroup:

Division 30 — (Reserved)

Division 31 — Earthwork

Division 32 — Exterior Improvements

Division 33 — Utilities

Division 34 — Transportation

Division 35 — Waterway and
Marine Construction

Division 36 — (Reserved)

Division 37 — (Reserved)

Division 38 — (Reserved)

Division 39 — (Reserved)

Process Equipment Subgroup:

Division 40 — Process Interconnections

Division 41 — Material Processing and
Handling Equipment

Division 42 — Process Heating, Cooling, and
Drying Equipment

Division 43 — Process Gas and Liquid Handling,
Purification, and Storage Equipment

Division 44 — Pollution and Waste
Control Equipment

Division 45 — Industry-Specific
Manufacturing Equipment

Division 46 — Water and Wastewater Equipment

Division 47 — (Reserved)

Division 48 — Electrical Power Generation

Division 49 — (Reserved)

13.5.3 Numbering

MasterFormat® uses three pairs of digits as a
numbering structure and allows for an additional
optional pair of digits for expansion.

Using the following MasterFormat® number and
title as an example, the paragraph explains how the
numbering system is organized.

- Section 03 20 00 — Concrete Reinforcing

The first two digits represent Level 1 Divisions, in
this case, Division 03 — Concrete. The next pair of
numbers, in this case, 20, represents Level 2. The
third pair, 00, represents Level 3 numbers. As pairs of
numbers represent each classification level, there is
room for expansion if required.

Items within the Procurement and Contracting
Requirements Group, Division 00, are not
specifications; they are documents. However,
MasterFormat® assigns standard locations and
numbers for these documents because they are usually
included in the project manual. For the remainder
of the project manual, Divisions 01 through 49 are
specifications and form the Specifications Group.
Divisions 02 through 49 are also referred to as
technical specifications.

It is not the intent of MasterFormat® to assign a
single standard location for materials, products,
or assemblies. Instead, MasterFormat® is a list of
titles representing construction practices or *work
results* that occur from the application of skills and
procedures to the materials, products, or assemblies.
Thus, different applications of the same product
can be found in different locations. For example,
plywood panels can be placed in Division 03 for
their function as concrete forms, in Division 06
for their application as interior finish paneling,
in Division 07 for their function as exterior
siding for weather protection, or in Division 27
as a telephone board. MasterFormat® provides a

fixed yet expandable framework for organizing specifications, a standard sequence for arranging specification sections, and an easy means for retrieving information.

MasterFormat® is typically updated on a biennial cycle. The specifier should stay apprised of CSI/CSC adjustments to numbers and titles.

13.5.4 Using MasterFormat®

A random designation system does not fulfill the needs of those who wish to standardize portions of their specifications, nor does it meet the requirements of those who use electronic media for data retrieval and automated processing. MasterFormat® provides an order that helps everyone involved in a construction project avoid this outcome and these potential communications disconnects.

13.5.5 Keyword Index

An alphabetical subject index is included in MasterFormat® as a convenient means of guiding the user in locating the proper grouping of titles for construction products and activities. References within the index use the six-digit classification number that designates the Level 1, 2, or 3 titles.

13.5.6 Applications

MasterFormat® is an organizing system with the flexibility to meet any particular company's needs, professional discipline, or project type. It is used by A/Es to organize project manuals and to help users of project manuals find information in standard locations. Estimators use it for organizing cost data, and it is suitable for either manual or electronic data management operations. It is used by A/E firms specializing in particular types of projects. Manufacturers and suppliers also use MasterFormat® to organize and identify product literature and market their products to users.

13.5.6.1 Specifications

MasterFormat® is most widely used for the purpose that drove its initial development: organizing specifications. Titles are provided in a logical sequence for the most common specification sections required for a construction project.

Use of the numbers and titles shown in MasterFormat® allow easy cross-referencing within the project manual because a section always has the same number and title. Sections can be written and reproduced at any time

DOMAIN 1
Planning,
Development,
& Organization

DOMAIN 2
Coordination

DOMAIN 3
Procurement,
Contracting,
& General
Requirements

DOMAIN 4
Research

DOMAIN 5
Analysis
& Evaluation

DOMAIN 6
Production

without renumbering the other sections in the project manual—one of the major advantages of using MasterFormat®.

Assembly of the final document in numerical sequence ensures the correct grouping of sections. For contractors and suppliers familiar with MasterFormat®, the retrieval of information during bidding and construction is faster, easier, and more thorough than with a non-standardized set of specifications.

The A/E using MasterFormat® can specify material or system work results or a combination of both. A system may be specified in a single Level 2 section, or the general system may be specified in a Level 2 section and its materials in several Level 3 sections. MasterFormat® has been developed to provide the A/E with a standard yet flexible system for organizing specifications and construction information.

MasterFormat® sections are not intended to correspond to a single trade or subcontractor work assigned by the contractor.

13.5.6.2 Data Filing

The system of numbers and titles serves to file and retrieve technical data and product literature organized by work results. Data filing under MasterFormat® is primarily concerned with the rapid retrieval of technical data related to products or work results being specified. Because the same system is used for data filing as for organizing specifications, it is easy to relate the filed material to the specifications being written for a project. MasterFormat® is used by many construction product manufacturers for their product literature, allowing their products to be related to the work result sections in which they are used.

13.5.6.3 Cost Classification

The number and title system serves as the basis for the organization of construction costs and parallels the organization of specifications. Familiarity with MasterFormat® and UniFormat® allows users to relate a specification section to product information and cost data.

13.5.6.4 Product Data

MasterFormat® has contributed significantly to standardization within the construction industry and is widely used to organize specifications, product literature, and cost information under a single classification system based on work results or construction practices. For a detailed discussion on the use of MasterFormat®, refer to the Introduction and Application Guide to MasterFormat®— Master List of Numbers and Titles for the Construction Industry.

13.5.7 Translating UniFormat® to MasterFormat®

There is a point during design when the written construction information needs to switch from UniFormat® to MasterFormat®. This point usually is at the design development phase when the PPDs, prepared during the schematic design phase, are used as a resource when preparing the outline specifications. Fortunately, UniFormat® provides a cross-reference to MasterFormat® Level 1 and 2 numbers within the document.

The specifier needs to be aware that systems and assemblies described in a PPD include materials, products, and components that are likely to be specified in several specification sections. For example, a curtain wall system may be described in the PPD under B2010.40— Fabricated Exterior Wall Assemblies. In reading the description, it is determined that it is a two-sided structural-sealant system on an aluminum framing system. It also includes aluminum-framed entrances with panic hardware and low-E insulated glazing. Per UniFormat®'s cross-reference to MasterFormat®, this system would be located in Section 08 44 00, which is titled Curtain Wall and Glazed Assemblies. Within MasterFormat®, Section 08 44 00 includes a Level 3 number and title, 08 44 13— Glazed Aluminum Curtain Walls.

Although the curtain wall framing, entrances, hardware, and glazing could be specified in a single section (08 44 13— Glazed Aluminum Curtain Walls), the entrances, hardware, and glazing may be used by other assemblies, such as a storefront system or hollow metal doors.

If that is the case, then 08 44 13 — Glazed Aluminum Curtain Walls is used for the curtain wall framing, 08 42 13 — Aluminum-Framed Entrances for the entrances, 08 71 00 — Door Hardware for the panic hardware, and 08 80 00 — Glazing for the low-E insulated glazing.

13.6 SectionFormat®

A uniform standard for arranging specification text in a project manual's sections is SectionFormat®. SectionFormat® is a three-part format. It reduces the chance of omissions or duplications in a specification section. (See Appendix E for a copy of SectionFormat®.)

13.6.1 Basic Organization

SectionFormat® provides a uniform approach to organizing specification text contained in a project manual. SectionFormat® assists in the organization of specification sections by establishing a structure consisting of three primary parts. These parts organize text consistently within each section. Although the format was developed to assist with the preparation of sections in Divisions 02 through 49, the principles also apply to sections in Division 01 — General Requirements (refer to Figure 13.2). A section is intended to cover one portion of the project requirements. It describes particular materials, products, systems, assemblies, installation, and administrative or procedural requirements. Individual sections with related items are grouped under the appropriate divisions within MasterFormat®. Specific sections are included in a project manual specification only as needed to meet the project requirements.

13.6.2 Parts

Written material within sections are divided into three parts:

PART 1 — GENERAL. This part describes the administrative, procedural, and temporary requirements unique to the section. PART 1 is an extension of subjects covered in Division 01 and amplifies information unique to the section.

PART 2 — PRODUCTS. This part describes products, materials, equipment, fabrications, mixes, systems, and assemblies required for incorporation into the project. Materials and products are included with their quality requirements.

PART 3 — EXECUTION. This part describes installation or application, including preparatory actions and post-installation cleaning and protection. Site-built assemblies and site-manufactured products and systems are included.

Sections are not intended to stand alone. They function with other portions of the procurement and contract documents and must relate to them. For example, PART 1 — GENERAL describes administrative and procedural requirements specific to the subject being covered. The requirements described in PART 1 should not duplicate statements that are contained in sections of Division 01. Each article and paragraph within PART 1 should supplement and coordinate with the applicable sections of Division 01 to avoid repetition or conflicting requirements.

13.7 PageFormat®

There are advantages to standardizing the way information is presented on a page. A standard page format provides an orderly and uniform arrangement of text for each page of a specification section. The standard page format has three objectives:

- To present text clearly and at a density best suited for easy reading and rapid reference
- To provide an acceptable standard suitable for use in specifications throughout the construction industry
- To provide a flexible format compatible with most current production techniques and electronic software

Uniformity of presentation eases preparation, review, and publication tasks and saves the specification user time and effort when searching for information. (See Appendix E for a copy of PageFormat®.)

DOMAIN 1
Planning,
Development,
& Organization

DOMAIN 2
Coordination

DOMAIN 3
Procurement,
Contracting,
& General
Requirements

DOMAIN 4
Research

DOMAIN 5
Analysis
& Evaluation

DOMAIN 6
Production

Figure 13.2
SectionFormat®
Outline

SECTIONFORMAT® OUTLINE

Standard Article titles in a section. **BOLD UPPERCASE**: Primary titles. Title Case: Subordinate titles that may be elevated to primary Article titles.

PART 1— GENERAL

SUMMARY
- Section Includes
- Products Furnished [OR] Supplied But Not Installed Under This Section
- Products Installed But Not Purnished [OR] Supplied Under This Section
- Related Requirements

PRICE AND PAYMENT PROCEDURES
- Allowances
- Unit Prices
- Alternates [OR] Alternatives
- Measurement and Payment

REFERENCES
- Abbreviations and Acronyms
- Definitions
- Reference Standards

ADMINISTRATIVE REQUIREMENTS
- Coordination
- Preinstallation Meetings
- Sequencing
- Scheduling

SUBMITTALS
ACTION SUBMITTALS/INFORMATIONAL SUBMITTALS
- Product Data
- Shop Drawings
- Samples
- Certificates
- Delegated Design Submittals
- Test and Evaluation Reports
- Manufacturers' Instructions
- Source Quality Control Submittals
- Field [OR] Site Quality Control Submittals
- Manufacturer Reports
- Sustainable Design Submittals
- Special Procedure Submittals
- Qualification Statements

CLOSEOUT SUBMITTALS
- Maintenance Contracts
- Operation and Maintenance Data
- Bonds
- Warranty Documentation
- Record Documentation
- Sustainable Design Closeout Documentation
- Software

MAINTENANCE MATERIAL SUBMITTALS
- Spare Parts
- Extra Stock Materials
- Tools

QUALITY ASSURANCE
- Regulatory Agency Sustainability Approvals
- Qualifications
  - Manufacturers
  - Suppliers
  - Fabricators
  - Installers/Applicators/Erectors
  - Testing Agencies
  - Licensed Professionals
- Certifications
- Sustainability Standards Certifications
- Preconstruetion Testing
- Field [OR] Site Samples
- Mock-ups

DELIVERY, STORAGE, AND HANDLING
- Delivery and Acceptance Requirements
- Storage and Handling Requirements
- Packaging Waste Management

FIELD [OR] SITE CONDITIONS
- Ambient Conditions
- Existing Conditions

WARRANTY [OR] BOND
- Manufacturer Warranty
- Special Warranty
- Extended Correction Period

Figure 13.2
SectionFormat®
Outline
(continued)

SECTIONFORMAT® OUTLINE

Standard Article titles in a section. **BOLD UPPERCASE**: Primary titles. Title Case: Subordinate titles that may be elevated to primary Article titles.

PART 2—PRODUCTS

OWNER-FURNISHED [OR] OWNER-SUPPLIED PRODUCTS
- New Products
- Existing Products

[SYSTEMS]/[ASSEMBLIES][MANUFACTURED UNITS]/[EQUIPMENT]/[COMPONENTS]/ [PRODUCT TYPES]/[MATERIALS]/[USER-DEFINED HEADING]

Manufacturers
- Manufacturer List
- Substitution Limitations
- Product Options

Description
- Regulatory Requirements
- Sustainability Characteristics

Performance/Design Criteria
- Capacities

Operation
- Operators
- Controls
- Operation Sequences

Materials

Assembly [OR] Fabrication
- Factory Assembly
- Shop Fabrication
- Assembly [OR] Fabrication Tolerances

Mixes

Finishes
- Primer Materials
- Finish Materials
- Shop Finishing Methods

ACCESSORIES

SOURCE QUALITY CONTROL
- Tests and Inspections
- Non-Conforming Work
- Manufacturer Services
- Coordination of Other Tests and Inspections

PART 3—EXECUTION

INSTALLERS
- Installer List
- Substitution Limitations

EXAMINATION
- Verification of Conditions
- Preinstallation Testing
- Evaluation and Assessment

PREPARATION
- Protection of In-Place Conditions
- Surface Preparation
- Demolition/Removal

[ERECTION]/[INSTALLATION]/ [APPLICATION]/[USER-DEFINED PROCESS]
- Special Techniques
- Interface with Other Work
- Systems Integration
- Tolerances

[REPAIR]/[RESTORATION]

REINSTALLATION

FIELD [OR] SITE QUALITY CONTROL
- Field [OR] Site Tests and Inspections
- Non-Conforming Work
- Manufacturer Services

SYSTEMS STARTUP

ADJUSTING

CLEANING
- Waste Management

CLOSEOUT ACTIVITIES
- Demonstration
- Training

PROTECTION

MAINTENANCE

ATTACHMENTS

END OF SECTION
- Schedules
- Tables
- Illustrations
- Forms

Chapter 14

SPECIFICATION METHODS

14.1 Methods of Specifying

There are four methods of specifying: descriptive, performance, reference standard, and proprietary.

Descriptive. Specifies properties of materials and methods of installation without using proprietary names. A descriptive specification is a detailed description of the characteristics, physical properties, and workmanship required to install a product or material. It generally requires technical knowledge and experience on the part of the architect/engineer (A/E).

Performance. Specifies the required results, the criteria by which the performance is judged, and the method by which it can be verified. The contractor is free to choose materials and methods complying with the performance criteria. A performance specification is a description of the required end result of a product or system and includes the criteria for verifying proper installation and performance. It is generally written to encourage the use of innovative techniques.

Reference Standard. Specifies products or processes by established standards. A reference standard specification uses recognized industry standards rather than individually written product or installation criteria. Standards must be reviewed carefully to avoid duplications and contradictions and to select required options.

Proprietary. Specifies products and materials using brand names, model numbers, and other proprietary information. Closed proprietary specifications do not allow for substitutions, but open proprietary specifications allow alternative products that meet the specified product's requirements.

Both the descriptive and proprietary specifying methods are used for prescriptive specifications; that is, the products and processes are specified, but not the results. Reference standards specifying can be used for prescriptive and performance specifications. However, performance specifications specify results and not the means to achieve them. Project specifications typically employ more than one

DOMAIN 1
Planning,
Development,
& Organization

DOMAIN 2
Coordination

DOMAIN 3
Procurement,
Contracting,
& General
Requirements

DOMAIN 4
Research

DOMAIN 5
Analysis
& Evaluation

DOMAIN 6
Production

specifying method. All four methods may be used in a single specification section. There is no clear rule for using either one method or a combination of methods. However, the A/E should be careful about combining methods in the specification of a single product. This approach can create redundancy or may result in a conflict incapable of resolution.

14.1.1 Descriptive Specifying

A descriptive specification is a detailed, written description of the required properties of a product, material, or piece of equipment, including the workmanship required for its installation. Proprietary names of manufacturers are not used.

A concrete mix of four-part coarse aggregate, two-part fine aggregate, and one-part cement with a 0.5 water-cement ratio is a descriptive specification. Performance strength of 3000 psi (20,684 kPa) after 28 days is implied in the design mix but not specified. Suppose concrete conforming to the descriptive specification was supplied but did not withstand a 3000 psi (20,684 kPa) load. In that case, the contractor could not be held responsible because only the design mix was specified. The burden of performance is assumed by the A/E when a descriptive specification is used. Once widely preferred, the descriptive method is being used less frequently as projects become more complex and better reference standards become available. Writing a descriptive specification is a lengthy and tedious process. However, when proprietary names are prohibited by law, and adequate reference standards do not exist, a descriptive specification may be the only logical choice.

14.1.1.1 Preparing Descriptive Specifications

There are five basic steps for preparing descriptive specifications:

1. Research available products.

2. Research essential features required. Analyze and compare requirements with available products.

3. Determine which features are best specified and which are best shown on the drawings.

4. Describe important features. State the requirements and ascertain that they can be met. Selecting and specifying unique features from several manufacturers' products may result in the description of a non-existent product. Avoid specifying irrelevant features.

5. Specify only information about submittals, testing, and other procedures necessary to ensure that acceptable products are provided. Do not require extensive shop drawings if catalog information is adequate. Do not require tests if a product certification suffices.

Figure 14.1 shows a portion of a descriptive specification for a shelf support assembly. Information on the location, length, and spacing of the supports would be shown on the drawings.

14.1.2 Performance Specifying

A requirement of 3000 psi (20,684 kPa) concrete strength is a performance specification. The end result, rather than the means-to-the-end result, is specified. A performance specification is defined as a statement of required results with criteria for verifying compliance but without unnecessary limitations on the methods for achieving the required results.

A statement of required results means that desired end results must be spelled out. An incomplete performance specification may lead to a significant loss of quality control over the materials, equipment, and workmanship for a project.

With criteria for verifying compliance means that the criteria are capable of measurement, test, evaluation, or other acceptable assurances. Measurement and testing may be done before production, at the time of production, in place at the site, or after a period of service.

Without unnecessary limitations on the methods for achieving the required results means that only essential restrictions are placed on the system. Limitations on the means should be avoided. Performance specifying should keep specific material and process descriptions to a minimum to encourage new means to achieve desired results.

Figure 14.1
Sample of a
Descriptive
Specification

PART 2—PRODUCTS

2.01 SHELF STANDARDS

A. Standards:

1. Surface-mounted, projecting 25mm (1 inch) maximum from finished surface.
2. Mounting screws spaced 300mm (12 inches) apart maximum.
3. Slots for shelf adjustment on approximate 25mm (1 inch) centers.
4. Finish: Gold anodized aluminum.

B. Mounting Screws:

1. Size: No. 8 by 40mm (1-1/2 inch) long.
2. Type: Steel wood screws.
3. Finish: Match standards.

C. Shelf Brackets:

1. Size: Suitable for 200mm (8 inches) wide shelves.
2. Depth at Butt: 75mm (3 inches) maximum.
3. Depth at Tip: 25mm (1 inch) maximum.
4. Attachment: Rigid engagement of lugs into 2 slots of standard.

DOMAIN 1
Planning,
Development,
& Organization

DOMAIN 2
Coordination

DOMAIN 3
Procurement,
Contracting,
& General
Requirements

DOMAIN 4
Research

DOMAIN 5
Analysis
& Evaluation

DOMAIN 6
Production

14.1.2.1 Application of Performance Specifying

The term performance specifying as related to project specifications has two applications. First, simple performance criteria can be incorporated into any specification, even one that generally describes what is wanted. A ceiling hanger may be performance specified as "non-sag" rather than descriptively as "straightened No. 11 wire, tightly wrapped two times."

In its second and broader application, performance specifying is a way of obtaining improved products and methods by stating the desired result and leaving the means to the innovative producer or contractor. What is often specified in this case is a systems approach.

Where performance specifying is the primary mode of design and contracting, specialized contract documents are often required. Contract procedures are more complex and often involve a variety of participants. Performance specifying could include complete project manuals using performance specifications for the design-build project delivery method. (See Section 14.2 for preparing performance-based specifications and project manuals.)

It is possible to successfully combine performance specifying and descriptive specifying in the same project. Some products may be specified with descriptions of components, and other products with performance statements.

Suppose it is known how a specific item performs. In that case, it is not difficult to work backward and describe its performance in sufficient detail so that bidders or proposers exactly know which product is desired. In such cases, the specification's writing takes much more time and effort and secures nothing better than what would result from descriptive or proprietary specifying. It is much easier to ask for a "10-gage galvanized, annealed steel wire" than to specify each performance criterion.

It is crucial that the performance requirements stipulated can be met. Establishing criteria that no manufacturer can meet would result in unachievable requirements.

14.1.2.2 Decision to Use Performance Specifying

Early in the planning process, the owner and the A/E should determine the project's suitability for the use of performance specifying. The owner's needs may make performance specifications feasible for several reasons:

- To expedite construction and access a wide range of options using existing technology and systems techniques

- To utilize technology that has not yet become standardized within the construction industry

- To develop new technology

- To delegate technical design responsibilities to industry specialists

Performance specifying is a method of indicating characteristics and requirements with measurable properties. Performance specifying can be extended from a single attribute to an entire project, with numerous variations in between. By specifying the end result, performance specifying provides flexibility in optional solutions that meet the same requirements. Various codes and standards are moving toward more performance criteria.

14.1.3 Reference Standard Specifying

Reference standard specifying establishes material, product, and installation requirements by referencing an industry-accepted standard rather than writing detailed requirements in the specification section. Many product manufacturers are familiar with the reference standards that shape and steer the development of products. By referencing a standard to establish minimum requirements, the specifier has more confidence in the outcome of a product's use in the project. However, once it is determined through product research that a reference standard is to be used within a specification (see Section 8.11), the specifier must properly incorporate it into the specification section.

14.1.3.1 Incorporate the Standard Properly

Properly incorporating standards requires the use of designations that distinguish each standard from all the others. A complete designation includes the following:

- Name of the issuing organization

- Number of the standard

- Title of the standard

- Date of issue of the standard

- Citation of applicable requirements, unless the entire standard is required

A standard's issuing organization is often indicated by its initials or abbreviation. Many organizations and their abbreviations are well known; others are not so widely recognized. It is appropriate to spell out the organization's name and its initials or abbreviation in parentheses when it is first mentioned in the specification section (see Figure 14.2, Option 1). A second option is to define all abbreviations of reference standards organizations in Division 01, Section 01 42 00 — References (see Figure 14.2, Option 2). Section 01 42 00 may also include the organizations' addresses whose standards are referenced in the project manual. The reference standard should be designated as it is printed on the actual standard.

Incorporating a standard into the specifications by reference takes advantage of an established body of industry knowledge and saves the A/E from writing detailed and lengthy specifications. When using a reference standard in the specifications, caution should be exercised according to the following criteria:

- Reference standards can create duplication and contradiction within the contract documents.

- Reference standards can contain embedded options.

- Reference standards generally refer to minimum requirements.

- Reference standards might contain undesired requirements.

- The authorities having jurisdiction (AHJs) may enforce different editions of the same reference standard, which might have conflicting requirements.

When the standard is referenced in a specification section, its complete designation should be included in the "References" article in PART 1 — GENERAL as described in SectionFormat®. Subsequent references to the standard in PART 2 — PRODUCTS and PART 3 — EXECUTION are referenced only by the number. The complete listing of standards referred to in PART 2 and PART 3 under the "References" article facilitates the gathering of reference materials. This listing of references can contain addresses to websites where the standards are available for view or purchase. The shorter references in PARTS 2 and 3 save time, effort, and space. The standards shown in Figure 14.2 would be referenced in PARTS 2 and 3 of the specification section as ACI 301, ACI 304R, ASTM C33/C33M, and ASTM C150/C150M.

14.1.3.2 Use of Dates

Standards are revised periodically. The revisions are dated with the year and sometimes the month of issue. As shown in Figure 14.2, Option 1, for ASTM C33/C33M-18 and ASTM C150/C150M-20, the "18" and "20" indicate that the standards were revised and republished in 2018 and 2020, respectively. There are two approaches to setting the dates of reference standards. One is to include the dates of reference standards (see Figure 14.2, Option 1). The A/E implies that the standard referenced edition fulfills the project's requirements by including the dates. It is the A/E's responsibility to determine the date of the applicable or latest edition. This task is made easier because standards organizations typically publish periodic catalogs. The A/E should not merely alter a publication date without reviewing the changes that have been made to the standard. A possible problem with stating dates is that standards current when the specification is prepared may be revised by the time the project is bid or construction begins. Additionally, AHJs might not have adopted or enforced the latest edition of a standard.

The second approach (see Figure 14.2, Option 2) is not to list publication dates for reference standards. This action alone is not recommended, as numerous editions of the same standard could result in

DOMAIN 1
Planning,
Development,
& Organization

DOMAIN 2
Coordination

DOMAIN 3
Procurement,
Contracting,
& General
Requirements

DOMAIN 4
Research

DOMAIN 5
Analysis
& Evaluation

DOMAIN 6
Production

Figure 14.2
Alternative
Methods for
Incorporating
Reference
Standards

OPTION 1

1.05 REFERENCES

A. American Concrete Institute International (ACI):

   1. 301-16   Specification for Structural Concrete for Buildings.
   2. 304R-00   Guide for Measuring, Mixing, Transporting, and Placing Concrete.

B. International (ASTM):

   1. C33/C33M-18   Standard Specification for Concrete Aggregates.
   2. C150/C150M-20 Standard Specification for Portland Cement.

OPTION 2

1.05 REFERENCES

A. ACI 301   **Specification for Structural Concrete for Buildings.**
B. ACI 304R   **Guide for Measuring, Mixing, Transporting, and Placing Concrete.**
C. ASTM C33/C33M   **Standard Specification for Concrete Aggregates.**
D. ASTM C150/C150M **Standard Specification for Portland Cement.**

Note: It is recommended that if "Option 2" is used, a general statement in Division 01 - General Requirements should be included to establish the dates of the standards referenced.

contradictions. A solution to this problem is to use the following statement in Section 01 42 00 — References: "The date of the standard is that in effect as of the date of receipt of bids for the project or as adopted by the authorities having jurisdiction." With such a statement, the contractor becomes responsible for checking for compliance.

14.1.3.3 Tentative Draft Standards

Standards listed as "tentative" have been approved by the sponsoring organization but are awaiting final approval by its membership or other concerned stakeholders. Tentative draft standards usually represent the latest thoughts and practices of the sponsoring organization. Tentative draft standards are usually not accepted by AHJs. A/Es should use tentative standards with caution because of their unofficial status.

14.1.3.4 Quoting Selected Parts of Standards

The practice of referencing a standard and then quoting supposedly pertinent portions of it should be avoided since it may be incorrectly quoted. Further, the reader may believe that only the quoted parts

apply. Similarly, a specific clause in a standard should not be referenced unless the specification modifies that clause's requirements.

14.1.3.5 Enforce the Requirements of the Standard

Once specified, effective means must be provided to ensure conformance with the requirements of the standards. Usual methods include checking shop drawings, samples, manufacturer's literature, test reports, and other required submittals, plus periodic on-site observations by construction contract administrators or knowledgeable design team members.

14.1.4 Proprietary Specifying

Proprietary specifications identify the desired products by manufacturer's name, brand name, model number, type designation, or other unique characteristics. However, when a manufacturer's name is not stated, a specification is still considered proprietary if the product specified is available from only one source. Advantages of proprietary specifications are as follows:

DOMAIN 1
Planning,
Development,
& Organization

DOMAIN 2
Coordination

DOMAIN 3
Procurement,
Contracting,
& General
Requirements

DOMAIN 4
Research

DOMAIN 5
Analysis
& Evaluation

DOMAIN 6
Production

- Product selection can be closely controlled.

- More detailed and complete drawings can be prepared based on precise information obtained from the selected manufacturer's data.

- Reduced cost and time benefits may be obtained by using shorter specifications and minimizing drawing production effort.

- Bidding might be simplified by narrowing competition and removing product pricing as a major variable.

Disadvantages of proprietary specifications include the following:

- Competition for products is reduced or eliminated.

- Products may be specified with which the contractor may have had little or a negative experience.

- Certain products and manufacturers may be favored over others.

- An error might occur when specifying model or product designations.

- Product may no longer be available.

Proprietary specifications can be issued in two forms: closed proprietary and open proprietary. The fundamental distinction between closed and open proprietary specifications is how they handle substitutions. Closed proprietary specifications generally prohibit substitutions, whereas open specifications permit them. Different specifying objectives are served by each method. In the closed specification, the A/E is sure that the named products are provided. On the other hand, using named products in open specifications indicates the desired properties and minimum requirements.

Closed Proprietary Specification:

- Only one product is named.

- One or more products are named as options.

- Substitutions are not allowed.

Open Proprietary Specification:

- One or more products are named.

- The bidders may propose substitutions.

- A/E approves acceptable substitutions.

14.1.4.1 Closed Proprietary Specifications

The closed proprietary specification permits the design to be completed to a high level of detail. This detailed level reduces variables and promotes accurate pricing; however, it does not offer protection against possible higher costs. The supplier of a specified proprietary product could take unfair advantage of being the sole source and increase its price. Another difficulty occurs when a contractor is obliged to use a product with which it has had an unsatisfactory experience, such as slow delivery, lack of proper technical services, or difficult payment arrangements. Claims of collusion between the A/E and a sole-source supplier could also be raised.

A closed proprietary specification can list one product or name several products as options. In either case, substitutions are not allowed. The control of the products and substitutions is accomplished by cross-reference in the instructions for procurement to Section 01 25 13—Product Substitution Procedures, which provides statements similar to the following:

> **One Product.** Where a product is specified by naming only one manufacturer, no substitute product will be considered. Bids must be based on the named product.

> **Optional Products.** Where products are specified by naming several manufacturers, no substitutes will be considered. Bids must be based on one of the named products.

Under the optional product approach, the successful contractor may be required to submit a product selection list when the bids are received or within a few days after the bid opening.

The listing of several optional products overcomes many of the objections raised when only one product is specified. If at least three products are named, competition may be achieved; however, the A/E must ensure that the named products are comparable and acceptable.

14.1.4.2 Open Proprietary Specifications

Open proprietary specifications may alleviate the problem of overpriced sole-source items.

Requested Alternates. There are several ways that proprietary specifications can be opened to allow alternate products. One method is to request proposals for alternate products. This form of proprietary specification defines the materials in the same way as a closed specification (i.e., only one brand is named for each material or item of equipment specified). Alternates to the specified products are named in the specification. The proposals submitted must be for the base-bid items, but the bidder may list prices for specified alternates. Space for quoting alternates should be provided on the bid form. A statement similar to the following might be used in the instructions for procurement:

- Where a product is specified by naming only one manufacturer, substitute products will not be considered.

- Where alternates to the base-bid products are requested, bidders may list prices for alternates on the bid form. Bid price for each alternate product must include amount required to incorporate alternate product in the project. Requests for additional money for alternates after execution of agreement will not be considered.

This method allows the bidder/proposer to select alternates and quote prices for preferred items. It may or may not be mandatory for the bidders/proposers to quote on all requested alternates.

The terms alternate and substitute are often misused. An alternate is something that is named for which alternative pricing is requested; a substitute is something that is requested to replace an item specified.

Proposed Substitutions. This form of open proprietary specification is prepared in much the same way as a specification requesting alternates. However, no alternates are named in the specifications. The bid/proposal must be based on the specified materials. However, the bidder/proposer is permitted to submit requests for substitutions, provided the bidder/proposer indicates the difference in cost if the substitutions are accepted. Substitutions must include product name, nomenclature, manufacturer name, and complete specifications and descriptive data. If the number of substitutions is unlimited, the task of evaluating and analyzing bids/proposals may become quite large.

A page should be included with the bid form for listing proposed substitutions. The following paragraphs in the instructions to bidders help to eliminate the indiscriminate listing of products that the A/E must evaluate and help to ensure that the proposed substitutions are worth considering:

- Bids shall be based on the specified products. However, bidders are encouraged to quote on substitute products by listing them on the substitution page of the bid form and by indicating the cost increase or decrease. Substitutions will not be considered after award of contract.

- The specified products have been used to prepare the drawings and specifications and establish minimum qualities that substitutions must meet to qualify as acceptable.

- Proof of comparability rests with the bidder, and adequate supporting information must accompany the bid.

- The bid price for each proposed substitution shall include all costs required to incorporate the substitution into the project. Later requests for additional money for substitutions will not be considered.

Controlled Substitutions. In this type of open proprietary specification, specific products are named, but substitutions are allowed under procedures specified in Section 01 25 13 — Product Substitution Procedures. A requirement may be met with the specified item or a similar product that is not necessarily identical but similar in performance (i.e., a comparable product). This method saves time during the development of a specification because only one product needs to be investigated and specified for each requirement.

The principal problem associated with this type of proprietary specification is that attempts are often made to substitute materials of different characteristics or requirements than those specified.

DOMAIN 1
Planning,
Development,
& Organization

DOMAIN 2
Coordination

DOMAIN 3
Procurement,
Contracting,
& General
Requirements

DOMAIN 4
Research

DOMAIN 5
Analysis
& Evaluation

DOMAIN 6
Production

This problem can occur when the time to submit proposed substitutions is improperly or inadequately specified. A weak specification is one that allows the contractor to propose substitutions after the contract award. This practice leads to additional bid shopping and pressure on the A/E to accept many substitutions. The owner may sometimes end up with substitute products with different characteristics. However, the owner may request that substitutions be allowed after contract execution. In that case, Section 01 25 13 should stipulate a minimum length of time that substitutions may be considered after contract execution.

The A/E's control over substitutions can be enhanced by including provisions in the instructions to bidders/proposers that address the following requirements:

- Substitution requests from bidders/proposers are in writing.

- Requests from manufacturers and suppliers are not considered.

- A definite deadline for the submittal of requests for substitutions is established.

- Submittal of supporting data by the bidders/ proposers is required.

- A written acceptance of substitutions is issued to all bidders/proposers by an addendum.

Establishing the deadline for requests is the prerogative of the A/E. For many projects, the established date indicated for accepting substitutions determines the time limit for product substitution requests. At least three days between the deadline and addendum publication should be allowed for proper consideration.

The requirements and procedures for requesting substitutions are best specified in Section 01 25 13—Product Substitution Procedures. This section can be used to define limitations on substitutions, contractor's representation in requesting substitutions, the method for requesting substitutions, and submission procedures. While some government agencies require that proprietary names used in the specifications be followed by phrases such as "or approved equal," "or equivalent," and "or equal," this is redundant if the project manual contains a comprehensive Section 01 25 13. The Construction Specifications Institute (CSI) principle of "say it once and in the right place" again applies.

The instructions to bidders/proposers should state times for submitting requests for substitutions during the bid/proposal period; however, they should cross-reference to Section 01 25 13 for other requirements and procedures.

The following statement may be used in the instructions to bidders/proposers for this purpose:

> The specified products establish minimum requirements that substitutions must meet to be considered acceptable. To obtain acceptance of unspecified products, submit written requests at least 10 days before the [bid] [proposal] date. Requests received after this time will not be considered. Refer to Section 01 25 13 — Product Substitution Procedures for requirements and procedures for requesting substitutions.

The proprietary specification may be extended by including descriptive requirements of the specified products in addition to the brand name and nomenclature. Substitutions must meet these requirements. When the characteristics of products are specified in this manner, they establish a basis for acceptance or rejection of proposed substitutions within the specifications.

14.1.4.3 Selection of Proprietary Methods

Many useful proprietary techniques consider the bidder/proposer's right to select products. The closed method generally gives the bidder/proposer little or no choice. The open method gives the bidder/proposer a broader choice.

The acceptance of substitutions opens the project to the possibility of accepting unknown and perhaps inferior products. If the specified item is part of a vital system, the situation may call for a proprietary specification prohibiting substitutions entirely. However, if keen competition and low construction cost are more critical than assured performance, then substitutions should be permitted.

Open specifications generally place a more significant workload on the A/E, increasing in direct proportion to the degree of choice available to the bidders/proposers. From the standpoint of reducing the design and specifying effort, the closed proprietary method is best. Because only one product is named for each application, the drawings and specifications can be completed quickly and

precisely. There is no need to accommodate several combinations or construction options.

When substitutions are allowed, competition is keenest. Material costs are nearly certain to be less, but this method is conducive to permitting products of lesser requirements. For example, the apparent savings can easily be lost through subsequent high maintenance and replacement costs. These considerations reinforce the conviction that the A/E should carefully word the procurement documents to provide a definite, controllable method for exercising review and approval over what is accepted as a substitution.

Specifying a proprietary item establishes a basis for determining quality, including performance, appearance, and cost. A proprietary name also indicates that the designer considered the specified product's characteristics, decided upon its incorporation into the project, and used its dimensions to prepare the drawings. Any coordination effort resulting from the use of a contractor-proposed substitution should be the responsibility of the contractor.

14.1.4.4 Non-restrictive Specifications

The federal government and some other public authorities restrict using proprietary or exclusionary specifications except under exceptional circumstances. A typical public law — in this case, the one providing for federal participation in the financing of wastewater treatment plants — includes the following language:

> Reference in the specifications to equipment, material, articles, or patented processes by trade name, make, or catalog number shall be regarded as establishing a standard of quality and shall not be construed as limiting competition. The Contractor may, at its option, use any equipment, material, article, or process that, in the judgment of the Contracting Officer, is equal to that named in the specifications, unless otherwise specifically provided in this contract.

Non-restrictive specifications may be developed from descriptive, performance, reference standard, proprietary specifications, or any combination of

Construction
Specifications
Practice Guide

DOMAIN 1
Planning,
Development,
& Organization

DOMAIN 2
Coordination

DOMAIN 3
Procurement,
Contracting,
& General
Requirements

DOMAIN 4
Research

DOMAIN 5
Analysis
& Evaluation

DOMAIN 6
Production

these four methods. Descriptive and performance specifications can easily be used for non-restrictive specifications. However, care must be taken to ensure that several manufacturers or suppliers can meet descriptive and performance requirements. Failure to do so makes the specifications restrictive, even though a proprietary name has not been used.

A proprietary specification masquerading as a performance specification is not non-restrictive. This specification is created when the A/E deletes the product's identifying name and then lists the salient qualities verbatim from the manufacturer's literature as product requirements. Since no ranges of characteristics and performance are given, this method results in a fully proprietary, closed specification and is not a suitable solution for a non-restrictive project. Several methods of converting a closed proprietary specification into a non-restrictive specification have been used by A/Es practicing in public works fields. Public agencies usually require a minimum of three brand names followed by the words "or equal," along with descriptions of the salient characteristics of the item specified to provide a basis for judging equality.

Another method is the appendage of "or equal" to every manufacturer's name. This method is awkward and redundant. A single paragraph in Division 01 is more effective than the repetition of "or equal" throughout the specifications. A paragraph covering substitutions should be included in the instructions to bidders and Section 01 25 00 — Substitution Procedures. The following paragraph is typical:

> Whenever a product is specified using a proprietary name or a particular manufacturer or vendor's name, the specific item mentioned shall be understood as establishing type, function, dimension, appearance, and quality desired. Other manufacturers' products might be accepted, provided sufficient information is submitted to allow the A/E to determine that products proposed are comparable to those named.

14.2 Performance Specifications

As stated in Section 14.1.2, performance specifying indicates characteristics and requirements with measurable properties. Performance specifying can be extended from a single attribute to an entire project, with numerous variations in between. By specifying the end result, performance specifying provides flexibility in optional solutions that meet the same requirements. However, describing performance specifying is easy — putting it into an actual application, such as an entire specification section, can be challenging for those with little experience in performance specifying.

14.2.1 Construction Systems and Assemblies

Performance specifying can be used to specify complete systems and assemblies as well as components and construction products. Performance specifying might be applied in this context for a variety of reasons. The owner may need to expedite construction by seeking complete construction systems and assemblies or seeking the broadest range of products and construction methods available. Increased competition for products and the use of efficient construction technology may also provide cost savings. Using available products and systems for conventional project requirements is a primary advantage of performance specifying. By utilizing existing technology, performance specifying is practical even for smaller projects and can apply to a complete project or portions of a project. Entire systems and assemblies may require specialized engineering and performance-based criteria. This level of performance specifying may be subject to licensure and regulation by AHJs.

14.2.2 Utilizing Non-standard Technologies

Many products and systems emerge from research and development before they evolve into standard configurations or solutions. Although they may not be entirely new technologies, their development and use may be at a stage where no alternatives

DOMAIN 1
Planning,
Development,
& Organization

DOMAIN 2
Coordination

DOMAIN 3
Procurement,
Contracting,
& General
Requirements

DOMAIN 4
Research

DOMAIN 5
Analysis
& Evaluation

DOMAIN 6
Production

are similar enough to specify descriptively without excluding other variations of that system. Some examples include alternative energy systems, environmental control systems, building monitoring systems, and data and communication systems. When the A/E is not familiar with specialized products to describe the best solution, performance specifying may help. As sustainable design certifications such as Leadership in Energy and Environmental Design (LEED) for structures and Envision for infrastructures become more commonplace, alternative solutions to the traditional construction are required. Green roofs are an example of non-traditional roofing and require reconsideration of traditional roofing requirements.

14.2.3 Developing New Technology

Where existing products, techniques, or processes do not suit the owner's needs, innovation must be encouraged. Shortcomings in available technology may relate to technical capabilities, construction cost, or expediency. Performance specifying in this context gives the owner the advantage of attracting research-and-development expertise and resources from many construction industry elements. New technologies and products are being developed to meet the performance requirements of sustainable and green projects. New technologies include materials consisting of recycled pre-consumer and post-consumer waste. These new materials can be utilized by providing performance requirements describing the salient characteristics.

There are also disadvantages for the owner involving the time and expense of developing requirements, solicitation, research, design and development, and prototype tests. The requirements must also gain economies of scale of the newly developed technology because considerable expense might be incurred in producing a unique product, system, or assembly. The feasibility of using performance specifications to develop new technology is generally limited to large corporate owners or public agencies with a high volume of construction. Specifying a new technology that has not been previously developed does include a risk that some companies might not be willing to take.

14.2.4 Delegating Responsibilities

In many instances, an owner may not wish to assume full involvement in the facility's design and construction. Many owners with extensive, ongoing construction programs maintain architectural or engineering departments but do not assume full design or construction responsibilities and may pass those responsibilities to the supplier. An owner can utilize performance specifying to establish the owner's requirements for a project using the design-build project delivery method. The owner delegates the final design and construction tasks to the design-builder using performance criteria, ensuring the owner's needs are met through well-developed performance specifications.

14.2.5 Roles of Participants

Performance-oriented design, construction documentation, procurement, and contracting may alter some of the traditional roles and responsibilities customarily assumed by participants in the construction delivery process.

14.2.5.1 Owner

The owner's project requirements and needs are the primary concerns regardless of the project type, specifying method, or project delivery method selected. Depending on the project type, the owner may begin the project by defining the project requirements via performance criteria. The performance criteria might then be utilized to prepare a request for proposals using the design-build project delivery method. Under other delivery methods, performance specifying may provide flexibility and alternative solutions through traditional construction documents. Using performance criteria, the owner relinquishes some control over the solution. Under this process, the owner must be willing to accept the results of performance criteria. Therefore, to ensure satisfaction with results, the owner must be able to communicate the criteria thoroughly. This performance specifying feature may encourage the owner to perform a more comprehensive analysis of needs than might be done in a traditional relationship.

14.2.5.2 Architect/Engineer

Depending on the project delivery method, the A/E might be a part of a design-build entity providing design in response to the owner's performance-based project requirements. In the traditional design role, the A/E may determine that particular elements are performance specified. The A/E must know what performance levels result in a satisfactory solution and know standards, tests, and verification methods. Performance specifying may also be a form of design transfer. This situation is frequently the case with engineered elements such as wood or metal trusses, precast concrete, and certain foundations. Some states may have regulations that limit the transfer of design from the A/E of record.

14.2.5.3 Construction Manager as Advisor/Agent

When a construction manager as advisor/agent is involved in the project delivery, the CM-advisor/agent might assume the task of coordinating multiple-prime contracts. The CM-advisor/agent might deal with both performance elements and the descriptive items' interface with those performance elements. Details of some items may not be known before releasing the documents for procurement. Thus, the CM-advisor/agent is involved in administering the procurement of performance items, interfacing these with traditionally designed items, and coordinating with the A/E on design matters.

14.2.5.4 Contractor

Contractors have different responsibilities when responding to performance criteria. The contractor might be a part of a design-build entity where an A/E is also part of that entity and involved in providing solutions to the owner's performance criteria. The contractor or design-builder must be able to generate solutions within the bounds of performance criteria. This solution generation requires design and engineering capabilities and may also require closer collaboration with suppliers and manufacturers to acquire additional engineering support for particular solutions.

If a contractor is bidding or proposing only on a specific system or component as one of the multiple-prime contracts, there may be unknown interfaces with other systems. The successful contractor is then responsible for resolving these details after awarding the contract and completing traditional detailing. Generally, performance-based requirements will not significantly affect labor participation. A possible exception would be the extensive use of prefabricated systems built mostly in the factory rather than on-site. The overall amount of work to be performed, however, is essentially unchanged. Many systems, assembly, and component manufacturers retain erection and installation workers whose work must be coordinated with other systems and assemblies.

14.2.5.5 Manufacturer

Performance specifications affect manufacturers by placing competing products on the common ground of performance. Manufacturers are responsible for submitting proof of the product's compliance with specified performance criteria through contractual lines. A product's use is based on performance rather than on an effective advertising campaign. Manufacturers might be placed in a situation in which they provide additional assistance such as design services. Manufacturers of systems or products may, for example, provide engineering to size their products and meet specific criteria or codes. In some cases, the manufacturer might also provide specialized installation.

14.2.5.6 Authorities Having Jurisdiction

In performance-based procurement, AHJs generally do not have complete construction documents for review at the time of permit application or code reviews. Final documentation is often not completed until sometime after the contract is awarded and construction has begun. In such cases, AHJs review the available definitive materials and the performance specifications for code conformance. If no conflicts are in evidence, they may be asked to issue permits contingent on inspection and final documentation approval.

Construction
Specifications
Practice Guide

DOMAIN 1
Planning,
Development,
& Organization

DOMAIN 2
Coordination

DOMAIN 3
Procurement,
Contracting,
& General
Requirements

DOMAIN 4
Research

DOMAIN 5
Analysis
& Evaluation

DOMAIN 6
Production

14.2.6 Determining the Extent

Determining the extent of a performance specification involves two interdependent decisions:

- The elements (pieces, parts, components, assemblies, and systems) to be performance specified

- The extent to which those elements are performance specified

Entire structures can be performance specified. Some projects may have only selected subsystems specified in performance terms, whereas other specifying methods are better suited for the project's remainder. The extent of performance specifying that best suits the owner's needs should be determined early in the project life cycle.

14.2.7 Performance Specifying of Project Elements

The first determination is which elements of a project, if any, should be specified in performance terms. Which elements provide a range of available options where competition among those options provides optimum solutions? The question applies to any project element scale (i.e., part, component, assembly, or system). For example, a performance specification might permit any material components that support specific wind loads. Performance specifying might also permit a choice of load-bearing structural systems. Where a range of options is available, the following conditions favor the use of performance specifications:

- No single, distinct solution is recognized as an exclusive choice in terms of material, configuration, or technique.

- Costs of options are reasonably competitive.

- A system or assembly is a substantial portion of the entire project and does not necessitate a configuration or require such specificity to preclude options.

Performance specifications may also offer advantages under the following conditions:

- A project element embodies a technology where the current state-of-the-art has not yet provided a standard solution for a given situation.

- Development beyond the current state-of-the-art is required of an existing product or construction item.

- Nothing exists on the market that satisfies the owner's design or construction needs.

14.2.8 Levels of Performance Specifying

Figure 14.3 shows a range of specifying modes from full descriptive to full performance specifications. The broadest levels of performance specifying (H and J) are generally used only in design-build contracts.

The middle levels (D through G) are the broadest practical levels typically used in traditional construction documents. Functional elements of the project are identified as systems, subsystems, assemblies, or components. Statements of functional requirements are attached to these elements and qualified with technical criteria.

The narrowest levels of performance specifying (B and C) are practical for use in most construction but, in some cases, that might be too restrictive to allow the manufacturers to be innovative. Specific components or products are identified, and technical criteria are tailored to that type of component. Specifications based on MasterFormat® and UniFormat® should not be combined into a single project manual. MasterFormat® Section 01 80 00 can be utilized to specify overall performance requirements.

14.2.8.1 Establishing the Level of Performance Specifying

Establishing the level of performance specifying depends on how much latitude is permitted in the results. Figure 14.3 also illustrates the range of control the A/E may exercise for any given construction item. Greater control over the element's configuration is retained by using a narrow degree of performance specifying. In this case, the particular type of subsystem, component, or item — such as

Figure 14.3
Levels of
Performance
Specifying

		Performance/Descriptive Mixture	Sample Text
Typical Specification Using *MasterFormat*®	Conventional Specifying Degree to which sample support requirements can be performance specified	**A** Total project specified in descriptive terms.	10-gage galvanized annealed steel wire hangers spaced 4 ft.o.c. both ways.
		B Descriptive with performance criteria.	Galvanized annealed steel wire hangers of size and attachment sufficient to support 60 lb. each and spaced 4 ft. 0 in.o.c. both ways.
		C Descriptive with performance criteria.	Galvanized annealed steel wire hangers of size spacing and attachment sufficient to support a uniform ceiling load of 7.5 lbs/s.f.
		D A major assembly specified in *MasterFormat*® as a self-contained component.	Integrated ceiling… capable of supporting based load + 6 lbs/s.f. live load.
		E Several major assemblies specified in *MasterFormat*® with interface required.[1]	Integrated ceiling… capable of supporting dead load + 6 lbs/s.f. live load … with key slots along building module lines in order to receive top rail of partitions.
Design-Build statement of system based on *UniFormat*®	Degree to which systems projects can be performance specified	**F** Major components specified as UniFormat® systems with interface required.	Ceiling/illumination/HY AC component… capable of supporting dead load + 6 lbs/s.f. live load … capable of supporting partitions at any building module line capable of…etc.
		G Descriptive with performance criteria.	Ceiling/illumination/HY AC component… capable of supporting dead load + 6 lbs/s.f. live load… capable of supporting partitions at any building module line capable of…etc.
		H Total project(s) specified to be developed as systems solely according to general statements of performance.	Ceiling/illumination/HY AC component… capable of supporting all dead and live loads necessary to structural integrity and the safety of the occupants … capable of receiving partitions universally along a building module grid … capable of…etc.
	Specifying by Determinates	**J** Total project(s) specified according to human requirements alone, requiring translation into suitable design, systems, and technical performance requirements.	… Building occupants shall be provided with adequate light for common office tasks, without harshness or deadening uniformity; attractive ceilings that absorb undesirable noise levels without denying sharpness of voice communication; constructed in such a way that partition may be attached and relocation can be accomplished with disturbance limited to the immediate area and of not more than a day's duration.

Construction
Specifications
Practice Guide

DOMAIN 1 — Planning, Development, & Organization
DOMAIN 2 — Coordination
DOMAIN 3 — Procurement, Contracting, & General Requirements
DOMAIN 4 — Research
DOMAIN 5 — Analysis & Evaluation
DOMAIN 6 — Production

Figure 14.3
Levels of
Performance
Specifying
(continued)

	Technical Input	Source of Components	Testing/Inspection	Specification Type
A	No design input required. (2)	Off-the-shelf products. (2)	Check sample. Observe executed work.	Typical Specification Using *MasterFormat*®
B	Propose size.		Check sample and proposed size. Observe executed work.	
C	Propose, size, spacing, attachment.		Check sample, proposed size, and spacing. Observe executed work.	
D	Propose many particulars of assembly and interface, depending on degree of performance specifying.	Assembled largely from available products.	Check mockup and standard test data. Observe executed work.	
E		Assembled largely from rationalized available products.		
F	Contractor must have design capability and ability to modify or produce components.	Assembled from rationalized available components or from project-designed components.	Design needed tests, test mockups, and prototypes for performance. (3) Check executed work for performance.	Design-Build statement of system based on *UniFormat*®
G	Contractor must have highly developed design and manufacturing capability.	Assembled largely from project-designed subsystems. (4)		
H	None, until architect/engineer has translated general statements down to the degree of Line G.			
J				

(1) At about this degree consider switch to UniFormat®.

(2) Off-the-shelf includes products traditionally fabricated for each project using existing technology.

(3) Move testing as much as possible to the factory for intermittent production-line sampling or prototype destructive testing, conducted by national certifying organizations to replace on-site testing and review by local authorities and project architect/engineer. On-site testing will still be needed but at reduced levels.

(4) As first-generation systems develop into second-generation systems over a number of years, more and more project-designed products become off-the-shelf items.

structural-steel framing, integrated light/ceiling system, or aluminum curtain wall—is identified. Performance criteria are based on characteristics intrinsic to that type of component. Latitude in devising a solution within the constraints of the element's required performance is inherently allowed. This greater latitude in configuration, material, and process is possible through a broad degree of performance specifying.

UniFormat® provides a breakdown of project elements that can be used in performance specifications to integrate functionally related items on a subsystem level. However, describing subsystems or components in broad terms (e.g., B20—Exterior Vertical Enclosures) and functional criteria in broad terms (e.g., thermal transmission or weather resistance) allows the provider to respond with various solutions. For example, glass curtain walls, insulated metal panels, composite panels, precast panels, cementitious panels, or brick veneer may all provide satisfactory and acceptable "exterior vertical enclosures." Project conditions may sometimes necessitate greater control over selected elements. For example, narrowing the scope of B20—Exterior Vertical Enclosures to include curtain walls may be further specified as B2010.40—Curtain Wall Assemblies. If the A/E wants to limit the framing materials, the specification could list acceptable materials or unacceptable materials such as the following:

> Acceptable Framing Materials:
> 1. Aluminum.
> 2. Steel.
>
> Unacceptable Framing Materials:
> 1. Bronze.
> 2. Timber.
> 3. Fiberglass.

In some cases, the A/E may wish to increase specificity in the performance criteria to be more consistent with the described component. For example, maximum wind deflection for an "Exterior Vertical Enclosure" might be performance specified as follows:

> Design exterior vertical enclosures using load conditions per ASCE/SEI 7, "Minimum Design Loads and Associated Criteria for Buildings

and Other Structures," with the following deflection limitations:
> 1. Plaster and Stucco Finishes: l/480.
> 2. Other Finishes: l/240.

However, the same criterion for "Curtain Wall Assemblies" might be performance-specified this way:

> Deflection of any metal framing member in direction normal to wall plane, when tested per ASTM E330, "Standard Test Method for Structural Performance of Exterior Windows, Doors, Skylights and Curtain Walls by Uniform Static Air Pressure Difference," not to exceed 1/175 of clear span, or 3/4-inch, whichever is less, except when plastered surface is affected, in which case deflection not to exceed 1/360 of span.

14.2.8.2 Response to Performance Criteria

The local construction community's likely response must also be considered when establishing the level of performance specifying. The response is a critical factor in performance-oriented procurement. A sufficient number of bidders or proposers must be capable of responding to performance criteria and be willing to participate in a performance-based project solicitation. The advantages of performance specifying can be negated by insufficient participation. Performance-based requirements include administering contracts, designing and engineering performance-specified items, acquiring appropriate systems products, and coordinating installation as necessary. Bidders or proposers may provide necessary services in-house or may retain them on a project-by-project basis as needed. In either case, the level of performance specifying must be established according to the construction community's capabilities.

14.2.8.3 Means of Evaluation

The level of performance specifying also depends on evaluating the submitted proposals, whether objectively or subjectively, and the constraints imposed by the criteria. A subjective evaluation allows a broader level of performance specifying. The ability to accept or reject a proposal or to

DOMAIN 1
Planning,
Development,
& Organization

DOMAIN 2
Coordination

DOMAIN 3
Procurement,
Contracting,
& General
Requirements

DOMAIN 4
Research

DOMAIN 5
Analysis
& Evaluation

DOMAIN 6
Production

negotiate particular items might provide greater latitude in performance specifying. If absolute objectivity in evaluation is demanded (a "complies/ does not comply" basis), a narrower level of performance specifying may be best. A broad level of performance specifying does not necessarily mean longer proposal development time or a more involved evaluation. However, a broad level of performance specifying requires more time for the A/E to design proposed solutions that use the performance specification to meet the design intent.

A contractor who uses systems building components regularly may readily respond to broad-level performance specifications. However, narrow-level performance specifications may serve only to exclude otherwise acceptable options.

14.2.9 Resources

Once the extent of performance specifications has been established, and the attributes applicable to appropriate project elements have been selected, performance criteria must be established for those attributes. Familiarity with related data such as previous performance specifications, performance standards, industry standards, design guides, and federal regulations is essential in developing performance specifications. Trade associations can

also provide standards and data that are oriented to specific products and materials. The referenced standards or tests must be performance oriented. Many standards and tests were developed for a specific material under specific conditions and do not apply to other materials or conditions. However, other material-oriented tests may have valid applications to other materials and conditions, despite their material-specific origins.

Familiarity with particular standards and tests is vital to ensure their validity, applicability, and usefulness in evaluating the end result. Specified standards or tests should reflect project conditions. It serves no purpose to overspecify by requiring compliance with standards having no real utility. Such overspecifying also increases costs by placing an unnecessary burden on the bidder or proposer.

Avoiding specification conflicts is critical in performance specifying. Do not specify the same item in both descriptive and performance terms. This situation creates a potential conflict between specified performance criteria and the actual performance of the described component. Specifying a concrete mix by mix proportions as well as by properties of strength might create a conflict. The bidder or proposer might have the option of complying only with the lesser requirement.

14.2.10 Drawings and Specifications Coordination

Most performance specifications are accompanied by drawings that supplement written performance criteria. The drawings may include schematic diagrams, layouts, plans, maximum and minimum dimensions, nominal dimensions, critical dimensions, modular increments, and component arrangements. A broad level of performance specifying dictates that these drawings be diagrammatic in composition and content. Conversely, a narrower level of performance specifying requires more definitive drawings.

Any drawings representing only a suggested definition and that do not require strict adherence to a particular configuration should be noted. Contradictions between written and graphic material must be avoided. Requirements that cannot be communicated verbally should be conveyed graphically, with performance criteria presented clearly and consistently. The procurement documents clarify who is responsible for coordinating the design based on the final performance product characteristics.

14.2.10.1 Extent of Drawings

The level of detail on drawings depends on the level of performance specifying and the procurement method being used. Bidders/proposers are provided with definitive drawings that contain blanks where performance-specified items occur. The bidder/proposer fills in the blanks with proposed solutions. A drawing, an outline without detail, or any similar indication may represent the occurrence of a performance-specified element (system or component). However, the A/E must definitively indicate the elements with which the system or component must interface. This information is important to the bidder/proposer. The bidder/proposer then develops detailed drawings showing proposed performance-specified items and their relationship to other work.

When several major systems are performance specified, definitive site drawings may be developed, whereas structural drawings, plans, elevations, sections, and details allow for completion by the successful bidder/proposer. Definitive plans may sometimes be drawn, but with only nominal dimensions indicated where alternative solutions might result in different dimensions. Likewise, foundation drawings and structural layout drawings must accommodate the alternatives allowed by the performance specifications.

Where materials or configurations are optional, they should be drawn only as generic or schematic representations. Elevations and sections may illustrate the arrangement of elements, but only nominal dimensions and abstract material representations should be indicated wherever these vary according to the proposed solutions. Details of definitively described items should be drawn, indicating their interface with generically illustrated, performance-specified items. The successful bidder/proposer completes the drawings, indicating proposed solutions to performance-specified items and their interfaces with the traditionally designed elements drawn by the A/E. A wide range of performance specifying allows the bidders/proposers to develop a proposal for most, if not all, elements of the project.

The construction drawings may consist of site drawings showing the project outline and design drawings showing schematic plans, elevations, and sections. The successful bidder/proposer develops definitive drawings for the project.

If the bidder/proposer develops the design, the construction drawings might include only a definitive location plan. Because the project's final design is not yet determined, the site plan should include a blank area or footprint to indicate where the project is to be located. The design criteria and schematic drawings can be included as part of the performance specifications. The successful bidder/proposer then develops documentation to substantiate the solution. At the broadest level of performance specifying, such as a turnkey or design-build project, drawings consist only of existing condition drawings.

Design guidance should be communicated primarily through design criteria included in the performance requirements, supplemented only with schematic drawings. The successful bidder/proposer develops construction drawings for the project.

DOMAIN 1
Planning,
Development,
& Organization

DOMAIN 2
Coordination

DOMAIN 3
Procurement,
Contracting,
& General
Requirements

DOMAIN 4
Research

DOMAIN 5
Analysis
& Evaluation

DOMAIN 6
Production

If multiple-prime contracts are awarded for several performance-specified components or systems, each bidder/proposer may offer a solution for only one particular system. The A/E provides definitive construction drawings for all descriptive items, indicating only generically the performance-specified items. The successful bidder/proposer develops a performance-based system solution, indicating its interfaces with the descriptive items. Where multiple performance-based elements interface, those details have to be coordinated after each interfacing system has been selected.

If a prime contract is awarded for each of several systems assembled before delivery, no definitive drawings accompany the performance specifications. The A/E provides only a schematic project design to each bidder/proposer. These drawings should provide enough information to determine the system's configuration, details, and quantities, thus enabling the development of a solution. Bidders/proposers submit definitive drawings for their respective systems. Not until the final selection of each system has been made will the A/E begin to develop definitive construction drawings, integrating performance-specified items with each other and with descriptive items.

14.2.11 Performance Specification Format

The three-part SectionFormat® should be used in performance specifying to maintain consistency and flexibility in developing a project manual. Figure 14.4 shows SectionFormat® as it might be applied to a performance specification. Some article headings have not been listed because they typically would not apply to performance specifications. One additional broad article title has been added as well as several narrow article titles. This method is in keeping with the concept that all article titles are optional and should be carefully selected to meet the specification section's exact requirements. The detailed descriptions of the articles are presented in SectionFormat® and are also applicable to performance specifications. The following sections address the unique circumstances of performance specifying. Figure 14.5 is a sample performance specification.

For page layout of performance specifications, PageFormat® can be used for either narrow- or broad- level performance specifying. For broad-level performance that specifies using UniFormat® as the organizational format for the project manual, the section title would include the applicable UniFormat® number and title in place of a MasterFormat® number and title.

14.2.11.1 PART 1—GENERAL

Most of the administrative and procedural requirements used in PART 1—GENERAL are possible criteria for a performance specification. The "Summary" article should be used to define the specified system's interface with systems or products specified in other sections.

The "Submittals" article is an essential part of the performance specification concept. The types of submittals required for performance verification include shop drawings, product data, samples, test reports, certificates, and design data. Some submittals may require review and approval, whereas others are forms of documentary evidence or for information only. These submittals can be separated into quality assurance and quality control submittals, with provisions to ensure correct design liability responsibility. Submittals may be requested at several points in time: before bid or proposal, with bid or proposal, before fabrication, before installation, and before final acceptance.

Under the broad "Quality Assurance" article, the qualification requirements must include credentials for entities involved, such as manufacturer, contractor, designer, installer, and testing agency. These credentials may require engineering expertise and licensure by AHJs.

14.2.11.2 PART 2—PRODUCTS

The generic term *products* refers to building elements, including systems, assemblies, and components. Since the end results, rather than the means of achieving the end, are specified, the article titles "Manufacturers," "Materials," "Manufactured Units," "Equipment," "Accessories," "Mixes," and "Fabrication" are seldom used in a performance specification. This type of information might

Figure 14.4
SectionFormat®
as Applied to
Performance
Specifications

PART 1—GENERAL

SUMMARY
  Section Includes
  Products Supplied But Not Installed
    Under This Section
  Products Installed But Not Supplied
    Under This Section
  Related Requirements

PRICE AND PAYMENT PROCEDURE
  Allowances
  Unit Prices
  Alternates

REFERENCES
  Definitions

ADMINISTRATIVE REQUIREMENTS
  Coordination
  Preinstallation Meetings
  Sequencing
  Scheduling

SUBMITTALS
  Prior to Bid
  With Bid
  Prior to Fabrication
  Prior to Installation
  Prior to Final Acceptance

MAINTENANCE MATERIAL SUBMITTALS
  Extra Materials
  Maintenance Service

QUALITY ASSURANCE
  Qualifications
  Manufacturer Qualifications
  Bidder Qualifications
  Designer Qualifications
  Installer Qualifications
  Testing Agency Qualifications

DELIVERY, STORAGE, AND HANDLING

PROJECT OR SITE CONDITIONS
  Environmental Requirements
  Existing Requirements
  Field Measurements

WARRANTY
  Manufacturer's Warranty
  Special Warranty

PART 2—PRODUCTS

PERFORMANCE/DESIGN CRITERIA
  Attributes
  Requirements
  Criteria
  Tests

COMPONENTS
  Attributes
  Requirements
  Criteria
  Tests

FINISHES

ACCESSORIES

SOURCE QUALITY CONTROL

PART 3—EXECUTION

EXAMINATION

PREPARATION
  Protection of In-Place Conditions
  Surface Preparation

[ERECTION]/[INSTALLATION]/[APPLICATION]

FIELD QUALITY CONTROL

ADJUSTING

CLEANING

PROTECTION

END OF SECTION

SCHEDULES

DOMAIN 1
Planning,
Development,
& Organization

DOMAIN 2
Coordination

DOMAIN 3
Procurement,
Contracting,
& General
Requirements

DOMAIN 4
Research

DOMAIN 5
Analysis
& Evaluation

DOMAIN 6
Production

Figure 14.5
Sample
Performance
Specification using
SectionFormat®

SECTION 06 10 00
ROUGH CARPENTRY

PART 1—GENERAL

1.1 SUMMARY

    A. Section Includes:
        1. Wood grounds, nailers, furring, blocking, and sleepers.
        2. Plywood backer panels.

1.2 REFERENCES

    A. Lumber Standard: Comply with PS-20 and with applicable rules of the respective grading and inspecting agencies for species and products indicated.
    B. Plywood Product Standards: Comply with PS 1 (ANSI A199.1) or, for products not manufactured under PS 1 provisions, with applicable APA Performance Standard PRP-108 for type of panel indicated.

1.3 DEFINITIONS

    A. Rough carpentry includes carpentry work not specified as part of other Sections and generally not exposed, unless otherwise specified.

1.4 SUBMITTALS

    A. Product Data:
        1. Chemical treatment manufacturer's instructions for handling, storing, installation, and finishing of treated material.
        2. Treating plant's certification of compliance stating type of preservative used and method of treatment employed, net amount of preservative retained, and compliance with applicable standards.
        3. For waterborne treated products, include statement that moisture content of treated materials was reduced to levels indicated prior to shipment to project site.
    B. Certification that chemical treatment complies with specification for each type of treatment.

1.5 QUALITY ASSURANCE

    A. Ensure all preservative is adequately fixed in wood. Reject lumber with surface residues of white salts. Provide wood that is kiln-dried after treatment or prefinished with a sealer.
    B. Obtain approvals from Building Official for alternative wood preservative treatment.
    C. No products used within the interior of the building shall contain urea formaldehyde glue.

1.6 FIELD CONDITIONS

    A. Examine substrates and supporting structure and the conditions under which work is to be installed. Do not proceed with the installation until unsatisfactory conditions have been corrected.

1.7 DELIVERY, STORAGE, AND HANDLING

    A. Keep materials under cover and dry. Protect against exposure to weather and contact with damp or wet surfaces. Stack lumber as well as plywood and other panels; provide for air circulation within and around stacks and under temporary coverings including polyethylene and similar materials.
        1. For pressure-treated lumber and plywood, place spacers between each bundle to provide air circulation.

(Project name)   ROUGH CARPENTRY   06 10 00

Figure 14.5
Sample
Performance
Specification using
SectionFormat®
(continued)

SECTION 06 10 00
ROUGH CARPENTRY

PART 2—PRODUCTS

2.1 LUMBER, GENERAL

A. Lumber Standards: Furnish lumber manufactured to comply with PS 20 "AmericanSoftwood Lumber Standard" and with applicable grading rules of inspection agencies certified by American Lumber Standards Committee's (ALSC) Board of Review.

B. Inspection Agencies: SPIB - Southern Pine Inspection Bureau.

C. Grade Stamps: Provide lumber with each piece factory-marked with grade stamp of inspection agency evidencing compliance with grading rule requirements and identifying grading agency, grade, species, moisture content at time of surfacing, and mill.

D. Nominal sizes are indicated, except as shown by detail dimensions. Provide actual sizes as required by PS 20, for moisture content specified for each use.
   1. Provide dressed lumber, S4S, unless otherwise indicated.
   2. Provide seasoned lumber with 19 percent maximum moisture content at time of dressing and shipment for sizes 2 inches or less in nominal thickness, unless otherwise indicated.
   3. "Standard" grade.
   4. Southern Pine graded under SPIB rules.

2.2 WOOD GROUNDS, NAILERS, BLOCKING, AND SLEEPERS

A. Provide lumber for support or attachment of other construction including rooftop equipment curbs and support bases, cant strips, bucks, nailers, blocking, furring, grounds, stripping, and similar members.

B. Fabricate miscellaneous lumber from dimension lumber of sizes indicated and into shapes shown.

C. Grade: "Standard" grade light-framing-size lumber of any species or board-size lumber as required. No. 2 boards per SPIB rules.

D. Wood grounds, nailers, and sleepers shall be pressure treated as specified herein.

2.3 PLYWOOD PANELS

A. Construction Panel Standards: Comply with PS 1 "U.S. Product Standard for Construction and Industrial Plywood" for plywood construction panels and, for products not manufactured under PS 1 provisions, with APA PRP-108.

B. Trademark: Furnish construction panels that are each factory-marked with APA trademark evidencing compliance with grade requirements.

C. Electrical or Telephone Equipment Backing Panels: DOC PSI, exposure I, CD plugged, fire retardant treated; Thickness: Minimum 15/32 inch. Painting requirements per work described in Division 26.

2.4 FASTENERS

A. Provide fasteners of size and type indicated that comply with requirements specified in this article for material and manufacture.

B. Nails, wire, brads, and staples: FS FF-N-105.

C. Power driven fasteners: NER-272.

D. Wood screws: ANSI B18.6.1.

E. Lag bolts: ANSI B18.2.1.

F. Bolts: Steel bolts complying with ASTM A307, Grade A; with ASTM A563 hex nuts and, where indicated, flat washers.

(Project name)   ROUGH CARPENTRY   06 10 00

DOMAIN 1
Planning,
Development,
& Organization

DOMAIN 2
Coordination

DOMAIN 3
Procurement,
Contracting,
& General
Requirements

DOMAIN 4
Research

DOMAIN 5
Analysis
& Evaluation

DOMAIN 6
Production

Figure 14.5
Sample
Performance
Specification using
SectionFormat®
(continued)

SECTION 06 10 00
ROUGH CARPENTRY

2.5 MISCELLANEOUS MATERIALS

A. Water-Repellent Preservative: NWWDA-tested and -accepted formulation containing 3-iodo-2-propynyl butylcarbonate (IPBC) as its active ingredient.

2.6 PRESSURE TREATMENT OF WOOD

A. Preservative Treatment:
1. ACQ-Ammoniacal Copper Quartemary Compound: Pressure-injected.
2. Use 0.25 lb/cu ft retention.
3. Kiln dry after treatment to 19 percent maximum moisture content for lumber and 18 percent for plywood.
4. Optional Preservative Treatment: CDDC: Copper dimethyldithiocarbamate

B. Fire Retardant Treatment (for plywood backing panels only): AWPA C27 Type A.

PART 3—EXECUTION

3.1 INSTALLATION, GENERAL

A. Discard units of material with defects that impair quality of rough carpentry construction and that are too small to use in fabricating rough carpentry with minimum joints or optimum joint arrangement.

B. Set rough carpentry to required levels and lines, with members plumb and true to line and cut and fitted.

C. Fit rough carpentry to other construction; scribe and cope as required for accurate fit. Coordinate location of furring, nailers, blocking, grounds, and similar supports to allow attachment of other construction.

D. Securely attach rough carpentry work to substrate by anchoring and fastening as indicated.

E. Use screws, unless otherwise indicated. Select fasteners of size that will not penetrate members where opposite side will be exposed to view or will receive finish materials. Make tight connections between members. Install fasteners without splitting of wood; predrill as required.

F. Use IPBC-treated products at interior locations and ACQ- or CDDC-treated products at exterior locations.

3.2 INSTALLATION OF WOOD GROUNDS, NAILERS, BLOCKING, AND SLEEPERS

A. Install wood grounds, nailers, blocking, and sleepers where shown and where required for screeding or attachment of other work. Form to shapes as shown and cut as required for true line and level of work to be attached.

B. Attach to substrates as required to support applied loading. Countersink bolts and nuts flush with surfaces, unless otherwise indicated. Build into masonry during installation of masonry work. Where possible, anchor to formwork before concrete placement.

C. Install permanent grounds of dressed, preservative-treated, key-beveled lumber not less than 1-1/2 inches wide and of thickness required to bring face of ground to exact thickness of finish material involved. Remove temporary grounds when no longer required.

3.3 INSTALLATION OF CONSTRUCTION PANELS

A. Comply with applicable recommendations contained in Form No. E30, "APA Design Construction Guide-Residential & Commercial," for types of construction panels and applications indicated.

B. Fastening, Plywood Backing Panels: Nail, bolt, or screw to supports.

END OF SECTION

(Project name)   ROUGH CARPENTRY   06 10 00

typically be determined by the manufacturer, fabricator, supplier, or contractor. However, they could be used to narrow the list of possible products to those that are acceptable or unacceptable (see Section 14.2.8.1).

The "Performance/Design Criteria" article is intended to describe the specified element's design requirements and desired performance. This article is used by listing each element's performance attribute and stating the discrete needs or expected results. These requirements must be limited by criteria statements that set limits or give standards. Related to each criterion is a test by which the performance is evaluated. Standard criteria tests include the following:

- Review of drawings
- Review of design calculations
- Review of computer simulations
- Independent testing laboratory certification
- Supplier certification
- Tests of mock-ups and prototypes
- Field inspection

There may be more than one requirement for each attribute and, similarly, there may be several criteria for a single requirement. Also, more than one test may be applicable for a single criterion. A useful reference for the specifier is provided in Figure 14.6, which lists various attributes along with sample requirements, criteria, and tests. The attributes are grouped into the following categories:

- Safety and protection
- Functional
- Sensible
- Practical

It may be necessary to define the attributes of major components and those of the total system in more complex systems. This subdivision of attributes provides a better-organized document reflecting more detailed information and makes the specification easier to understand and respond to with a solution. "Components" is a generic article title used to list a system or assembly components' performance attributes. The actual name of the component may be used as the article title. Because a system or assembly is composed of more than one component, several component articles can be provided. For example, "Suspension Grid," "Acoustical Panels," and "Luminaires"

Construction
Specifications
Practice Guide

DOMAIN 1 — Planning, Development, & Organization
DOMAIN 2 — Coordination
DOMAIN 3 — Procurement, Contracting, & General Requirements
DOMAIN 4 — Research
DOMAIN 5 — Analysis & Evaluation
DOMAIN 6 — Production

Figure 14.6
Suggested
Attributes/
Requirements/
Criteria/Tests

Attribute		Requirement (R)/Criteria (C)	Test

HEADING 1: SAFETY AND PROTECTION

11 Fire Safety

(01) Fire Areas	R:	Control fire hazard neighboring structures.	
	C:	Limit distance between structures: limit area within fire barriers; limit ceiling height.	
(02) Fire Barriers	R:	Control the spread of fire.	1
	C:	Require fire walls, fire stops, fire-resistance separation between egress openings; require that barrier penetrations maintain rated fire endurance; require fire dampers.	1
(03) Egress Means	R:	Provide means for emergency evacuation.	
	C:	State minimum number of exits, maximum travel distance to exits and other means of egress; require minimum width for public corridors and public stairways; limit obstruction by door swing or equipment installation; require exit signs.	1
(04) Protective Devices	R:	Provide warning devices and automatic fire extinguishing equipment.	
	C:	State conditions under which automatic fire detection systems, smoke detection systems, sprinkler systems, extinguishing systems, or other protection devices should be provided.	1.5
(05) Fire Resistance/ Combustibility	R:	Maintain integrity for sufficient time to permit evacuation or control of fire.	
	C:	Require use of noncombustible materials, state minimum hours of fire resistance or classification.	1.3
(06) Fire Load/Fuel Contribution	R:	Control fuel contribution of materials.	
	C:	State maximum potential heat (contribution to fire load) in BTU per hour or BTU per square foot of material.	3
(07) Surface Spread of Flame	R:	Control surface spread of flame.	
	C:	State maximum flame spread or flammability of rating.	3
(08) Flame Propagation	R:	Control propagation of flame through enclosed spaces.	
	C:	C: State maximum flame propagation index.	1.3
(09) Smoke Generation	R:	Control amount and toxic effect of smoke produced.	
	C:	State maximum smoke development rating; state maximum optical density and maximum time to reach critical density; limit toxicity of smoke, require that smoke be non-noxious.	3
(10) Smoke Propagation	R:	Control propagation of smoke through enclosed spaces.	
	C:	Require smoke-tight joints, provide for venting of smoke areas.	1.3
(11) Accidental Ignition	R:	Protect against accidental ignition of fire.	
	C:	Design to prevent spark formation; limit equipment overheating; require equipment mounting to permit adequate ventilation.	1

12 Life Safety (other than fire)

(01) Physical Safety	R:	Protect against physical hazards.	
	C:	Require guardrails, handrails, protective covers on moving parts; slip-resistant surfaces.	1
(02) Electrical Safety	R:	Protect against electrical hazards.	
	C:	Require protective cover, insulation, and grounding: require safety controls and interlocks.	1
(03) Toxicity	R:	Control dangerous materials and substances.	
	C:	Limit toxicity of materials, surfaces, and finishes; limit toxic emissions below stated temperatures; limit toxic venting and leakage.	3
(04) Chemical Safety	R:	Protect against hazard from chemical substances.	
	C:	Identify chemicals and agents, including concentration and anticipated frequency of use, to which the system will be exposed; indicate the level of atmospheric pollution permitted.	1

Figure 14.6
Suggested
Attributes/
Requirements/
Criteria/Tests
(continued)

Attribute		Requirement (R)/Criteria (C)	Test
(05) Azoic Protection	R:	Protect against infection from biological sources.	
	C:	Identify insects, vermin, fungi, microorganisms, and other biological contaminants likely to be encountered and state level of protection to be provided.	1

13 Property Protection

Attribute		Requirement (R)/Criteria (C)	Test
(01) Theft Security	R:	Protect equipment and contents against theft.	
	C:	Design to control unauthorized entry and access.	1
(02) Security against Vandalism	R:	Protect against malicious damage.	
	C:	Design to resist malicious damage.	1.5
(03) Resistance to Misuse	R:	Protect against accidental or deliberate misuse.	
	C:	Design to prevent improper usage. Design for failsafe operation. Perform factory adjustment. Provide instructions.	1.5

14 Accessibility Considerations

Attribute		Requirement (R)/Criteria (C)	Test
(01) Physical Access	R:	Provide for physical access by impaired individuals.	
	C:	Design to provide at least one means of ingress and egress for individuals in wheelchairs.	1
(02) Mobility-Impaired Usage	R:	Provide for building usage by mobility-impaired individuals, if appropriate.	
	C:	Design to permit mobility-impaired individuals access to and use of facilities and equipment, such as restrooms, drinking fountains, vending machines, elevators.	1
(03) Vision-Impaired Usage	R:	Provide for building usage by vision-impaird individuals, if appropriate.	
	C:	Design to permit vision-impaired individuals access to and use of facilities and equipment, such as restrooms, drinking fountains, vending machines, elevators.	1
(04) Hearing-Impaired Usage	R:	Provide for building usage by persons with hearing deficiencies, if appropriate.	
	C:	Design to permit hearing-impaired full usage of building services, such as, fire alarm systems, door bells, and audible signals system.	1

HEADING 2: FUNCTIONAL
21 Strength

Attribute		Requirement (R)/Criteria (C)	Test
(01) Static Loading	R:	Sustain gravity loads and superimposed and specified vertical and lateral loads.	
	C:	State dead loads to be supported, including forces transmitted from other systems. Specify how and where loads shall be transmitted from other systems.	2
(02) Live Loading	R:	Sustain dynamic loads.	
	C:	Describe live loads to be supported, including snow load. Identify concentrated loads and state design floor loads.	2
(03) Horizontal Loading	R:	Sustain wind loads and other lateral loads.	
	C:	For exterior walls, state design wind speeds and other live loads. State typhoon or hurricane conditions. For partitions, state lateral design load per square foot of partition area.	2
(04) Deflection	R:	Limit deflection.	
	C:	State maximum acceptable deflections.	2
(05) Thermal Loading	R:	Sustain loads due to temperature change.	
	C:	State the temperature extremes to be used for design.	2
(06) Structural Serviceability	R:	Retain serviceability under load and deflection.	
	C:	Require structure to sustain design loads without causing local damage.	2

DOMAIN 1
Planning,
Development,
& Organization

DOMAIN 2
Coordination

DOMAIN 3
Procurement,
Contracting,
& General
Requirements

DOMAIN 4
Research

DOMAIN 5
Analysis
& Evaluation

DOMAIN 6
Production

Figure 14.6
Suggested
Attributes/
Requirements/
Criteria/Tests
(continued)

Attribute		Requirement (R)/Criteria (C)	Test
(07) Seismic Loading	R:	Sustain earthquake loads.	
	C:	State the seismic zone to be used for design.	2
(08) Impact Loading	R:	Sustain impact loads and forces.	
	C:	C: Describe the source and magnitude of any impact loads to be sustained.	2
(09) Penetration Resistance	R:	Protect against damage from concentrated loads.	
	C:	Describe magnitude and location of concentrated loads.	2

22 Durability

Attribute		Requirement (R)/Criteria (C)	Test
(01) Impact Resistance	R:	Resist surface degradation due to point impact.	
	C:	Limit surface indentation due to specified impact load.	3
(02) Moisture Resistance	R:	Resist degradation when exposed to water or water vapor.	
	C:	Design for use in specified range of humidity. Limit permanent effect to exposure to water, water retention, and absorption.	3
(03) Thermal Resistance	R:	Resist degradation when exposed to temperature ranges expected in normal use.	
	C:	Limit physical change when exposed to specified temperature range.	3
(04) Corrosion Resistance	R:	Resist degradation when exposed to corrosive agents.	
	C:	Limit corrosive effect observed after specified exposure to salt spray or fog; require corrosive-resistant surface treatment; design to avoid contact of dissimilar metals.	3
(05) Chemical Resistance	R:	Resist degradation when exposed to chemicals. Resist staining or damage from soluble and insoluble salts, alkali attack, and oxidation.	
	C:	Limit changes in appearance or other specified property after exposure to specified chemicals.	3
(06) Weather Resistance	R:	Resist degradation when exposure to specified period of simulated weathering.	
	C:	Limit changes observed after exposure to specified period of simulated weathering.	3
(07) Ultraviolet Resistance	R:	Resist degradation due to exposure to ultraviolet light.	3
	C:	Limit discoloration after ultraviolet exposure.	
(08) Surface Serviceability	R:	Resist cracking, spalling, crazing, blistering, delaminating, chalking, and fading.	
	C:	Limit surface changes observed after exposure to simulated conditions of use.	3
(09) Stain Resistance	R:	Resist permanent discoloration when exposed to staining agents and chemicals.	
	C:	Limit visual evidence of permanent stains due to treatment with identified agents.	3
(10) Absorbency	R:	Resist tendency to absorb and retain water.	
	C:	Limit quantity of water retained after specified exposure.	3
(11) Cleanability	R:	Resist damage from routine maintenance and cleaning; permit removal of identified stains.	
	C:	Limit discoloration or surface change after simulated cleaning with specified cleaning agents.	3
(12) Color Resistance	R:	Resist fading over time.	
	C:	Limit discoloration after stared period.	3
(13) Friability/Frangibility	R:	Resist crumbling and brittle fracture.	
	C:	Limit damage observed after specified loading.	3
(14) Abrasion Resistance	R:	Resist degradation due to rubbing.	
	C:	Limit weight loss after specified number of abrasion cycles.	3
(15) Scratch Resistance	R:	Resist degradation due to scratching.	
	C:	Limit rating on pencil hardness scratch scale.	3

Figure 14.6
Suggested
Attributes/
Requirements/
Criteria/Tests
(continued)

Attribute		Requirement (R)/Criteria (C)	Test
(16) Dimensional Stability	R:	Control dimensional changes resulting from changes in environment.	
	C:	Limit volume change and movement under specified exposure to moisture and temperature variation.	3
(17) Cohesiveness/ Adhesiveness	R:	Resist peeling and delamination.	
	C:	Limit peeling or delamination failures under specified simulated loading.	3
(18) System Life	R:	Function properly for identified period.	
	C:	Limit failure under accelerated life test. Design life of components consistent with specified life of system.	3,4

23 Transmission Characteristics

Attribute		Requirement (R)/Criteria (C)	Test
(01) Heat	R:	Control heat transmission.	
	C:	Design for specified Thermal Transmittance ("U" value).	2
(02) Light	R:	Control light transmission.	
	C:	Design for specified percentage of light or radiation transmission.	2
(03) Air Infiltration	R:	Resist leakage of air.	
	C:	Limit infiltration under specified pressure or wind load. Design for specified maximum leakage.	2, 3,4
(04) Vapor Penetration	R:	Resist vapor penetration.	
	C:	Design vapor barrier for minimum vapor permeability.	2, 3,4
(05) Water Leakage	R:	Resist water leakage.	
	C:	Limit infiltration under specified pressure or wind load design for specifiedmaximum leakage.	2, 3,4
(06) Condensation	R:	Control admission and condensation of moisture.	
	C:	Design to provide moisture barriers and thermal breaks.	2,4

24 Waste Products and Discharge

Attribute		Requirement (R)/Criteria (C)	Test
(01) Solid Waste	R:	Control production of solid waste. Provide for elimination or emission and prevent undesired accumulation.	
	C:	Design to accommodate waste produced or accumulated. Require identification of wastes produced.	1,2
(02) Liquid Waste	R:	Control production of liquid waste. Provide for elimination or emission and prevent undesired accumulation.	
	C:	Design to accommodate waste levels produced, accumulated or omitted. Require identification of waste produced.	2
(03) Gaseous Waste	R:	Control production of gases. Provide for elimination and prevent undesired accumulation.	
	C:	Design to accommodate levels of gas accumulated or emitted. Require identification of gaseous waste emitted.	1,2
(04) Odor	R:	Control formation and persistence of odors.	
	C:	Design to prevent odor formation.	1
(05) Particulate Discharge	R:	Control production of particulate wastes. Provide for collection of waste and prevent undesired accumulation.	
	C:	Design to accommodate amount of particulate waste produced. Limit particulate concentration.	1,2
(06) Thermal Discharge	R:	Limit of thermal energy and vibration. Provide for control or reabsorption.	
	C:	Design to control thermal discharge produced below specified levels.	2
(07) Radiation	R:	Limit emission of radiation. Provide for control or reabsorption.	
	C:	Design to control radiation discharge produced below specified levels.	2

DOMAIN 1
Planning,
Development,
& Organization

DOMAIN 2
Coordination

DOMAIN 3
Procurement,
Contracting,
& General
Requirements

DOMAIN 4
Research

DOMAIN 5
Analysis
& Evaluation

DOMAIN 6
Production

Figure 14.6
Suggested
Attributes/
Requirements/
Criteria/Tests
(continued)

Attribute		Requirement (R)/Criteria (C)	Test
25 Operational Characteristics			
(01) Method of Operation	R:	Provide operating methods consistent with function.	1,2,
	C:	List desired operating modes.	3,4
(02) Results of Operation	R:	Provide output consistent with function.	
	C:	List desired output quantities and rates.	1,2,5
(03) Cycle Time/Speed of Operation	R:	Provide cycle times to accommodate functional requirements.	
	C:	List desired repetition rates.	1,2,5
HEADING 3: SENSIBLE			
31 Aesthetic Properties			
(01) Arrangement	R:	Provide order, organization, or relationship appealing to visual perception.	
	C:	Design for pleasing relationships between elements and components.	1
(02) Composition	R:	Provide unified appearance appealing to visual perception.	
	C:	Design for pleasing overall appearance.	1
(03) Texture	R:	Provide surface finishes appealing to tactile perception.	
	C:	Design surface finishes pleasant to touch and feel.	1,4,5
(04) Color/Gloss	R:	Provide finishes with pattern or luster appealing to visual perception.	
	C:	Design surface finishes for pleasing appearance.	1,4,5
(05) Uniformity/Variety	R:	Provide appropriate consistency or variety of visual environment.	
	C:	Design to provide pleasing variety of colors, textures, and glosses. Limit visual confusion.	1,4,5
(06) Compatibility/Contrast	R:	Provide appropriate consistency or variety of visual environment.	
	C:	Design appearance of elements in a pleasing and harmonious combination.	1,4,5
32 Acoustical Properties			
(01) Sound Generation	R:	Control production of solid waste. Provide for elimination or emission and prevent undesired accumulation.	
	C:	Design to accommodate waste produced or accumulated. Require identification of wastes produced.	2,3, 4,5
(02) Sound Transmission	R:	Control transmission of sound.	
	C:	Design for specified sound transmission classification. Provide STC or SPP rating.	1,2,3, 4,5
(03) Reflectance	R:	Control reflection, reverberation, and echo production.	1,2,
	C:	Design for specified reverberation time, and sound path length.	3,4
33 Illumination			
(01) Level	R:	Control production of liquid waste. Provide for elimination or emission and prevent undesired accumulation.	
	C:	Design to accommodate waste levels produced, accumulated or omitted. Require identification of waste produced.	2,5
(02) Color	R:	Control production of gases. Provide for elimination and prevent undesired accumulation.	
	C:	Design to accommodate levels of gas accumulated or emitted. Require identification of gaseous waste emitted.	
(03) Shadow/Glare	R:	Control formation and persistence of odors.	
	C:	Design to prevent odor formation.	2, 3,4
(04) Reflection	R:	Control production of particulate wastes. Provide for collection of waste and prevent undesired accumulation.	
	C:	Design to accommodate amount of particulate waste produced. Limit particulate concentration.	2, 5

Figure 14.6
Suggested
Attributes/
Requirements/
Criteria/Tests
(continued)

Attribute		Requirement (R)/Criteria (C)	Test

34 Ventilation

(01) Air Quality — R: Control air quality.
C: Design for specified natural ventilation. Design to control rate of air removal and supply design to control odors. — 1,2

(02) Velocity — R: Control air movement.
C: Design to maintain air motion between specified limits. — 1,2

(03) Distribution — R: Control temperature gradients.
C: Design to control temperature gradients within specified limits. — 1,2

(04) Pressurization — R: Control pressure differential.
C: Design to limit air leakage. — 2

(05) Temperature — R: Control air temperature content.
C: State exterior design conditions. Design to control rate of change of mean radiant temperature within specified range.

(06) Moisture — R: Control air moisture content.
C: State exterior design conditions. Design to provide specified range of relative humidity. — 2

35 Measurable Characteristics

(01) Levelness — R: Control deviation from identified horizontal.
C: Require level installation. Design for case of level installation. — 5

(02) Plumbness — R: Control deviation from identified vertical.
C: Require plumb installation within specified tolerance. Design for case of plumb installation. — 5

(03) Dimension/Tolerance — R: Control spatial extent for installation or fit within available space.
C: Conform to specified spatial dimensions and tolerances. — 5

(04) Volume — R: Control volumetric measure or capacity.
C: Conform to specified limits of volume or capacity. — 5

(05) Flatness — R: Control planar surface characteristics.
C: Limit deviation from flat, smooth, or planar surface. — 5

(06) Shape — R: Control surface configuration, contour, or form.
C: Conform to specified shape limitations. — 5

(07) Weight/Density — R: Control weight or density.
C: Conform to specified weight or density limitations. — 5

36 Material Properties

(01) Hardness — R: Control resistance to penetration.
C: Limit penetration under specified load. — 3

(02) Ductility/Brittleness — R: Control capability to shape by drawing. Control tendency to shatter.
C: Limit percentage elongation or percent change in cross section before rupture. — 3

(03) Malleability — R: Control capability to shape by hammering.
C: imit choice of materials.

(04) Resilience — R: Control capability to store energy.
C: Limit residual deformation after impact load. — 3

(05) Elasticity/Plasticity — R: Control capability to retain original shape when load is removed.
C: Limit residual deformation after removal of load. — 3

DOMAIN 1
Planning,
Development,
& Organization

DOMAIN 2
Coordination

DOMAIN 3
Procurement,
Contracting,
& General
Requirements

DOMAIN 4
Research

DOMAIN 5
Analysis
& Evaluation

DOMAIN 6
Production

Figure 14.6
Suggested
Attributes/
Requirements/
Criteria/Tests
(continued)

Attribute		Requirement (R)/Criteria (C)	Test
(06) Toughness	R:	Control capability to change shape without rupture.	
	C:	Limit energy absorption before rupture.	3
(07) Viscosity	R:	Control fluid resistance to flow.	
	C:	Limit coefficient of viscosity.	3
(08) Creep	R:	Control permanent change in shape after prolonged exposure to stress or elevated temperature.	
	C:	Limit permanent deformation under specified load or temperature conditions.	3
(09) Friction	R:	Control tendency of two bodies in contact to resist relative motion.	
	C:	Limit coefficient of friction.	3
(10) Thermal Expansion	R:	Control change in unit dimension resulting from change in temperature.	
	C:	Limit coefficient of thermal expansion.	3

HEADING 4: PRACTICAL

41 Interface Characteristics

Attribute		Requirement (R)/Criteria (C)	Test
(01) Fit	R:	Control size and shape of interface elements.	
	C:	Design for physical compatibility with specified elements. Control	1,4,5
(02) Attachment	R:	physical and electrical connection at interface.	
	C:	Design to use specified connections.	1,4,5
(03) Tolerance	R:	Control variation in interface dimension.	
	C:	Design to accommodate specified tolerance.	1,4,5
(04) Modularity	R:	Control standardized unit dimensions or repeating dimension.	
	C:	Design for compatibility with the specified module.	1,4,5
(05) Rotability	R:	Control orientation at interface.	
	C:	Design to provide or permit specified orientations.	1,4,5
(06) Relocatability	R:	Control ability to disassemble move or relocate.	
	C:	Design to provide specified flexibility to dismount and re-erect.	1,4,5
(07) Erection Sequence	R:	Control order of erection or installation.	
	C:	Design to provide specified flexibility to dismount or re-erect.	1,4,5

42 Service

Attribute		Requirement (R)/Criteria (C)	Test
(01) Repairability	R:	Provide for repair or replacement of damaged or in-operative elements.	
	C:	Design for ease of repair. Limit use of special tools, limit amount of labor required.	1,4,5
(02) Interchangeability	R:	Provide for interchangeability of elements.	
	C:	Design for interchangeability.	1,4,5
(03) Accessibility	R:	Provide access for service and maintenance.	
	C:	Design with access panels. Avoid placing connections in inaccessible locations	1,4,5
(04) Replaceability	R:	Provide for substitution of equivalent elements.	
	C:	Design to permit substitution.	1,4,5
(05) Inconvenience	R:	Limit disturbance during maintenance and repair.	
	C:	Design to minimize inconvenience. Provide backup or alternate elements.	1,4,5
(06) Extendibility	R:	Provide for capability to increase capacity.	
	C:	Design to permit or accommodate extension or expansion.	1,4,5
(07) Adaptability	R:	Provide for alteration or modification.	
	C:	Design to use industry standard connectors and interface elements.	1,4,5

Attribute		Requirement (R)/Criteria (C)	Test
(08) Replacement Sequence	R:	Provide for identified order for removal and replacement.	
	C:	Design for identified replacement sequence.	1,4,5
(09) Service Frequency	R:	Control repair and maintenance frequency.	
	C:	Design for identified failure rates and maintenance schedules.	1,4,5
43 Personnel Needs			
(01) Maintenance Personnel	R:	Control skill levels required for maintenance.	
	C:	Design for maintenance by personnel with identified skills.	2
(02) Training	R:	Control availability of trained personnel.	
	C:	Require provision for training operators and maintenance personnel.	2

Figure 14.6
Suggested
Attributes/
Requirements/
Criteria/Tests
(continued)

are all components of an integrated ceiling system. Each component is provided a separate component article that specifies the appropriate attributes, requirements, criteria, and tests specific to that component. When using performance specifications, the A/E must be aware of the state of technology involved in the systems and components being specified.

A requirement to advance the specified element's state-of-the-art-technology may produce a limited response unless there is enough volume of work to support the research and development costs. If the A/E is looking for the most cost-effective solution using existing technology, care must be exercised to not overspecify.

14.2.11.3 PART 3 — EXECUTION

This part of a performance specification section covers execution provisions pertinent to the systems and components specified in PART 2 — PRODUCTS. The articles typically found under PART 3 — EXECUTION are generally applicable for performance specifying as well. The "[Erection]/[Installation]/[Application]" article may or may not be included to describe the installation, depending on the extent of the system being specified. The installation or erection may be dependent on the actual product developed by a manufacturer for the project.

However, several products may meet the performance specification, each with its own application; or, the installer may be allowed to implement some other installation options. In some situations, only a statement requiring compliance with the manufacturer's installation instructions is necessary. Extra care should be taken to avoid conflicts caused by specifying both the performance requirement in PART 2 and a method of achieving the requirement in PART 3. Division 01 — General Requirements includes Section 01 80 00 — Performance Requirements with numerous Level 2 and 3 numbers and titles for various building elements if a narrow level of performance specifying is used. For a broad level of performance specifying that uses UniFormat®, the Level 1 and 2 numbers and titles could be used for sections addressing broad-scope building element requirements. This approach to performance specifying establishes requirements for an end result for a building element without referencing specific products. Additionally, both MasterFormat®'s Section 01 80 00 and UniFormat®'s taxonomy (but not together in the same project manual) are well-suited for the design-build project delivery method allowing alternative products, solutions, or technologies that are not able to be specified elsewhere.

**DOMAIN 6:
PRODUCTION**

Chapter 15

PREPARING THE SPECIFICATIONS

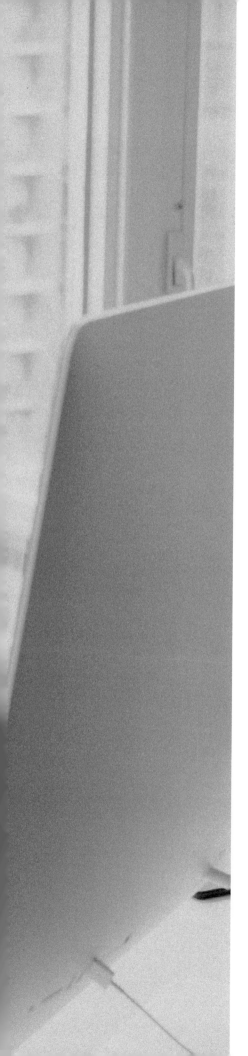

15.1 Section Title List

Once the project's basic scope and requirements are known, the specifier develops a list of section titles along with the scope of work associated with each. This list should also indicate related work that is specified in other sections. The section title list serves as a device for coordination among the sections and helps prevent overlaps or omissions in the specifications. MasterFormat® can serve as a checklist for developing the section title list and ensuring that all required sections are included. Because the list of sections is usually distributed to the owner and other design team members, it is preferable to list other documents and forms included in the project manual. Such a list in its final form can become the table of contents for the project manual.

If a master guide specification system is used, the list of proposed section titles should be compared with the master guide specification system's contents. Sections that can be developed or edited from the master guide text and those that must be custom-prepared should be indicated. Attention should be given to products or work that might be specified in more than one section. When a master guide specification is used, care should be taken when changing section numbers, as cross-references may be included in other sections of the master. Other sections of the specifications should be referenced as needed for proper coordination of the requirements. References should be made to section numbers only rather than to article or page numbers, which may change with subsequent revisions of the specifications.

15.2 Writing/Editing Preparation

The specifier should review project requirements for the scope of work covered in each section. Preliminary project descriptions (PPDs) and outline specifications prepared during the early design phases may be helpful. It is also important to thoroughly review the drawings, details of construction, and schedules. Local conditions and governing codes must also be considered, as both proprietary and master guide specifications may not address local project conditions or may contain

DOMAIN 1
Planning,
Development,
& Organization

DOMAIN 2
Coordination

DOMAIN 3
Procurement,
Contracting,
& General
Requirements

DOMAIN 4
Research

DOMAIN 5
Analysis
& Evaluation

DOMAIN 6
Production

references that do not apply. Although Division 01 sections should be prepared as early as possible and drafts distributed for review, as a general rule, sections of Divisions 02 through 49 should be written before finalizing the Division 01 sections.

The most effective writing sequence for an individual specification section is as follows:

1. PART 2 — PRODUCTS is most frequently the first step in the writing process. Sometimes it is necessary to skip over secondary materials and fabrication methods until PART 3 — EXECUTION has been written.

2. PART 3 — EXECUTION follows typically unless the installation process dictates the type of materials. After PART 3 is completed, return to PART 2, verify products are correct for the installation specified, and edit content for secondary materials and fabrication methods.

3. PART 1 — GENERAL can be done most effectively after the substance of the other two parts has been established. By putting PART 1 last, the summary; submittals; quality assurance; delivery, storage, and handling; and warranty articles can be correctly edited for the products and installation methods specified.

15.3 Illustrations in Specifications

Although illustrations and drawings are usually included in the contract drawings, this does not preclude using illustrations within the specifications. The old cliché states, "A picture is worth a thousand words," and one illustration can help minimize extensive descriptions and prevent misunderstanding. The illustrations can also assist the owner, contractor, and supplier in understanding the intended product. Typical items that would benefit from illustrations are hardware, toilet accessories, furniture, lighting fixtures, and many accessory items. Illustrations are sometimes presented as photographs or in an isometric view, simulating a three-dimensional view and providing a good understanding of the specified product.

The use of illustrations, graphics, and photographs may require permission or copyright release

from the graphics owner or originator. Some graphics may include proprietary or patented designs, which could imply additional specification requirements.

Graphics should be used in specifications only with due consideration and text that clarifies the graphics' status within the documents. Such text may be included in the supplementary conditions under definitions of contract documents. Many manufacturers provide data and other informational sheets that can be included to illustrate the products being used as the basis of design in the project. The datasheets can also be referenced in the individual section or, as suggested by SectionFormat®, they can be inserted in the project manual following the individual section.

15.4 Specification Language

As briefly stated in Chapter 11, specifications need to follow the four Cs for effective communication: clear, concise, complete, and correct. The specification language stands alone when compared to all other types of writing. Specifications are highly technical, but at the same time they have the force of a legal contract. In essence, the words used in specifications matter.

15.4.1 Writing Style

A good writing style is characterized by accuracy, brevity, and clarity. Long, complex sentences and stilted language do not contribute to effective communication. Follow these simple rules for a good specification writing style:

- Use simple sentences.

- Maintain sentence structure in simple declarative or imperative statements.

- Avoid complicated sentences in which inadvertent omission or insertion of punctuation could change the meaning or create ambiguity.

- Choose words and terms that are simple and clearly understood.

15.4.2 Vocabulary

Words should be carefully selected and used for precise meaning. Once a word is selected, use it consistently throughout the specifications whenever the same meaning is intended. The following are some examples of misused or ambiguous terms commonly found in specifications:

Amount and Quantity: *Amount* should be used when writing about money. *Quantity* should be used when writing about numbers, linear measure, area, or volume.

Any: *Any* is imprecise in number, permitting discretion by the reader. "Repair any cracks" could mean some cracks selected by the contractor, but "repair cracks" means all cracks.

And, Or, And/Or: *And* connects elements that are to be taken jointly. It may also mean "plus" or "added to the preceding quantity." *Or* is used to introduce any of the possibilities in a series. The two words together, *and/or*, represent a hybrid term often used in legal and business documents as a grammatical shortcut. The term *and/or* is not recommended for specifications because it allows the contractor to decide whether the term means *and* or *or*.

Balance and Remainder: *Balance* should be used when writing about money. *Remainder* is preferred for "that which is left over."

Either and Both: *Either* implies a choice between two options, whereas *both* is all-inclusive. Make clear whether the intent is to have "glass sidelights on either side of the door" or to have "glass sidelights on both sides of the door."

Flammable and Inflammable: *Flammable* and *inflammable* have exactly the same meaning, even though they sound opposite. *Flammable* is preferred.

Furnish, Install, and Provide: *Furnish* means to supply and deliver to the project site, ready for installation. *Install* means to place in position for service or use. *Provide* is commonly accepted in specifications to mean *furnish* and *install*, complete and ready for the intended use. These definitions should be placed in the supplementary conditions or Division 01 — General Requirements.

Insure, Assure, and Ensure: To *insure* is to issue or procure an insurance policy. *Assure* is to give confidence to or convince a person of

DOMAIN 1
Planning,
Development,
& Organization

DOMAIN 2
Coordination

DOMAIN 3
Procurement,
Contracting,
& General
Requirements

DOMAIN 4
Research

DOMAIN 5
Analysis
& Evaluation

DOMAIN 6
Production

something. *Ensure* is to make certain in a way that eliminates the possibility of error.

Observe and Supervise: *Observe* means to watch or view the execution or performance of work, whereas *supervise* means to oversee and to have control and direction of the work.

Party and Entity: *Party* refers to a signer of a contract, such as an owner and contractor in an owner-contractor agreement. When the intent is to include persons or companies — such as subcontractors and others involved in the construction process but who are not signers of the contract — the generic *entity* should be used.

Replace and Remove and Provide New: *Replace* can be construed as requiring reinstallation of removed materials rather than furnishing and installing new materials as *remove and provide new* implies. Be specific as to what is required for the replaced material.

Shall and Will: *Shall* is used as an imperative in reference to the work required to be done by a contractor. In specifications, *will* is considered less obligatory and is used in connection with acts and actions required of the owner or the architect/engineer (A/E).

Must and Is To: Neither of these is recommended for use in specifications.

15.4.3 Spelling

Spelling should be correct and consistent, based on a particular dictionary designated as the office standard for spelling. A supplemental list of technical terms may be needed for words not contained in the dictionary selected as the standard. In cases where two spellings are considered equally correct, the shorter of the two spellings is preferred for use in contract documents (e.g., facia not fascia, gage not gauge, molding not moulding, and catalog not catalogue). However, unacceptable spellings produced by attempts at brevity or simplification should be avoided (e.g., thru instead of through).

15.4.4 Sentence Structure

Two basic grammatical sentence moods can be used to convey specification requirements clearly:

- Imperative mood
- Indicative mood

15.4.5 Imperative Mood

The *imperative mood* should generally be maintained throughout a specification. The verb that clearly defines the action becomes the first word in the sentence. The imperative sentence is concise and readily understandable:

- Spread adhesive with notched trowel.
- Install equipment plumb and level.
- Apply two coats of paint to each exposed surface.

15.4.6 Indicative Mood

The *indicative mood* in specifications typically requires the use of *shall* or *will*. This sentence structure can cause unnecessary wordiness and monotony.

Traditionally, the word *shall* has come to mean "has a duty to." There are many examples of specification sections that begin nearly every sentence with "Contractor *shall*," which can be correctly interpreted to mean "Contract *has a duty to*" do something.

Because the contractor and owner are the only parties to the owner-contractor agreement, all instructions are addressed to the contractor. The words "Contractor shall" are generally omitted in favor of the imperative mood. However, when the contractor and owner or contractor and A/E are mentioned in the same article or paragraph, "The Contractor shall," "Owner will," and "A/E will" could be used for clarity. Although *will* has the same legal meaning as *shall*, when used in specifications, *will* is considered to be the less obligatory variant (see Section 15.4.2).

When it comes to specifying products and their installation, the usage of *shall* is also viewed negatively. In each of the following examples, the use of *shall* fails to conform to the traditional meaning since none of the subjects in these examples legally "has a duty to" do anything:

- Adhesive shall be spread with notched trowel.
- Equipment shall be installed plumb and level.
- Two coats of paint shall be applied to each exposed surface.

15.4.7 Abbreviations

Abbreviations should be used only on drawings and schedules where space is limited. Well-known and industry-accepted abbreviations are a shorthand that helps the communication process only if the meaning is easily recognized and understood. Abbreviations should be defined on the drawings or in Division 01. Abbreviations with multiple meanings should be avoided unless used in different disciplines where their meaning is clear from the context in which they are used.

Abbreviations should be limited to five or fewer letters. Abbreviations of short words that save only one or two characters should be avoided. Ensure abbreviations are consistent between the drawings and the specifications. A list of abbreviations is included in the United States National CAD Standard (NCS). When in doubt, spell it out. The exceptions to these guidelines include the following:

- Part of a company's legal name (Co., Inc., LLC)
- Names of organizations (ASTM) with no periods
- Time (a.m., p.m.)
- Time Zones (EST)
- Temperatures (degrees F)
- Units of measure (psi, mph) with no periods

15.4.8 Symbols

The cautions and guidelines for abbreviations apply to symbols substituted for words or terms. Two additional factors that limit the use of symbols are their conflict with use as command characters in software programs and potential translation of font problems when converting from one software program to another. Small symbols may also bleed together and become unreadable in poorly printed text. Following are some of the symbols that should not be used in specifications:

- % for *percent*
- ° for *degree*
- + for *plus*
- − for *minus*
- × for *by*, as in 2 × 4

DOMAIN 1
Planning,
Development,
& Organization

DOMAIN 2
Coordination

DOMAIN 3
Procurement,
Contracting,
& General
Requirements

DOMAIN 4
Research

DOMAIN 5
Analysis
& Evaluation

DOMAIN 6
Production

- / for *per*

- @ for *at*

The use of parentheses and quotation marks should be minimized or avoided; underlines should not be used. When including dimensions in the text of a specification section, apply the following rules:

- Spell out feet when no inches are used (e.g., 8 feet).

- Spell out inches when no feet are used (e.g., 8 inches).

- When feet and inches are both used, use symbols (e.g., 8′-8″ or 8′-2-1/2″).

- A complete dimension should appear on one line.

Designations from industry standards (e.g., ASTM C270, ANSI/ASME A17.1, ACI 318) and MasterFormat® numbers (e.g., Section 01 42 19) should appear on the same line. Use a non-breaking space character to keep them together.

15.4.9 Numbers

The use of Arabic numerals rather than words for numbers is recommended per the following rules:

- Use numerals whenever possible because they are easy to identify. However, when numbers are used to define both size and quantity, the written word should be used for the quantity (e.g., three 1/2-inch holes; five 2 by 4s).

- Always use figures for dimensions, degrees of temperature, percentages, and dollars and cents (e.g., 3 inches by 5 inches, 10 degrees C (50 degrees F), 20 percent, $5.50).

- Clock times and dates should be expressed in figures (e.g., 2:10 p.m. on June 15 [omit the "th"], 2021). Exceptions to this are the use of the words *noon* and *midnight*. The same rules apply to a 24-hour clock as well.

- Decimals should be expressed in figures (e.g., 6.235). For quantities less than one, a zero should be used before the decimal point (e.g., 0.235).

- Fractions should be typed using individual keys and not converted to superscript/subscript fonts or special characters (e.g., 1/4, not ¼; and 1/2, not ½).

- Omit unneeded zeroes in time and money references (e.g., $200, not $200.00; and 9 p.m., not 9:00 p.m.).

15.4.10 Capitalization

Capitalization should be consistent throughout the contract documents. Capitalizing the initial letter of certain specific nouns and proper names defined in the conditions of the contract is appropriate. Following are some examples of words that should be capitalized:

Agreement. When referring to the specific form signed to execute the contract.

Architect. When referring to the architect who is a party to the owner-architect agreement.

Article. When referring to an article in the specifications or conditions of the contract.

Authorities Having Jurisdiction (AHJs). When referring to any regulatory entity that has enforcement responsibilities over the project.

Change Order. When referring to a contract modification.

Contract. When referring to the specific contract for which the specifications are written.

Contracting Officer. When referring to the representative of a government agency with authority to make decisions on behalf of the agency.

Contractor. When referring to the contractor who is a party to the owner-contractor agreement.

Division. When referring to a specific division within the project manual.

Drawings. When referring to the graphic portions of the contract documents.

Engineer. When referring to the engineer who is a party to the owner-engineer agreement.

General Conditions. When referring to the specific general conditions of a contract.

Government. When a government agency is a party to the contract.

Owner. When referring to the owner who is a party to the owner-contractor or owner-architect agreement.

Paragraph. When referring to a paragraph in the specifications or other contract documents.

PART. When referring to one of the three parts of SectionFormat®.

Project. When referring to the specific project of which the work is a part.

Project Manual. When referring to the bound volume that is part of a specific set of construction documents.

Room Names. For example, Library, Science Room, or Chemistry Laboratory.

Section. When referring to a specific section of the specifications.

Shop Drawings, Product Data, and Samples. When referring to submittals required for the specific project.

Specifications. When referring to the sections in Divisions 01–49.

State or Commonwealth. When referring to a specific state (e.g., the State of Missouri, the Commonwealth of Pennsylvania).

Supplementary Conditions. When referring to the specific modifications to the general conditions of a contract.

Work. When referring to the work of a specific contract.

No capitalization is required when the preceding examples are used in the general sense. Directions such as *east* or *northwest* are not capitalized unless they form a proper noun. The words subcontract and subcontractor are not capitalized because they do not apply to a specific party defined in the contract agreement. The words subparagraph and clause are usually not capitalized.

15.4.11 Punctuation

Because specifications are legal documents, the formal rules of punctuation must be observed. Sentences should be constructed so that the misplacement or elimination of a punctuation mark does not change the meaning. Use a comma in locations where the clarity of the statement is improved. Employ the Oxford comma, which uses a comma after each item in a series, including the item preceding a conjunction (e.g., clean walls, floors, and ceilings).

All paragraphs should be ended with either a period or colon. Use a colon at the end of a parent paragraph when it is necessary to link subparagraphs to the parent paragraph. For paragraphs that include subparagraphs forming lists, each item in the list should be terminated with a period to indicate no content is missing.

15.4.12 Grammar

The clarity of writing is heavily reliant on the usage of proper grammar. Employ the use of grammar-checking applications if you have limited grammar skills; however, many of these applications may not recognize the technical language used in specifications.

15.4.12.1 Subject/Verb Agreement

The subject and the verb must agree in number. Singular verbs should be used with singular subjects and plural verbs with plural subjects. An error in number is easy to make when a sentence is long and complicated. The singular subject of a sentence can be confused with a plural modifier.

> **Incorrect:** One of the elongated central fasteners are to be placed around the eye of the panel and bolted.

> **Correct:** Place one elongated central fastener around eye of panel and bolt.

> **Preferred:** Bolt one elongated central fastener to panel eye.

The incorrect example uses the singular subject *one* with the plural verb *are*. The grammatically correct example has number agreement between subject

DOMAIN 1
Planning,
Development,
& Organization

DOMAIN 2
Coordination

DOMAIN 3
Procurement,
Contracting,
& General
Requirements

DOMAIN 4
Research

DOMAIN 5
Analysis
& Evaluation

DOMAIN 6
Production

and verb but is a lengthier sentence. The preferred language has number agreement and is a simple, direct instruction statement — that is, it is clear, concise, correct, and complete.

15.4.12.1 Parallel Construction

Good grammar also requires using an identical grammatical structure in both parts of a compound subject or predicate. An identical grammatical structure in a series of nouns, adverbs, or prepositional phrases is also recommended.

Compound:
Incorrect: Tests shall be performed to determine strength and establish qualities.
Correct: Tests shall be performed to determine strength and to establish quality.
Preferred: Perform tests to determine strength and to establish quality.

Series:
Incorrect: Heating, ventilation, and air-conditioning.
Correct and Preferred: Heating, ventilating, and air-conditioning.

15.4.13 Inappropriate Terms

Avoid using phrases that have missing objects:

- As allowed
- As appropriate
- As approved
- As directed
- As indicated
- As necessary
- As required

Avoid these adverbs:

- Hereinafter
- Hereinbefore
- Herewith
- Wherein

Avoid these articles:

- Any
- All
- Such

Avoid these words and expressions:

- Etc.
- As per
- In a workmanlike manner
- To the satisfaction of the architect/engineer
- Shall function as intended
- Also

Do not use foreign language terms or expressions.

Incorrect: In lieu
Correct: Instead

15.4.14 Pronoun Reference

The use of pronouns in specifications should be minimized or avoided. Personal pronouns should not be used. Repeating the noun is better than risking possible misunderstanding.

Poor: Apply coating with pneumatic equipment when it is above 40°F.

Better: Maintain pneumatic equipment above 40 degrees F (5 degrees C).

- or -

Apply coating when ambient temperature is above 40 degrees F (5 degrees C).

Which and other relative pronouns should be used sparingly, if at all.

Poor: Contractor shall install bathroom accessories which are to be purchased under an allowance.

Better: Install bathroom accessories to be purchased under an allowance.

Preferred: Install bathroom accessories purchased under allowances specified in Section 01 21 00.

DOMAIN 1
Planning,
Development,
& Organization

DOMAIN 2
Coordination

DOMAIN 3
Procurement,
Contracting,
& General
Requirements

DOMAIN 4
Research

DOMAIN 5
Analysis
& Evaluation

DOMAIN 6
Production

The word *same* should not be used as a pronoun.

Poor: If materials are rejected, the contractor shall replace same at no additional cost.

Better: If materials are rejected, replace with acceptable materials at no additional cost.

Preferred: Remove rejected materials and provide acceptable materials at no additional cost.

15.4.15 Unnecessary Words

Definite article *the* and indefinite articles *a* and *an* need not be used in most instances.

Poor: Apply an oil paint with a brush to the wall.

Better: Apply oil paint with brush to walls.

The use of the word *all* is usually unnecessary.

Poor: Store all millwork under shelter.

Better: Store millwork under shelter.

Avoid using *contractor* as the subject of the sentence.

Poor: Contractor shall lay brick in common bond.

Better: Brick must be laid in common bond.

Preferred: Lay brick in common bond.

15.4.16 Prepositional Phrases

Sentences may be shortened in specification language by using modifiers in place of prepositional phrases.

Correct: Top of platform.

Preferred: Platform top.

Correct: Within the time recommended by manufacturer.

Preferred: Within manufacturer's recommended time limit.

15.4.17 Streamlining

Attempts to reduce verbiage in specifications are recommended if the meaning can still be conveyed. Although difficult to adapt to descriptions or instruction, streamlining is used to list products,

materials, reference standards, and other itemized specifications. This technique places the subject first and provides keywords for quick reference.

- Adhesive: Spread with notched trowel.
- Equipment: Install plumb and level.
- Portland Cement: ASTM C150, Type 1.
- Aggregate: ASTM C33.
- Air-Entraining Agent: More-Air Brand, More-X Manufacturing Company.

When using the streamlining method, A/Es often include the following explanatory statement in Division 01 or the supplementary conditions:

- These specifications are written using imperative mood and streamlined form. The imperative language is directed to Contractor unless expressly noted otherwise. The words "shall," "shall be," and "shall comply with," as applicable to context, are included by inference where a colon (:) is used within sentences or phrases.

15.4.18 Specification Detail

Language style should not be confused with specification detail. Specification detail should be commensurate with the requirements of the project and method of project delivery. Specifications for a large housing project may be more complicated than those for a small vacation cottage, but the same general rules for clarity and conciseness apply to both projects.

The degree of detail is a matter of judgment and is often tempered by economic considerations. A specification is complete when it covers important details without elaborate or unnecessary language.

15.5 Specifying Quality Assurance and Quality Control

Divisions 02 through 49 are composed of individual sections, each addressing a distinct subject area or work result. The issues and requirements concerning quality assurance and quality control specific to that section are addressed. The contract documents are so interrelated that none of them can stand alone. An examination of SectionFormat® helps clarify the interrelationships between article requirements within individual sections in Divisions 02 through 49 and Division 01 specification sections. The requirements in Division 01 are dependent on provisions in the conditions of the contract.

15.5.1 PART 1—GENERAL

Three articles in PART 1 that deal specifically with quality are "Administrative Requirements," "Submittals," and "Quality Assurance."

Administrative Requirements. This article includes preinstallation meetings requiring complex installations that require coordination and understanding between several participants.

Submittals. Quality assurance and quality control submittals are generally in response to requirements specified in the articles "Quality Assurance," "Source Quality Control," and "Field [or] Site Quality Control."

Quality Assurance. Requirements include prerequisites, standards, limitations, and criteria that establish an overall quality for products and workmanship and may include the following subjects:

- *Regulatory Agency Sustainability Approvals* include procedures and requirements for posting bonds, jobsite recycling requirements, restrictions on airborne pollution, requirements to submit a procedures plan, and securing review and approval by AHJs.

- *Qualifications* state the minimum expertise required of the manufacturer, supplier, fabricator, erector, applicator, or installer. They also include qualifications of testing agencies and design engineers employed by the contractor or manufacturer.

- *Regulatory Requirements* describe obligations for compliance with codes for contractor-designed items. They include the requirements of AHJs.

- *Certifications* may be required to verify that performance is equivalent to that of tested units or specified criteria. AHJs may also require certifications.

- *Field or Site Samples* are usually used to state requirements for sample field applications of finishes, such as paint or other finish materials and coatings. Accepted samples may establish a minimum standard of workmanship.

- *Mock-ups* state the requirements for full-size erected assemblies to ensure understanding and coordination of required construction. Mock-ups may also be used for testing and observation and establishing standards by which workmanship is judged.

15.5.2 PART 2—PRODUCTS

The following are several articles in PART 2 that specifically address quality assurance and quality control:

Assembly or Fabrication. This article includes tolerances to establish a statistical range of acceptability for products' properties before being incorporated into the project.

Source Quality Control. This article involves quality control of products during their manufacture. These controls become assurances of a product's quality.

Tests. These may include compression tests for verifying a concrete mix design, sieve analysis of natural materials such as aggregates or soil, and test curves for fabricated units such as electrical switchgear.

Inspections. These may include a checklist of items to be verified by inspection of products at their source. The inspector's qualifications are significant when inspections require judgments based on experience and knowledge of a particular field.

Non-Conforming Work. This article includes requirements for identification and correction of non-conforming work and final actions required to prepare installed products to perform correctly.

Manufacturer Services. These services may require coordination during manufacturing at the source for

DOMAIN 1
Planning,
Development,
& Organization

DOMAIN 2
Coordination

DOMAIN 3
Procurement,
Contracting,
& General
Requirements

DOMAIN 4
Research

DOMAIN 5
Analysis
& Evaluation

DOMAIN 6
Production

special inspections, including access by AHJs and other third parties.

15.5.3 PART 3—EXECUTION

The following articles in PART 3 relate to quality assurance and quality control:

Examination. This article is a quality assurance measure for required actions to determine that the conditions are acceptable to receive the primary products specified in the section.

Preparation. This article is a quality assurance measure for required actions to ensure the surface, area, or site is ready to receive the installation or application.

Tolerances. These are used to establish an acceptable range of deviation. Verification of dimensional tolerances may be required if the deviation appears unacceptable. Dimensional tolerances may involve such characteristics as surface flatness or alignment. The frequency of the deviation from tolerances is sometimes controversial. A tolerance that indicates the deviation shall not exceed 1/4 inch in 10 feet (6 mm in 3000 mm) may be questioned as to direction and whether the deviation is

cumulative, such as 3/4 inch in 30 feet (20 mm in 9100 mm); fragmentary, such as 1/4 inch in 1 foot (6 mm in 300 mm); or multiple, such as 1/4 inch every 6 inches (6 mm every 150 mm).

Field or Site Quality Control. This article addresses the final form of verification and may serve as the basis for identifying defective work during or after installation.

- *Field or Site Tests* usually involve quality control of variable conditions. Test methods, intervals between tests, and test sites are important issues. Field testing may include soil compaction, load tests, compression tests, and various other non-destructive testing forms. Field testing may not always be performed at the site and may be performed on samples taken from the site.

- *Field or Site Inspections* may involve visual observation for compliance with specified criteria. This visual observation may involve such items as joints and connections.

- *Non-conforming Work* may include requirements for identification and correction of non-conforming work and final actions required to prepare installed products to perform correctly.

- *Manufacturer's Services* may require a manufacturer's representative to visit the site to instruct an installer or owner's personnel in the proper installation of a material or the operation of specialized equipment. The manufacturer's field service may also be required to verify compliance with the manufacturer's instructions. A field report is an appropriate quality control submittal for these services.

15.6 Specifying Sustainability Requirements

Suppose the project is subject to a sustainability certification program with a specific certification level as its goal; however, the contractor is given the liberty to select which points to target (i.e., performance specifying). In that case, the performance requirements are established in Section 01 81 13 — Sustainable Design Requirements.

On the other hand, suppose the certification level is based on a select group of specific point targets (i.e., descriptive specifying). In that case, the general sustainability product requirements are specified in Section 01 35 63 — Sustainability Certification Project Requirements, and the particular product requirements should be specified within the affected sections.

With either of the two methods previously described, Section 01 33 29 — Sustainable Design Reporting and Section 01 35 66 — Sustainability Certification Project Procedures could be used. The former could be used to establish the tracking, recording, and submitting of sustainability information for the project. The latter could be used to address specific procedures the contractor must follow regarding managing the certification process.

Suppose recycling of packaging and construction waste is a requirement. In that case, Section 01 74 00 — Cleaning and Waste Management should be included to address the required general procedures and identify special procedures for specific types of materials. Also, Section 01 35 46 — Indoor Air Quality Procedures could be included if

building flush-out or controlling emissions within an occupied building is required.

If the project is not subject to a sustainability certification program but sustainability is a matter of practice for the A/E, client, or both, the general sustainability requirements can be specified in Section 01 35 00 — Special Procedures (or an appropriate Level 3 number and title), and the particular sustainable product requirements should be specified within the affected sections.

15.6.1 PART 1 — GENERAL

PART 1 of a specification section subject to sustainability requirements includes "Summary," "Submittals," and "Quality Assurance."

Summary. This article includes "Related Requirements," which may include references to the general sustainability requirements in Division 01.

Submittals. This article can include two different types of sustainable design submittals.

- *Sustainable Design Submittals* include product submittals that specifically address sustainable requirements. This type of submittal may be located under "Action Submittals" or "Informational Submittals," or they can be included in a completely separate submittal article.

- *Sustainable Design Closeout Documentation* includes information that is included in the package submitted for certification.

Quality Assurance. This article includes the following two articles specifically for sustainability:

- *Regulatory Agency Sustainability Approvals* are for specific approvals by AHJs regarding sustainability, such as emissions control, recycling procedures, or posting of bonds.

- *Sustainability Standards Certifications* include requirements for providing documentation indicating the specified items comply with a sustainable certification program (e.g., the Chain of Custody Certifications from the Forest Stewardship

Council [FSC] or the Cradle to Cradle Certifications from the Cradle to Cradle Products Innovation Institute).

15.6.2 PART 2—PRODUCTS

Although PART 2 is where most sustainability requirements are specified, the "Description" article is the only one that explicitly includes sustainability requirements.

Description. Within this article, "Sustainability Requirements" of the product or products are provided. Suppose the products being specified are subject to a general product sustainability requirement specified in Division 01 (e.g., VOC content for all sealants). In that case, you can reference that section instead of repeating the requirement here.

Materials/Mixes/Finishes/Accessories. If the umbrella article "Sustainability Requirements" is too limiting for the items specified, then item-specific sustainability requirements can be included with each item specified.

15.6.3 PART 3—EXECUTION

PART 3 sustainability content is limited but could include the following depending on the work result specified:

Installation/Application. Some actions during execution may include controlling chemical odors, runoff, or discharge.

Adjusting. Once the installation is complete, products may need to be adjusted to achieve the performance level specified to comply with a sustainability requirement (e.g., adjusting flow control faucets).

Cleaning. This article includes collecting recyclable packaging or construction waste specific to the work result specified. Suppose Section 01 74 00—Cleaning and Waste Management is provided, and the requirements within that section adequately address the waste generated in this section. In that case, it is unnecessary to repeat the requirements here. This section can also provide requirements for the flush-out of specific materials or products if no building flush-out is required in Division 01.

15.7 Specifying Workmanship

Workmanship is often confused with the term quality. As quality is a mirror of the requirements, the requirements need to reflect what is intended. Workmanship generally refers to precision and craftsmanship. These requirements have measurable properties and can be specified with a means to verify compliance. Workmanship can be controlled in several articles of a specification section. These articles specify qualifications, tolerances, and various other aspects of quality assurance and quality control. An excellent example of controlling workmanship is the North American Architectural Woodwork Standards (NAAWS), jointly published by the Architectural Woodwork Manufacturers Association of Canada (AWMAC) and the Woodwork Institute (WI). This publication establishes measurable tolerances for joinery, surfaces, and clearances, along with respective grades of premium, custom, and economy, which must be selected and specified. Workmanship can be divided into two main categories:

- Workmanship relating to the manufacturing and fabrication of products
- Workmanship relating to the application, installation, or erection of products

Workmanship relating to the fabrication should not be confused with the materials used in the product; that is, the fabrication of a product made of copper or stainless steel may not be any different from the fabrication of the same product made of carbon steel. Although materials have their own characteristics, they can be affected by both human and machine workmanship. It is a combination of materials and workmanship that results in the final characteristics of the product. Characteristics such as flatness, reflectivity, and finish may result from the thickness of the material and the fabrication techniques such as rolling or folding into specific shapes. The specified characteristics, including tolerances, determine the requirements and thus the required quality.

DOMAIN 1
Planning,
Development,
& Organization

DOMAIN 2
Coordination

DOMAIN 3
Procurement,
Contracting,
& General
Requirements

DOMAIN 4
Research

DOMAIN 5
Analysis
& Evaluation

DOMAIN 6
Production

Workmanship relating to the application and installation of products is equally important to ensure proper performance and aesthetically pleasing installation. In this area, the qualifications of the installer, applicator, and erector control the final execution. The A/E's knowledge and experience can be of special value. A mock-up or field sample can be specified to establish an acceptable level of workmanship.

When workmanship is specified, care should be taken to distinguish between product and installation items. Each workmanship requirement is placed under the proper heading in the specification section: product and fabrication workmanship in PART 2 — PRODUCTS and installation workmanship in PART 3 — EXECUTION. Product data usually contain adequate information for PART 2; however, the installation or application also needs special attention and can be of equal or even greater importance.

Construction projects are made from many interrelated products, requiring specialized skills to make each product a functional part of the project. Workmanship requirements should be specified to an appropriate level per the needs of the project. Project requirements should be specified without demanding conformance to unattainable standards or standards exceeding those necessary for the overall project's requirements.

Workmanship statements can be ambiguous if not properly worded. Workmanship requirements should be measurable. Avoid broad generalities such as "best possible workmanship." The word "best" is open to many interpretations by the contractors, subcontractors, and suppliers reading the specifications.

Appropriate methods for achieving desired workmanship include:

- Referring to applicable standards and codes
- Establishing qualifications of the manufacturer, fabricator, and installer
- Referring to workmanship requirements of trade associations
- Requiring samples to establish an acceptable level of workmanship and a basis for judging subsequent work

- Specifying tolerances and performance or physical requirements
- Establishing testing and inspection requirements

15.8 Specifying Closeout Documentation

Closeout documentation is broadly covered in the conditions of the contract and Section 01 78 00 — Closeout Submittals, and should include the specific submittals that the contractor is required to provide at the close of the project. Closeout submittals typically include the following:

- Maintenance contracts
- Operation and maintenance data
- Final survey
- Warranties
- Project record documents
- Spare parts
- Extra stock materials
- Sustainable design closeout documentation (see Section 15.7)

PART 1 of each section includes articles for "Closeout Submittals" and "Maintenance Material Submittals." These articles should address the unique requirements specific to that work result and not repeat the general requirements specified in Division 01.

15.9 Reviewing Specifications Prepared by Others

Careful coordination is required if others, such as consultants, write portions of the project manual. The A/E should assume responsibility for overall coordination of the specifications, including specifications prepared by engineering consultants, such as mechanical, plumbing,

electrical, structural, civil, landscape architectural, acousticians, or specialists such as roofing and waterproofing, elevator, architectural hardware, food service equipment, theater consultants, and lighting designers.

Conditions of the contract, along with Division 01 — General Requirements sections, should be made available to the consultants before they prepare any

of their respective sections. The consultants need to know the information in these documents to coordinate their sections properly and eliminate duplications and omissions. Input from them for Division 01 — General Requirements sections should be requested at this time. This procedure ensures that duplication of Division 01 requirements in consultant-prepared sections is avoided.

Index |